MAGNIFICENT WOMEN
AND FLYING MACHINES

MAGNIFICENT WOMEN AND FLYING MACHINES

THE FIRST 200 YEARS OF BRITISH WOMEN IN THE SKY

SALLY SMITH

First published 2021

The History Press
97 St George's Place, Cheltenham,
Gloucestershire, GL50 3QB
www.thehistorypress.co.uk

British Library Cataloguing in Publication Data.
A catalogue record for this book is available from the British Library.

ISBN 978 0 7509 9746 1

Typesetting and origination by The History Press
Printed and bound in Great Britain by TJ Books Limited, Padstow, Cornwall.

Trees for Life

CONTENTS

FOREWORD

I am indebted to Dr Alice Bunn who has kindly agreed to write a foreword for this book. Alice personifies the character of the women featured in Magnificent Women and Flying Machines *and is pursuing interests and a career that are still breaking barriers, from her roles as International Director at the UK Space Agency, Head of the UK Delegation to the European Space Agency, member of the World Economic Forum Future Council on Space Technology and Fellow of the Royal Aeronautical Society through to her current role as Chief Executive at the Institution for Mechanical Engineers.*

Sally Smith

***

Magnificent Women and Flying Machines is a fantastic celebration of the amazing achievements of women in the air and in space! For so long women were the invisible pioneers, and it is high time we took away that cloak of invisibility and applauded these wonderful women. All kudos to our foremothers who said 'knickers' to peril and prejudice and went ahead with their ambition regardless.

These women refused to be held back from realising their potential and their dreams just because society wasn't quite ready to recognise all the capabilities they possessed. There is a beautiful defiance in their firmly held beliefs that they should continue with their endeavours, regardless of support or recognition. This book provides a wonderfully entertaining and personal insight into the magnificent women who overcame many obstacles to break new boundaries and fly high. Enjoy!

Dr Alice Bunn
FRAeS FIMechE

INTRODUCTION AND ACKNOWLEDGEMENTS

Right from the beginning of the exciting world of flight, British women have wanted to be involved. Since 1785, when the first British woman took to the air in a flimsy unstable balloon, many other remarkable women decided to defy traditional society and public opinion to become pioneers in the fascinating and exhilarating world of aviation. Ballooning, parachuting, gliding, airships, fixed-wing flying and rockets: in every form of aviation British women have played their part.

Yet, amazingly, there is no proper record of many of these women. With lives full of excitement, adventure and bravery, these are stories that needed to be told, so I decided to make a start by concentrating on the women who had achieved real firsts in their area of aviation. The research was fascinating and there was a bonus: following the lives of these extraordinary ladies also illustrated the steady change that has taken place in the position of women in society over the years.

In some cases, trawling through very old media and records, it was hard to establish facts and to sort out reality from more creative styles of reporting and communicating. I have done my utmost to ensure that every fact is verified and that every picture painted is an accurate portrayal, but there was no way I could have achieved this alone.

I am therefore especially indebted to many people who have been willing to give their time and help in ensuring the best accuracy possible for all the information here. People such as David and Claire Ivison of the Royal Parks Guild who, thanks to their dedicated research, helped to finally confirm the very opaque background of early parachutist Sylva Boyden; and Bernard Vivier, the historian at the Pau Wright Aviation Association in France, who shared his infectious enthusiasm as well as his research material for Britain's first female pilot Edith Cook. Thanks also to Jim Bell who provided fascinating insights into exceptional pilot Winifred Spooner.

Descendants proved a valuable source of information, including Nick Thomas, whose mother was the outstanding airwoman Naomi Heron-Maxwell; and Gail Hewlett, who provided so much personal detail about her grandmother-in-law, Hilda, the first British woman to gain a pilot's licence. I also managed to talk to two women who have shown this pioneering spirit in more recent years: Britain's first commercial airship pilot, Kate Board, whose use of technology provides a stark contrast to the days when Rose Spencer took off in the simple family airship 120 years ago; and Helen Sharman, who helped me to understand what it's really like to train as an astronaut and to stare down at our vividly blue planet from space.

I am also grateful to my agent Andrew Lownie and to Amy Rigg and Jezz Palmer at The History Press for their dedicated assistance in bringing this book into reality. But most of all, I would like to say an enormous thanks to all the women mentioned in this book. Their entertaining stories demonstrate, sometimes in rather a dramatic fashion, what women can achieve in the sky. Ladies of the air, I salute you all.

Sally Smith
Somerset, 2021

1

LETITIA SAGE

1785
THE FIRST BRITISH WOMAN TO FLY

Looking up at the high sash windows of the old, yellowed brick buildings in London's Covent Garden, one can almost imagine the face of Letitia Sage peering out. After all, when Letitia woke up on the morning of that momentous day in June 1785, one of her first actions must have been to look outside to check the weather. Good visibility and low winds were vital to ensure her planned flight in a flimsy balloon would take place.

She probably wasn't fearful. As an exuberant actress just entering her thirties and someone who had been happy to be in an unofficial marriage, Letitia was a confident and independent woman. But underneath her carefully created buoyant personality she would have been more than aware that being lifted into the air by a thin fabric balloon entailed a certain amount of risk. Ballooning was, after all, still very new in Britain, and even in France, where development was further ahead, it was only eighteen months since the very first man had been lifted free off the ground.

That was in 1783, at a time when rumours and false ideas about flight were everywhere. When the Montgolfier brothers, based in Annonay in the south of France, had first shown that hot air could lift a solid object, many people didn't believe them. Undaunted, they kept going with their hot-air experiments, burning wool and straw in little bonfires under the mouths of carefully sewn balloons to get them to fly. On 21 November 1783, in the centre of Paris, a Montgolfier balloon was filled with hot air and took off with two male passengers. After a flight of over 5 miles, Pilâtre de Rozier and the Marquis d'Arlandes landed safety to write their names in the history books as the first people ever to fly.

The following summer, in Lyon, Frenchwoman Elizabeth Thible stepped into a hot-air balloon and was flown by the pilot for 2½ miles, becoming the first ever woman to take to the air.

For Letitia Sage, if she could become the first ever British woman to fly, there was a promise of fame and possibly even fortune; who knew what the future could bring? She hadn't had too much luck so far in her life. She was one of three daughters born to humble parents involved in provincial theatre. All three girls decided to go on the stage but while her two sisters did well, appearing in many plays and also making good marriages, poor Letitia had minimal success. After one mediocre performance at London's Covent Garden Theatre, one of the newspapers of the day commented that 'Mrs Letitia Sage's talents, unlike those of her sisters, are not sufficient to earn her a stage career'. For Letitia, with two successful siblings, reviews like that must have been very hurtful.

Her marriage stakes were no better. Letitia had lived for a while with Mr Sage, a haberdasher who dealt with lace, ribbons and other fine decorations from his establishment in London's Cheapside. Letitia took the name of Mrs Sage, although it appears there was no official wedding. There were no children either and something went wrong because Letitia soon moved back to what was then Charles Street, now called Wellington Street, in Covent Garden, taking whatever jobs she could in the nearby theatres.

So her life continued until, during an event with the local theatre crowd, she became close friends with a couple of young men interested in the new phenomenon of ballooning. Handsome and glamorous Italian Vincenzo Lunardi had teamed up with English aristocrat George Biggin to further their shared interests in the incredible concept of flight. Vincenzo had already achieved fame after making the first manned balloon flight in England in September 1784, taking off at Moorfields, north London, with a dog and a cat. George came from a traditional aristocratic background of Eton and Cambridge University and was following his education with involvement in fine art, music and the theatre in London. With Vincenzo's skills and George's money, the two of them decided to get together for a spot of ballooning.

When Letitia showed an interest not only in Vincenzo and George but also in balloons, the Italian quickly realised that taking the first ever Englishwoman up in the skies could enhance his fame. Also, if they charged spectators to watch the launch, it could bring in some very useful money too.

Once the plan was launched, Letitia immediately faced competition. Vincenzo was surrounded by many wealthy female admirers and the great beauties of the day who were willing to share the dangers and fame of going up in a balloon; the pleasure of being squeezed into a small basket with the glamorous Italian was an extra incentive. Letitia, though, clearly had great charm as well as determination, for she fought off all competition and, by May 1785, had become Vincenzo and George's firm choice for the first British woman to join them on a balloon flight.

The flight was initially planned to be a dramatic ascent from the Artillery Grounds in Moorfields with Vincenzo, George and Letitia on board. Unfortunately, like many of the early ballooning ventures at the time, this flight did not get off the ground. Vincenzo had chosen to use the latest idea of hydrogen as a safer way to lift a balloon rather than having a live hot fire on board, and on this first planned flight the balloon simply wouldn't lift. This may have been due to a lack of hydrogen, a badly sewn balloon or simply too much weight in the basket. Whatever the cause, the crowd had paid good money to see the spectacle and became angry, demanding their money back when nothing happened.

So, when the day of the second attempt dawned, on Wednesday 29 June 1785, Vincenzo knew he had to make this much-advertised first flight with a British woman a big success or his reputation would be lost forever. This time he chose a new launch site at St George's Fields, just south of the River Thames in Southwark.

Vincenzo and George had arranged the event with immense attention to detail and they got down to the site very early to check that this time everything would go to plan. Letitia was not needed until the balloon was nearly inflated, so she had time to prepare carefully. She treated the flight as another theatrical engagement, hoping this time for a lot of positive publicity, and she dressed carefully.

Stays were very much the fashion of the time with bodices strengthened with strips of whalebone to help produce a trim look and lift the bosom – a helpful style for the generously proportioned Letitia. On top of her undergarments and hooped petticoat she added a charming silk plum-coloured dress with a very low cleavage and a large hat finished with a mass of tall white feathers. The finishing touch would have been her make-up: white face powder (probably containing the dangerous lead that was commonly used in those days) and bright red cheeks from rouge made from vegetable matter. A final check in a small hand mirror and, by 9.30 a.m., she was ready.

Letitia left her house looking the best she could. The weather appeared kind. After a fine, warm spell it was clear, humid and muggy. There was low wind and no sign of the heavy thunderstorms which were beginning to build away to the west.

Together with two friends for support, she stepped into a horse-drawn carriage and clattered off through the crowded and noisy London streets. As they crossed the river to reach the wide expanses of St George's Fields, Letitia could see clearly that the filling of the balloon was going well. Vincenzo, developing steadily as a top showman, had built a low stage with poles so that the limp balloon hung in easy view of the growing crowds who were intrigued to see the fabric expanding bit by bit as it filled with hydrogen.

When Letitia arrived, the balloon was about a quarter full, giving a firm rounded top but loose sides which were gently flowing in and out and changing shape. The balloon was made of carefully oiled silk and had been spectacularly decorated with an enormous Union

Jack. Vincenzo was not going to miss a trick to make this flight a huge showstopping success.

Letitia was also on top of maximising publicity. Having seen that all was going well, she stayed hidden in the coach parked away from the centre of action, watching quietly as the balloon steadily expanded. Her plan was to make a grand last-minute entrance, the star of stage and balloon. But as she sat in her carriage the expansion of the balloon suddenly slowed and she must have had a moment of concern and quite probably anger. Not again! This time the crowd could well become vigorously hostile if they found they had paid their money and once more there was no action. The iron supply to make the hydrogen had become exhausted and then the water supply had become dangerously low. But new supplies of iron and water were quickly found, more hydrogen gas was made, and the balloon started to expand again. The crowd was rapidly expanding too as news got around that the flight might really happen.

The time was fast approaching for Letitia to make her entrance. In those final quiet moments in her coach, with the horses standing patiently in front, one wonders if she had a few moments of qualm. After all, just six months earlier the very first person to fly in a balloon, Frenchman Pilâtre de Rozier, had died after an attempt to fly across the English Channel had gone wrong. But that had been in a hybrid balloon which used both hot air and hydrogen, and the balloon had caught fire during the flight. Hydrogen on its own was surely much safer – a thought that would have buoyed Letitia's confidence as she stepped down from the carriage and pushed her way, smiling and gracious, through the thronging crowd to the stage.

Vincenzo and George had been having a frantic time, checking pipes and tether lines, calling out instructions to their eager band of helpers, checking the gas flow, the ballast, adjusting the release ropes and netting and even shooing away unwanted spectators who pushed too close to the activities. It had been noisy and chaotic, but the balloon was now filled and Vincenzo didn't want to hang around. Any small leak from the balloon would reduce buoyancy and could prevent lift-off. Time to get going.

As Letitia approached the stage where the filled balloon stood, swaying gently against its tethered lines, the crowd would have hushed. This was the woman who was going to fly. Was she brave or mad? Would she really get off the ground? Would they ever see her again? Letitia must have loved the attention; at last she was getting the sort of audience she had dreamed of for so many years.

Clambering up on to the platform in what should have been her moment of triumph, Letitia was aghast to see that there were already four people squashed into the tiny balloon basket. The design and style of the basket had not been left to chance. Vincenzo had ensured that with elegant wire netted sides and hanging drapes, it complemented the beauty of his balloon. Cushions on the wooden floor and provisions of various kinds were loaded on. But it had not been designed for five people and as Letitia got up on the platform she saw with horror that along with Vincenzo and George in the basket was their friend Colonel Hastings; and, even worse, there was also an unknown woman.

There was little room left in the basket, and squeezing in a woman of Letitia's generous proportions was out of the question. Letitia was having none of this. She had a prior claim to the flight, it had been agreed weeks before, and the poor hopeful female was quickly ejected. Then there were four in the basket. The order was given to release, and as the handlers on the tether ropes let go and Letitia took up her role of stardom, waving elegantly to the crowd, the balloon became free. The large pretty silk envelope started to sway above them but against some early gasps from the onlookers, the basket stayed firmly on the ground.

In what was rapidly becoming a chaotic scene, things took a turn for the worse when an order from George to adjust a rope to the valve of the balloon was incorrectly interpreted and it was reattached by enthusiastic helpers, leading to some gas inadvertently escaping. Suddenly it was all going horribly wrong – again. The balloon had lost some of its lift and the basket was refusing to move at all. The noise from the crowd was rising. Had they all paid good money to see this aerial spectacle only to be cheated again? Poor Vincenzo. In a moment of gallantry plus possibly sheer panic he stepped out of the basket. He certainly couldn't afford to refund the crowds this time if the flight did not happen. There were now three people in the swaying balloon, but the basket still stayed firmly implanted on the stage. It was no good: the balloon basket was still too heavy. Letitia stood firm. After all her preparations, excitement and anticipation, she was not going to take that humiliating step back down from the stage.

George too was determined. He had spent much of his free time studying flight and balloons; he was extremely knowledgeable and had put a lot of resources including his own money into getting Vincenzo's ventures off the ground. This time he wanted payback.

As Vincenzo urgently called that any further delay would jeopardise the entire project, the third passenger, Colonel Hastings, stepped out through the small door space in the wire netted sides, leaving just George and Letitia in the basket. Now, at last, the basket started to stir and lift. At 1.25 p.m. the balloon, with its prettily decorated basket below, started to edge upwards.

Lifting gently and quietly, for the first time ever, a British woman took to the skies.

After all the loud chaos, suddenly the world went quiet. Letitia looked down in amazement at the throng of white faces, all upturned to see the balloon gently rising into the sky. She hadn't really known or even thought about what to expect, but this was just amazing. The people, the trees, the little horse-drawn carriages parked around the edge of St George's Fields, the River Thames, everything was spreading out below her. Letitia was delighted at the peaceful stillness in the basket. No wind, no sensation of going up; it was as if the earth was just quietly dropping away. What an experience!

George was also flying for the first time but was more absorbed in the technicalities of controlling the balloon than looking at the sights, and he suddenly realised that, after an initial ascent, they were beginning to descend quite fast. George quickly selected a sand-filled ballast bag from the stack in the basket and emptied half of its contents over the side. The balloon stopped its rush earthwards but still continued to descend in a slow, leisurely fashion. They hadn't travelled far and, still over the wide expanse of St George's Fields, crowds were running up to catch the balloon as it came down. But George had other ideas. Calling down to the people to move away, he emptied the entire contents of the ballast bag over the side and then threw the bag down as well for good measure.

With so much weight gone, the descent was quickly arrested and soon the balloon was gently climbing again, with London and all its bustle and busyness steadily coming into view. As it climbed, the balloon slowly headed west, crossing over the River Thames near Westminster Bridge. With the flight now more under control, George checked out the balloon. In the panic to get away, the opening entrance to the balloon basket had been left wide open. He asked Letitia to lace it up. Generously proportioned Letitia was no athlete. She got down on her knees on to the cushions on the floor of the basket to complete the lacing and, once down there, she decided getting up again was going to be too much of a challenge, so she remained down there for much of the flight. Unfortunately, when she knelt down, she had accidently put her weight on the balloon's barometer and broken it. George had intended to use the barometer to check atmospheric pressure and ascertain their height above the earth, so now they could only estimate their height. With neither of them ever having been off the ground before, this was difficult, and reports of the height of the balloon cannot be accepted with any degree of accuracy.

But whatever the height, flying they were. There was little wind and the balloon slowly drifted towards St James's Park; Letitia reported that she could spot many houses she knew. As they flew on, people rushed out and some cheered wildly as they saw the balloon flying quietly above them. George took out a flag and waved it to the excited crowds below. This was what it was all about, what he had hoped for and imagined in his months learning all he could about flight.

Letitia was in a daze of happiness as the flight surpassed her expectations. She hadn't really known how she would react or how fearful she would be when the time came; she had even brought with her a bottle of smelling salts in case she had fainted. But, to Letitia's delight, all she felt was pleasure plus some detachment from reality. It was more like a dream. She was up in the sky and loving every minute of it.

The balloon was unlikely to have been more than a few hundred feet high at this point, because it caught the drift of air that can so often flow along water and it made a gentle change of direction following the path of the Thames towards Battersea Bridge. Again they spotted more clusters of people and again George waved his flag over the side.

Here Letitia noted that the balloon regained its absolute full shape, probably expanding from the continuous heat of the sun on this midsummer's day, and the balloon started to ascend once more. On George's instructions, Letitia dropped some small pieces of paper over the side of the basket to check their rate of ascent. All seemed to be going well and George began to relax.

There was ham, chicken and wine on board and the pair enjoyed a brief celebratory meal with George joining Letitia sitting down on the cushions. Then he threw their empty wine bottle over the side and turned to the experiments he had carefully prepared for this moment. This was an era of great experimentation as well as exploration; the Watt Steam Engine was just months from going into production; Captain Cook was just one day away from returning after his dramatic second voyage around the world. It was unthinkable for an educated and forward-looking man such as George to take to the skies without undertaking various experiments. As the balloon steadily climbed, he unpacked his equipment and began to work on several tasks to test magnetism, to test sound using a small tinkling bell, and to do an electrical experiment involving silver wire and sealing wax. Letitia willingly passed things and held things and assisted whenever she could, albeit with minimal idea of what the experiments were about.

As the balloon rose, they hit wisps of white cloud and Letitia was warned that it would get colder and the air pressure might begin to drop. The balloon also rotated, giving Letitia a view from various directions. The drift of the balloon changed with height and now started on a more north-westerly route, until the faintly visible shining thread of the River Thames finally disappeared in a fuzz of white haze to the south. They must have continued to climb steadily as it seems the surrounding misty cloud became denser; the cold became more intense and George suffered from problems with his ears. Letitia was a little chilled but otherwise fine, and continued to help out on anything that needed doing in the basket including a few more experiments.

The balloon had slowly been leaking small amounts of hydrogen and, like the passengers, was now beginning to cool. After around ninety minutes of flight, the inevitable descent started. It is unlikely that Letitia had given much thought to an actual landing in a balloon. The excitement of taking off in front of thousands of spectators and being the first ever British woman to fly had been enough; the actual landing was something she had not really considered.

George was prepared, though, and he threw out ballast, the remains of the meal and a few other disposable items to slow their descent as the earth came nearer and nearer. Looking out through her laced door, Letitia would have spotted that while there was a wonderful peace and no wind in the basket, there was clearly now some wind on the ground. It soon became apparent that the balloon was travelling quite rapidly. Letitia must have begun to suffer some anxiety as she watched the fields around Harrow, north-west of London, rushing past below her.

As they got nearer to the ground, George threw out a big grapple anchor attached to a long line from the basket. The plan was that it would catch in something and pull them to a halt as they landed. It was an optimistic idea. He also slowly emptied the last bag of ballast over the side to try to obtain a gentle final touchdown. It was not to be. In windy conditions the balloon continued to descend and then hit the ground with a sudden shattering blow. With both George and Letitia wedging themselves well down in the basket and hanging on tightly, the balloon bounced and took off again before hitting the ground once more. A local agricultural worker, after his initial astonishment, rushed after the basket and tried to grab it, but the force was far too much for one man to hold and he fell on his face as the balloon bounced on. More nearby labourers rushed to the scene and, after the balloon had cut a long rut through the field, it finally came to rest as the group all managed to grab the basket and helped to stop the flight.

The balloon had landed on common ground fully planted with crops and, as the pair shakily clambered out of the basket and got themselves together after such a rough landing, a furious local man, the Master of the Fields, quickly approached them. How dare they destroy his crops and his profit? The idea of flight was lost on him. Instead, he was beside himself to the point of almost physically attacking the miscreants. Dragging their basket across his field had cut a long, damaging furrow across the carefully nurtured crop; he wanted full compensation immediately. The labourers, still stoically hanging on to the balloon basket, kept their heads down.

Letitia must have been badly shaken by the landing and also upset by an injury she had sustained to her foot during the vigorous bouncing and jarring. But as more and more people tramped across the field to approach the balloon, she recovered enough to tidy herself up, adjust her large hat and regain some composure. Despite her aching foot, she had been the first woman in Britain ever to fly and now she was ready to accept the applause and acclaim. Chatting graciously to everyone who approached, she was soon recounting the amazing views and the feeling of flying high up above the earth to a very attentive crowd. It was beginning to dawn on her what she had done; she had been up in a balloon!

A local couple, Mr and Mrs Wilson, suggested she accompany them back to their house to relax, and Letitia accepted with gratitude. A comfortable chair and some refreshments were just what she needed. At the same time, a group of schoolboys and a gentleman approached the balloon. The gentleman was Rev. Dr Joseph Drury, headmaster of the nearby Harrow School, who had been pleased to see his students' delight and interest in the invention of balloon flight. He had happily rushed across with the boys to see the balloon land.

Seeing the confrontation taking place, the forceful and generous Dr Drury addressed the question of money for compensation with the angered Master of the Fields. Meanwhile, the Harrow boys were put to work helping to squeeze the remaining gas out of the balloon and compress the unwieldy fabric into a manageable ball before it was packed off in a cart back to London. George was then invited to accompany Dr Joseph Drury back to his Harrow home for dinner. Letitia was not included here, possibly because she had already accepted the invitation from the Wilsons, or possibly because after all George was an old Etonian while Letitia came from a somewhat different sphere of life.

Whatever the reason, the pair separated. Letitia, limping badly on her injured foot, was assisted by a very willing group of local and admiring gentlemen back to the home of the Wilsons, about a mile away from the landing place.

The Wilsons were very happy to act as hosts to the new star of the air, and soon their home was filled with friends and neighbours of all ages coming to find out about the balloon and meet the amazing female aeronaut. Sitting comfortably and resting her injured foot, Letitia was brought the best food and drink the Wilsons could find. She must have created quite a picture. Still ensconced in her flowing plum silk dress and hat, she talked happily to a large group of admirers of all ages. Letitia may have felt some connection to the group of local country girls who came in to hear about her exploits, for she gave them the smelling salts she had with her and one or two other bits and pieces she had taken on her flight.

It turned out to be quite a party, and later in the evening there was concern about how Letitia was going to get back home to London. But George hadn't forgotten his adventurous companion and sent a horse-drawn chaise to pick her up and transport her to join him at the headmaster's house at Harrow. Letitia arrived at Harrow at around 10 p.m., when it was only just fully dark in the English summer, and found that some friends had also arrived who had chased the balloon on their horses all the way from St George's Fields in London. More acclaim, more descriptions and celebrations, and Letitia and George finally set off home in their chaise at about 10.30 p.m. As they departed from the headmaster's house, a group of young Harrovians gave them repeated cheers and then followed them out of the village, stringing out along the road to cheer the pair as they headed south to London.

With both George and Letitia exhausted as well as exulted by the events of the day, it is likely they dozed rather than carried on animated conversation during the trip back to London, but when they arrived back at Letitia's Charles Street home, it was party time again. News had already got around and several friends had congregated to celebrate the bravery and accomplishments of this amazing pair.

Interestingly, it seems that Vincenzo Lunardi was not there to welcome the pair's return. The celebrations didn't last too long as both George and Letitia were tired out. George was soon on his way home to sleep. When Letitia finally removed her silk dress and her tight corset and collapsed on to her bed, she must have breathed a big sigh of relief. It had been a very, very long day, but that said, it really had been all she could have hoped for.

The following day reality began to catch up and Letitia stayed in bed all day because of the pain from her foot. She may well have had a bad sprain or even a small fracture; either way her foot was clearly causing her a significant problem. She spent some time greeting friends who came to visit her, no doubt bringing her food and drink, but she spent most of the day writing a long account of the flight. Despite the injury, Letitia hadn't lost any of her ambition for fame and money and she realised that publishing her personal account of the flight would enhance her celebrity and hopefully bring in some useful financial reward as well.

As Letitia's foot slowly improved and she got about again, she read with pleasure the stories about the flight which were beginning to appear in newspapers and magazines across the country. She was being described as brave, fearless, a real heroine. The next few days and weeks passed in a blur of acclaim and adulation. Enjoying celebrity status at last and praised for her courage and fortitude, Letitia met many of the important personalities of the time, going through again and again what it was like to go up in a balloon as a female. George, having shared a flight with a woman, was also in great demand. Vincenzo was quick to ensure that his part of the success was fully recognised, and rightly so: without his dedication and determination Letitia would never have got off the ground. Vincenzo set the balloon up in the Pantheon, a large public entertainment hall on the south side of Oxford Street in London's West End. It had a main rotunda, a large domed room, and the balloon was inflated and sat there still and shimmering, with no wind to ripple the fabric. It looked beautiful. At a cost of 5*s*, members of the public could examine the balloon and talk to Vincenzo and Letitia, asking all the questions they wanted about her flight.

But fame alone didn't bring in money, and Letitia also worked hard to finish her personal account of the flight. Handwritten in a flowery pose, it ran to just under 5,000 words and was entitled, in the long descriptive fashion of the day, *A Letter, addressed to a female friend. By Mrs. Sage, the first English female aerial traveller. Describing the General Appearance and Effects of Her Expedition with Mr. Lunardi's Balloon; Which Ascended from St. George's Fields on Wednesday, 29th June, 1785, Accompanied by George Biggin, Esq.*

Once it was complete, Letitia approached John Bell, one of the most successful publishers of the day, and arranged to pay for her pamphlet to be printed. In a small format, and running to thirty-two pages, Letitia's pamphlet sold for the price of 1*s*. Its reasonable price ensured the first edition was snapped up fast, and a further two editions were published before the end of the year.

Sadly, for Letitia Sage, her fame was very short lived. While trial and error with balloons of all sorts continued to advance, Letitia had made her only flight. Her acting career did not take off again either and, as new aeronautical performances hit the headlines, slowly but surely Letitia reverted back to her earlier life of earning money in work connected with the theatre, mainly as a dresser and wardrobe mistress.

There is some evidence she lived with, if not married, a Mr Robinson at some point, but twenty-five years later she was back in her old stomping ground, working in the wardrobe department of Drury Lane Theatre. It is very likely she would sometimes have walked down nearby Charles Street in the course of her normal activities. How often did she look back, recalling that amazing morning when she stepped into a carriage to start the most memorable day of her life? For a few months Letitia Sage was one of the top celebrities in Britain. Nothing can ever take that away, and she will now always be part of history as the first British woman ever to fly.

2

MRS HINES AND JANE STOCKS

MRS HINES, 1785
THE FIRST BRITISH WOMAN TO TAKE PART IN A NIGHT FLIGHT AND WATER LANDING

In 1785, in the weeks following Letitia's magnificent performance, there had been some more balloon flights in Britain by both French and English men. It was one of the hottest, driest summers on record and it was a time for great experimentation. Hot-air balloons with live fires in the baskets, gas balloons filled with lighter-than-air hydrogen, combined balloons involving the somewhat explosive mix of both live fire and hydrogen, and various other flying ideas and contraptions were all trialled with a range of successes – and a great number of failures!

Women were still very much out of it. Apart from normal social pressures, at the time there was also serious concern about the physical effect of these new activities on women. Would the reduced air pressure from going up in the sky damage the organs of the delicate female body? Would the weaker sex lose consciousness? Was it morally right for two people of different sexes to be in such close proximity in a balloon basket?

Quite. But despite this, there were some courageous and independent women who put all these terrifying concerns aside and, seeing the increasing general interest in flying, were keen to get off the ground themselves.

Just three months after Letitia had made her groundbreaking flight, a young lady, Mrs Hines, became the very first Englishwoman to make a night flight and a water landing. She very nearly became the first female balloon fatality as well.

None of this was in any way intentional. Local housewife Mrs Hines had joined a group of fascinated spectators on a large flat grassy field outside the small town of Beccles, 8 miles inland from the Suffolk coast, to watch a team of well-respected gentlemen from the town launch their own homemade balloon.

The gentlemen had pooled their scientific knowledge and financial input to construct a large hydrogen balloon with a fine basket lined with crimson satin and decorated with gold fringes. Whether they drew lots or how they determined who would fly is not known, but the passengers were set to be group members Rev. Peter Routh and Robert Davy, Esq. plus a local woman, Miss Fanny Shouldham.

They were an intelligent and honourable group who had tried to think of everything, even setting out a payment plan for local farmers to compensate any damage to the fields made by the crowds who would come to watch the balloon launch. This was a good consideration. Today, with the air above us being increasingly filled with flying hardware, it is hard to imagine what it was like in the late 1700s to see something heavier than a bird lift off from the ground. In those days, the concept of flight defied all logic and was a totally bewildering and amazing spectacle. Balloon launches drew big crowds.

In Beccles, after weeks of careful preparation, the afternoon of the launch finally arrived. It was Saturday 7 October 1785. The nights were drawing in, but the weather on that afternoon was clear and still, perfect for the first flight of the precious, carefully constructed balloon.

After being steadily filled with hydrogen for over three hours, the balloon was perfectly shaped and full. Into the lovely basket, in the semi-open wired net design of the day, stepped the three intrepid balloonists. There was a massive crowd of excited spectators. When everything was ready, on one firm call the balloon was released. Despite the tangible excitement and the breathtaking expectations among the attentive audience, not a lot happened. The balloon and basket gently stirred but remained firmly on the ground. It didn't take long to work out that despite its 36ft diameter, the balloon simply wasn't big enough to lift up the three passengers. The female passenger, Miss Fanny Shouldham, was not of a diminutive stature – in fact, in later media comments, she was described as being replaced by someone 'less corpulent'. Miss Fanny Shouldham was asked to step down.

The balloon enthusiasts would have been very aware of the publicity achieved by Letitia Sage just a few months before, and the plan had always been to take a woman. Standing towards the front of the crowd was the better proportioned and lighter Mrs Hines, very much a local Suffolk woman who possibly, without much forethought, quickly stated an enthusiasm for going for a flight. The two men in the basket knew it was imperative the balloon was launched without too much delay and the switch of women was quickly made. With the two gentlemen and now Mrs Hines in the basket, the balloon lifted off easily, rising gently and steadily up into the air above the field, above the madly cheering crowds and then, finally, above Beccles itself. The three adventurers waved their hankies over the side, clearly mesmerised by the vision of the expanding world below them as they made no attempt to release any gas to halt what was now becoming quite a rapid rate of ascent.

Being a few miles from the coast, and with virtually no wind on the ground, the team and the crowd of supporters probably expected to see the balloon rise gently, float over a few fields, and then put down at a not-too-distant spot. Instead, it climbed higher and higher and then it hit a north-easterly drift. In those days, there was limited information about wind shears or weather forecasting generally, certainly in Suffolk. While there would have been some observation of the movement of clouds, on this still sunny afternoon in Beccles no one had fully taken into account the fact that wind at height can be entirely different from that on the ground. There must have been some surprise in the basket as the balloon not only continued to gain height, but then headed off steadily on a north-easterly track towards Great Yarmouth, a distance of 15 miles. As the balloon travelled on, people rushed out to look at the spectacle as it passed overhead and descriptions afterwards say the balloon had quickly reached an immense height. It was heading towards the coast and, after that, there was only sea. As the balloon soared far above Yarmouth, there was concern in the town and talk of sending out boats to follow it, but it was decided the balloon was too high and going too fast and there would be no point. Evening was also approaching and most of the concerned throng who had rushed out to see what was going on probably assumed that this was the last they would see of the balloon and its passengers.

In hindsight, perhaps a gentle man of God, a gentleman recognised for his painting and knowledge of fine art, and a local housewife was not the most appropriate team to undertake such an adventurous trip, and their reactions as they saw the coast of England disappear behind them must have been one of total surprise and probably horror. The flight had clearly not been thought through to this extent or they would quickly have released gas to descend on land or at least near the coast in reach of boats and rescue.

Instead, off they soared further and further east as a gentle westerly breeze carried them out deep over the rugged North Sea. It had been a late afternoon take-off, and now night was falling. There is no record of what provisions they may have had on board. This was not a good situation. Furthermore, poor Mrs Hines, totally unprepared for a flight, would have been suffering from the increasing cold and, at some point, would no doubt have needed a toilet. Easy for the men, but what on earth was a properly brought up woman to do squeezed in a tight basket with two well-to-do males of possibly little acquaintance? As it became fully dark, it would not have been an easy time. Unlike a hot-air balloon, there was no source of light in a gas-filled balloon; they would have lost any idea of the track on which they were heading or indeed whether they were climbing or descending. It must have been a terrifying nightmare. Rev. Peter Routh had his faith to console him, and a poem he wrote afterwards sums up what it might have been like in the basket:

> When floating in the vast expanse, we owned Thy gracious care, for twas alone Thy providence that chased away our fear. Supported by Thy mighty arm, when dangers threatened around, composed we sat, secure from harm, and perfectly safely found.

It paints a lovely picture of the three of them sitting on the silk cushions, quietly awaiting their fate. Clearly Rev. Peter Routh helped to reduce any panic, and there they sat, feeling no wind in the basket, as they drifted along hour after hour, just quietly alone in the enormous black sky. Mrs Hines had been recognised back in Beccles for her cheery countenance and, with great bravery, it is reported she also helped to keep up the spirits of the little group during this impossible time.

As the balloon cooled in the night air and no doubt gas slowly leaked from the hand-sewn seams, eventually the balloon began to lose lift. The three passengers had spent all night in the basket and, as the darkness began to fade, they realised they were descending. As the light improved, they could see the sea below and soon it became apparent that they were actually descending quite rapidly towards the water. Still well short of the Dutch coast, the intrepid trio quietly resigned themselves to their fate. The sea got nearer and nearer and then, suddenly, they splashed down, with a gentle early morning breeze skimming them along the thankfully fairly calm surface. It would only be a matter of minutes, though, before the basket would become submerged and the passengers tipped into the heaving mass of the North Sea.

These waters were well populated by seagoing vessels, especially Dutch herring boats, but it was still amazingly lucky that a boat happened to be in the right place at the right time. When the crew of a small boat spotted the extraordinary spectacle of the balloon coming down, it was very likely to have been the first airborne vehicle any of them had seen. On the report of this strange sighting, kindly but bemused Captain Andrew Van Sweiten acted at once, turning the small sailing ship quickly to get as near as possible to the route of the balloon as it slowed and the basket began to sink deeper into the water. Lowering what was probably a small rowing boat, they chased and managed to somehow pick up the passengers; no doubt the chivalry of the two gentlemen lasted to the end and they insisted Mrs Hines be picked up first. It wouldn't have been an easy operation; it is most unlikely that any of them could swim. However, it was done and the three were soon on board the main vessel. Wet, cold and shaken, their relief must have been overwhelming.

Back home, the balloon party had been given up for lost. Beccles was only a small town, and the construction of the exciting new balloon had been big news for some time. The day after the balloon disappeared gracefully over the horizon, the town was quiet and the local people were very subdued. Was there any news? Was there any hope at all? The general consensus was no.

On board the rescue boat, Mr Davy, by some fortuitous coincidence, spoke a little Dutch; there was also a passenger on board who spoke a little English, and between them the captain got the whole picture. With an adjustment to course, the hugely relieved but still very shaken balloonists were dropped off on the Suffolk coast the next day. The welcome they received as they finally made it back to their home town of Beccles can be imagined. It seemed the whole town was out to greet them, and the three balloonists were each given a laurel crown inscribed on the front with the words: *The favoured of Heaven.*

It is a shame Mrs Hines did not write a full account of the voyage. This, like Letitia Sage's, would surely have become a top seller. Instead, she disappeared quietly back into domestic life, possibly happy for the memory of the most scary and dramatic day and night of her life to fade into a distant recollection.

JANE STOCKS, 1824
THE FIRST BRITISH WOMAN IN A SERIOUS FLYING ACCIDENT AND FIRST INTERNATIONALLY RECOGNISED BRITISH AVIATRIX

Neither Letitia Sage's nor Mrs Hines's trips had sparked off a mass interest or involvement from British women in the idea of flight, and the next forty years saw very little in the way of advancement. One still had to look to the Continent for leadership in aviation. Just fourteen years after Letitia took off in England, in October 1799, a Frenchwoman, Jeanne Genevieve Labrosse, became the first woman to make a parachute descent. But this wasn't parachuting as we know it today. Jeanne stood in a carefully constructed circular cage which was attached to a rigid open round parachute above it. This parachute was then suspended below a balloon which was taken up to around 3,000ft before the parachute was released. With Jean still safely in the basket below, the parachute descended gently to the ground.

It was a wonderful achievement but it was very much a one-off, and in the coming years even in aviation-minded France very few women were managing to get their feet off the ground. When Sophie Blanchard, the wife of famous French balloonist Jeanne-Pierre Blanchard, made a solo balloon flight in France in 1805, she was one of very few women who had made it into the air. When her fabulous ballooning career ended in a spectacular fatal crash in Paris in 1819, the world's first ever female aviation fatality, it simply helped to strengthen a general opinion that a woman's place was on the ground.

In the UK, rather than harbour dreams of flight, daily survival was the main concern for most women, so it was an even greater achievement than perhaps first appreciated when, after a gap of nearly four decades, in 1824 two British women, a Miss Jane Stocks and a Mrs Margaret Graham, both managed to make it into the air.

Jane Stocks was a surprising contender for early aviation. She had been born in Shoreditch in east London and her mother had died when she was just a young girl. As one of seven children, she left home as soon as possible to earn her own living, joining a household nearer central London as a domestic servant, working long hours for low wages and food.

Young Jane was a lively girl growing into a slim and attractive woman. Along with the drudgery of everyday life, she was keen to enjoy herself in vibrant London, at that time the biggest city in the world. On the morning of Tuesday 25 May 1824, when Jane was 18, she had a day off. She put on her best frock and set off to join some friends to watch the launch of a well-publicised pretty balloon called the *Royal George*. Little did she guess that, by the next day, she would be one of the most famous ladies in England.

The *Royal George* balloon was the ambitious project of Thomas Harris. Thomas was one of the large band of foresighted men of the time developing new ideas and pushing back boundaries in a fabulously exciting time of steam development and other inventions. He had watched several balloons take off and land and had also been a passenger on a balloon flight. He realised that once a balloon lands, because it is still so buoyant it could bounce up into the air again or, in windy conditions, it could be dragged across the ground causing injury to the occupants. An idea called a grapple hook had already been developed to try to catch something on the ground to help bring a balloon to a halt, but this wasn't a good solution. It often failed to catch anything or hooked on to something so firmly that it stopped the basket violently, tipping out and sometimes injuring the passengers. Thomas recognised that if there were a quick way to deflate a balloon once it landed, then everything would be much safer. He spent the winter of 1823–4 designing a new type of valve to be fitted into the top of the balloon which, when opened, would let out a mass of gas or hot air so quickly that a balloon would deflate almost instantly.

Despite a lack of money, and with a wife and daughter to support, he set about constructing a gas balloon featuring his new-style valve release. Then, of course, he wanted to test the balloon with a proper flight. To help pay the large bills involved in this enterprise, Thomas arranged a big public launch and advertised for a passenger to accompany him in the balloon basket for 50 guineas. There were very few offers. Even when the event was well underway and take-off time approached, no one had bid the full amount to fly with Thomas. As Jane excitedly shuffled among the crowds while the balloon was being inflated, she heard talk that the balloonist was still looking for an extra passenger. It was assumed this would be a man. In those days the occupations and lifestyles of men and women were especially defined; women were generally considered to be the weaker sex more suited to domestic and traditional female roles. It was extraordinary for someone with Jane's background to even think she could go up in a balloon, but that is what she decided she would like to do. Probably unaware of the fee involved, and possibly egged on by her friends, she made her way to a nearby room set up as a base for the committee involved in the launch. Approaching the group in the room, something that must have taken a bit of courage for a young domestic servant, Jane said she would be willing to accompany Mr Harris on the balloon flight.

Word of this reached Thomas Harris and he came over to see what it was all about. While Jane didn't have the necessary 50 guineas, or indeed any money at all, Thomas would quickly have realised that flying with a woman could be useful to help publicise his unique new valve system. Also, the young and enthusiastic girl, standing there in a pretty dress and hat, must have been an attractive proposition as a flying companion. So the deal was quickly done and young Jane Stocks was set to go for an amazing flight in a gas balloon high up over London.

Friends and members of the committee escorted Jane towards the balloon. Thomas left the final preparations to meet Jane, and the pair climbed up on to the launch stage together. They made a handsome pair, Thomas in a blue naval-style uniform with a white and gold hat and Jane in her simple white muslin dress with a light green shawl and straw hat. With the decorated silk balloon swaying gently in the background, it must have been a lovely sight.

It had all happened very fast, though. From the anticipation of a simple fun day out at a balloon launch, suddenly Jane found herself the centre of attention. She must have felt some slight nervousness as she finally entered the gondola-shaped basket and sat down on a small velvet-covered seat. It had all been rather an impulsive decision and Jane hadn't had time to really consider what she was letting herself in for. The immense crowd cheered as she settled herself and that probably brought it home to her that she was about to do something rather special. She had the presence of mind to suddenly call down from the basket to one of the committee members, asking them to let her parents know what she was doing. After all, she was only 18.

Thomas made a few adjustments and, at just on 4.30 p.m., he gave the instructions to release the ropes.

It was an exciting moment. At Thomas's command, the balloon was released as planned, rising a few feet into the air but then stopping as one especially long tether rope halted its lift. This was part of the dramatic launch plan to provide the crowds with a final look at the balloon, and the spectators gasped as the balloon rocked to a halt just above them. This caught Jane by surprise and she held on tightly. Then the final tether rope was let free and the beautiful *Royal George* balloon, with its two passengers, ascended into the sky.

To begin with all went well. The balloon steadily rose and headed off in a southerly direction. There was some light cloud around and, after about ten minutes, Jane was enveloped in a white mist, blocking all views of the earth below. But it soon cleared and the lovely *Royal George* balloon was seen from the ground heading over London towards Croydon. Thomas made a slight descent towards a field just outside the town and then, as he released a little ballast, the balloon rose again. After the excitement of the launch, the reality of what she was doing hit Jane and for the early part of the journey she sat there on her cushion in a nervous state. She commented later that she looked over the side only occasionally. However, after being aloft for 30 minutes or so, Jane started to relax a little and then began to enjoy the view.

The balloon was now over the lovely parkland of Beddington, a couple of miles west of Croydon, and it was time to bring it down.

Jane's subsequent report on the event mentions that Thomas took out his fob watch to check how long they had been flying. Then it seems Thomas put his watch away and without due thought pulled on a rope to release gas. Accidentally, though, he pulled on the wrong rope. Instead of opening the small valve to release just a little gas, the rope that Thomas pulled operated his new quick-release valve designed to collapse the balloon on landing.

Only of course they weren't landing, they were still hundreds of feet up in the air. The last thing Jane remembers is Thomas crying out, 'Good God, the gas is bursting through,' and indeed it was. Thomas's new quick-release valve had worked perfectly and the hydrogen gas in the balloon was quickly escaping, turning the balloon into simply a long streaming and flapping piece of material.

The basket, and the two terrified occupants, dropped fast down to the earth, gaining speed until they first smashed through a branch of a tree and then finally crashed hard and noisily into the ground.

It was a sorry sight. First to arrive was a nearby gamekeeper but quickly people from the adjacent villages, who had been watching the balloon, thronged to the scene. Both bodies were retrieved from under the folds of the balloon material; Thomas was clearly dead and Jane only semi-conscious but still breathing.

First aid wasn't as slick then as it is today, and it took twenty minutes for a nearby doctor to arrive. Both Thomas and Jane were carried to a nearby pub, the Plough, in Beddington. These premises have now been rebuilt, but at Jane's time it was a traditional eighteenth-century inn.

Jane was carried upstairs to one of the bedrooms; she wasn't expected to last beyond a few hours. The doctor applied leeches to let blood which would not have helped poor Jane's condition as she lay there in a semi-conscious state. The poor girl was groaning and complaining of excruciating pains in her limbs. It was a miracle she was up to complaining at all. Thomas's body was laid in an adjoining room.

Over the next few days Jane hung in there, seriously ill and in pain but still alive and conscious. Slowly, though, as the days went on, she started to improve. Eventually, she was well enough to be taken back to her parents' basic home in east London to start the long, painful road to recovery.

But recover she did, and as she got back to health she was astonished to find she had become nationally and internationally famous. In newspapers on the Continent as well as in Britain, she had been described as the girl who had cheated death. The story had become especially big news because it was linked to the new idea of a release valve, something that was then being discussed by all the leading balloon enthusiasts of the day. Many visitors came to see Jane as she recovered, and one of them was Charles Green. He was an experienced balloonist who lived nearby in London's Clerkenwell. He was full of encouragement and goodwill, and he offered to take Jane for a flight at an exhibition he had arranged in Leeds, all expenses paid, when she was fully recovered.

By spring 1825, a year after her accident, Jane had recovered physically and also mentally from the bad memories of the flight and was probably beginning to look for domestic work again. Charles's offer of a flight interested her a lot. There were few opportunities for a 19-year-old east London girl to have adventure, let alone achieve fame and admiration. There had been recent news of successful flights without a problem. Enormous credit to Jane that, despite her horrendous accident, she was up for Charles's offer and said she wanted to do it.

The railway system was not yet established, so for Jane the trip to Leeds meant a long journey in a horse-drawn coach. But Jane went, and when she stepped into Charles Green's latest balloon outside Coloured Cloth Hall in Leeds, she was still fairly confident even though the weather was not ideal.

As usual in those days, the balloon ascent attracted a massive crowd, and just after midday they took off. Again Jane was very nervous, but as the time went by she started looking around and was intrigued by the views of the earth below. How peaceful and beautiful it all was. After a forty-minute flight over the lovely Yorkshire countryside, Charles released some gas and brought the balloon down into a field in a gentle, well-controlled landing.

The flight had been very successful, and the aeronauts were taken to a nearby house where they were praised and given great hospitality. They then took a chaise and four back to Leeds for more celebrations and Jane enjoyed all the attention and applause as people crowded in to hear about the experiences. Again, reports of a woman taking to the sky appeared in the media and Jane loved the attention.

During the following year, though, life once again became fairly mundane for Jane as she went back to domestic duties. However, she remembered there was another balloonist, George Graham, who had been to see her after her accident and had also offered to take her for a flight when she recovered. Jane decided to contact him to see if he would honour that promise of two years before.

It was an opportune moment. George was always short of money and had been well aware of the attention given to Jane as a female balloonist. When George's young wife, Margaret, had shown a real interest in his aviation activities, he was quick to realise the potential; a woman involved in ballooning could bring in large fee-paying crowds. Margaret had occasionally been up with George on a few flights and had become more enthusiastic than ever. She felt she might even be able to take control of the balloon herself for a short easy flight.

When Jane approached George, he had a brilliant idea. What about the two women going up together, on their own? He could charge a lot more for entry to see this spectacle – it would be an enormous crowd-puller and big news. No woman had flown a balloon before in England; having two go up at once would be dramatic. Margaret felt she knew enough and was happy to give it a go. Jane tentatively agreed as well. She didn't know Graham's wife, and it wasn't ideal, but she was keen to get up in the air again.

The flight was set for 26 June 1826, and it all started off as planned, with George's balloon being filled slowly but steadily in gardens at White Conduit House in Pentonville, a new suburb of north London that was developing fast. The gardens were large and flat, perfect for a balloon take-off. Large crowds, attracted by posters and heavy advertising plus an affordable entrance fee, steadily accumulated throughout the day as George Graham went through the procedures of filling up the balloon.

Margaret, who was quick to learn the best ways to entertain crowds, was carefully dressed for the occasion in a white dress covered with a pink cloak and bright yellow lining, all set off with a big violet hat. Jane, with her modest income and lifestyle, dressed more conservatively in a simple frock. A big thunderstorm at 3 p.m. delayed the proceedings but by late afternoon the balloon was ready. Because of the delay, Margaret and Jane had gone off separately to have some tea before the flight, and the women were called back urgently. The balloon, having been filled, was now beginning to lose gas as it wafted around in a fairly strong breeze.

Margaret, with her husband directing proceedings, felt reasonably confident but Jane, as she hurried into the basket, was becoming slightly anxious at the final rush and urgency. Standing in the gondola, her nervousness increased and she hung on tightly as the balloon was released. As the crowd went silent, the balloon basket started rocking around as the breeze tugged at the balloon, but it didn't lift. With two passengers, the load was too heavy.

A quick decision was needed as the balloon was very slowly leaking gas and losing lift. There would have been an option to remove ballast from the balloon for a speedy lift-off, but instead Margaret called firmly to Jane to get out of the basket. Margaret was well aware she was about to become the first ever British female pilot of a balloon. Sharing the glory of the flight with another woman could dilute the achievement. The crowds were getting restless and there was a tension in the air. Once again, this time very firmly, Margaret told Jane to get out of the basket. It must have been an incredible and shattering disappointment for Jane, but faced with Margaret's fierce determination, poor Jane didn't put up a fight.

After all the exciting build-up, Jane Stocks got out of the basket and relinquished not only her claim of being Britain's most famous female balloonist, but also the opportunity to share the glory of being in the first ever all-female balloon flight. Instead, Jane quietly pushed her way out through the massive crowds to disappear from ballooning activities for ever. It was a sad, flat end for a plucky girl who had been through some dramatic events, horrific injuries and also unique and wonderful experiences. Jane gave up her ideas of flight for good, returning to her more traditional life with mixed memories and a wealth of stories to recount to her family and friends.

But for Margaret, now about to take off as the first ever female pilot in Britain, things were just beginning. Not only would she set a number of records for women in flight, but she would create diversions and stories that would keep Victorian England amused and enthralled for decades.

3

MARGARET GRAHAM

1826
THE FIRST FEMALE BRITISH PILOT

By 1826, it had been forty-one years since a British woman had first taken to the skies, yet in that time little progress had been made in aviation.

There were a few advances. Hot air from live fires to produce lift had been superseded by hydrogen or coal gas. Wicker and cane baskets were also being incorporated instead of the wooden and sometimes even iron-carrying vehicles that had been used in early balloons. But for members of the public, these advances were minimal and there were no innovations that made flying displays any more exciting than they had been in previous years.

Because of this, there wasn't the admiration and support for the second generation of balloonists that, looking back in history, might have been expected. There were also some additional factors that restricted public acclaim. Farmers having their valuable crops damaged by unexpected landings from the sky did not go down too well. Displays which charged high entrance fees and then failed to get off the ground attracted anger. There were serious accidents and deaths in France, America and Germany as well as in Britain, and people were concerned about the unnecessary loss of life. Finally, what was it all for? A few balloons had been used in the French Napoleonic wars for aerial observation, especially to see troop movements, but apart from prestige and possibly creating a little fear, there hadn't been a great deal of benefit. Overall, the general public was not totally behind the adventurous aviators of the day, seeing them more as flashy showmen rather than groundbreaking innovators.

But, nevertheless, the early aeronauts kept going. So far, the very few women who had actually made it into the air had done so thanks to the goodwill or patronage of male balloonists. By 1826, it was high time for a British woman to make a proper contribution to aviation.

There was no hint of an exceptional future when Margaret Graham was born in 1804 in Bath in Somerset. Margaret's maiden name was Watson, and the Watsons came from an industrial group of hard-working and law-abiding semi-skilled families based around the area. Many country girls ended up in London and, at some point, Margaret moved to the capital.

The early 1820s were exciting times in London, and Margaret would have found the town full of fascinating new ideas. How Margaret met balloonist George Graham is not clear; she may have attended an early balloon event where George was present, or perhaps she even met him at a lecture on the occult, a subject that was a massive preoccupation for George before he discovered ballooning.

Either way, meeting George transformed Margaret's life. He would have been a good catch, part of a group of energetic and exuberant men in London in 1823 who, while lacking high levels of formal education or personal finance, became knowledgeable about chemistry, engineering and the many other developments that were going on.

It must have been incredibly exciting for young Margaret, being involved with a man so enthusiastic about new ideas and with the potential to introduce her to a world full of adventure. George was nearly twenty years older than 19-year-old Margaret, but who cared about the age gap? She would have loved his attention and been so impressed by the fact that he was just about to take delivery of a wonderful new balloon.

George planned a big exhibition to show off his new balloon in August 1823, and Margaret quickly signed on as a dedicated assistant. The event, at White Conduit House in London's Pentonville, was advertised as 'a display of the most magnificent balloon, far exceeding the magnitude and splendour of any aerostatic machine hitherto made', and the thought of seeing this massive balloon, 60ft high and filled with 33,000 cubic ft of gas, certainly drew the crowds.

Margaret assisted in the launch of the balloon but it turned out to be a total fiasco, with gas-filling problems preventing the balloon lifting off, a furious crowd demanding their money back and George hiding in a nearby tavern. But this failure didn't put Margaret off; it may have just added to the extraordinarily exhilarating world she was now joining. Just a few days later they had another go, with only slightly more success as the balloon was torn during the launch and after rising to just around 400ft it descended fast, dumping George and the basket into a nearby gravel pit.

Despite the serious mishaps, Margaret was still enthralled by these aerial adventures – and also by George. By the end of September, the couple may well have been married; certainly she had moved in with him to his rented rooms at 41 Poland Street in London's Soho. She also found she was pregnant. With winter coming and a baby on the way, her dreams of going up in a balloon had to be put on hold, but perhaps not for as long as anyone expected.

Little Rebecca Graham arrived at the end of April 1824, and it was just five weeks later that Margaret finally managed to start her career in aviation. Even as a new young mother, just turning 20, she wasn't daunted by the risk of ballooning, and on 2 June 1824 she joined her husband on a flight; not only while her baby was so small, but also just one week after the British newspapers had been carrying the sensational story of the death of balloonist Thomas Harris and the terrible injuries to passenger Jane Stocks. Despite this, Margaret stepped enthusiastically into the basket attached to a beautiful new silk balloon, constructed for George during the winter months. It was to be Margaret's first and George's sixth flight.

The launch with Margaret as a passenger was planned as a big, money-making event, a very real necessity for the Grahams, and the programme included evening fireworks after the flight. This time things went according to plan. Taking off from the familiar White Conduit Gardens in London's Pentonville in reasonable conditions, the launch went smoothly and George, with Margaret beside him, rose gently into the air in the brand new balloon, passing west over Tottenham Court Road as crowds came out to wave and cheer the couple. Margaret was fascinated, looking down as familiar buildings moved gently past below her.

During the rest of that summer and the following year Margaret continued to mix looking after little Rebecca with assisting with the ballooning business, plus going for the occasional flight when it fitted in.

From London-based flights, launches were now planned in various parts of the country where ballooning was less frequent and they could attract, thrill and charge fresh crowds of onlookers. In November 1825 a display had been booked in Plymouth, but the first two planned events were cancelled due to the weather. A third event was planned, but the wind was blowing from the north-west. This wasn't ideal for a launch of a balloon on the south coast of England. It appears that it was Margaret who resolved not to disappoint the crowds for a third time and insisted they should fly. The balloon, with Margaret and George in the basket, took off and inevitably drifted out to sea, dropping into the water about a mile offshore. They were rescued and all ended happily, with a relieved Margaret going back to her 7-month-old daughter safely.

By June 1826, when George planned and energetically advertised Britain's first all-female ascent in his balloon at White Conduit House in Pentonville, Margaret Graham already had quite a lot of knowledge and experience and clearly felt she was capable of flying the balloon by herself. It was still, however, an extraordinary decision. It is not as easy to control the ascent and descent of a gas balloon as it is with a modern hot-air balloon; the gas in the envelope can become heated by the sun and expand, giving unexpected lift, or the gas can slowly leak through the fabric or escape through the seals so that lift is gradually lost with no way of recovering it. The only means of control Margaret had was ballast, which she could throw out, and a vent line to release gas; but the more gas she let out the less lift she would have. There was no proper weather forecast and the balloon was set to take off in the middle of a built-up area in central London. Yet Margaret, dressed in bright clothes and wearing a charming hat, was happy and confident. She may have been good at hiding a slight apprehension, or perhaps she didn't really appreciate the dangers, or maybe she had that unshakable confidence of youth. After all, she was still only 21. Either way, after ejecting hopeful fellow passenger Jane Stocks, she took up her position solo in the basket beneath her husband's enormous swaying balloon and declared herself ready to go.

The crowds, having waited patiently all afternoon, watched and cheered as the order was given to release and the balloon lifted slowly off the ground at just after 6 p.m. While it did indeed rise into the air, it was a slow ascent that gave the balloon insufficient height to clear the trees and a building at the edge of the launch area. The basket, travelling along in a steady wind, bounced off the side of a roof and then started to sink again. Margaret, showing an immediate appreciation of the problem, started throwing everything she could find out of the basket to gain some lift. The balloon started to respond, rising high enough to just avoid the steeple of an Islington church and giving Margaret her initial insight into being alone in the sky. She had little time to enjoy it, though, for she didn't have much height and after only a short while the balloon lost its lift again and started descending, finally coming down in a sheltered vegetable patch of a garden belonging to a tavern just over 2 miles away in Stoke Newington.

For Margaret, as she stepped out of the gondola and started gathering up all the fabric, it had been a speedy introduction to an activity that was going to take over her life. It was also one without fanfare. Rather than a big celebration of the first British woman to fly an airborne vehicle of any kind, Margaret was met by a furious landlord demanding money. Husband George arrived fairly quickly on the scene, and together they fought off the irate tavern owner and made it back home with their balloon in one piece. However, a couple of days later they found themselves in the police court in Old Street defending themselves. The charge, brought by the landlord of the tavern where Margaret had landed, was for compensation against damage the balloon had done to his vegetable plot. It was an inauspicious beginning for British women pilots!

During the following months, in the summer of 1826, the couple packed in a high number of flights, mainly with George flying and Margaret helping on the ground. However, like all aeronautical activities of the era, it was a very hit-and-miss activity and minor incidents and accidents were common. Nevertheless, in September 1826, George took delivery of yet another brand new silk balloon and Margaret would have felt her life, living in Poland Street, Central London, with her little girl and travelling around the country when possible with her husband and the balloon, was going well. George was becoming quite well known and occasionally Margaret managed to go up in the balloon as well, something she loved.

Then, in November, a problem occurred. George was arrested and put into prison over a dispute regarding payment on his lovely new silk balloon. While George Graham and a Mr Bailey were acknowledged as joint owners of the balloon, it seems there were two creditors who hadn't received the funds they felt they were due. There was argument over the value of the debt and argument over the value of the balloon and a dispute over payments, all resulting in a court case which was not finally resolved until the following June. Margaret had to battle through seven months of uncertainty and worry with a young baby to look after and no ready income. The case was finally settled in favour of the plaintiffs, meaning George had lost.

It was a financial blow but at least George was back home, and throughout early 1828 he sorted out his money enough to continue to fly. Margaret had been busy investigating possible shows, and now the couple confirmed they would give displays at places as far apart as Kent, Hereford and Northampton. This involved a lot of organisation and a lot of travelling, all by horse-drawn vehicle. Margaret was keen to step into the basket when she could and managed to get on a couple more flights; they also managed to supplement their income by occasionally taking up fare-paying passengers.

Overall, the rewards were good. A successful display, with big crowds paying for entry or donating towards the cost, could bring in a lot of money and a lift in their social status too. On a display in September 1828, for instance, George made a successful flight from Southampton, flying with his good friend Mr Pickering, and with Margaret following the balloon in a horse-drawn trap. On landing, they were given a lavish dinner by a group from the local aristocracy including Lord and Lady Calcroft. This was a lovely experience and a big social step up for Margaret.

In October of that year Margaret made her eighth ascent and second as the pilot in charge, taking the loyal Mr Pickering up for a flight from Chichester. She only flew for ten minutes, and the landing could have been better: she bounced off the ground and ended up caught in a walnut tree. But the couple climbed out and made their way back to Chichester town centre, where they were met by a band and big celebrations.

Gaining in confidence, the following month in Northampton Margaret made another solo ascent. Initially, on this display, it was planned that Margaret would act as ground crew while her husband and Mr Pickering ascended. However, a small rip had occurred during inflation, reducing the balloon's buoyancy, and at the last minute it was decided that the lighter Margaret should fly the balloon herself. When everything was organised and Margaret, prettily dressed as usual, was ready in the basket, the majestic balloon was released. It ascended slowly up into the air, catching a gentle breeze, and then floated straight into the upper side of a tall house surrounding the market square. Here the balloon snagged on a chimney. Margaret again showed enormous resilience, remaining cool and calm as she tried various ways to get out of this situation, despite being showered by bricks and mortar being dislodged off the roof as she pulled and pushed in her attempts to free the balloon. In the market square below, the public's cheering had diminished to a dramatic silence. It was no good and poor Margaret, in rather an undignified manner in her long skirt, had to climb out of the basket and managed to get through an upstairs attic window of the house. The balloon, now considerably lighter, was dragged off the roof by the wind and ascended gently into the sky and out of sight.

And so it went on, a busy life full of ups and downs and various incidents that caused minor damage and cost money. But ballooning was now their life; the Grahams described themselves as aeronauts and their entire lives revolved around flying displays. Margaret was a natural businesswoman and she quickly became very good at talking to the newspapers of the day. It all helped to draw the crowds for future shows.

Margaret also appeared to take motherhood in her stride. After Rebecca, Margaret gave birth to a series of children: Alice in 1829 and then, after a gap, Lydia, Frances, Jane, Edward and Margaret, all during the 1830s. Pregnancy did not stop her; she even did a couple of flights when she was many months pregnant, hiding her figure with a big colourful cloak that fitted in well with her love of dramatic performance.

Making a successful business from ballooning was no easier than it is today, for the weather in Britain is so often unsuitable. Generally, the low winds required for safe flight occur early in the morning or later in the evening, while paying crowds want displays in the middle of the day. The Grahams found this a continuing challenge. They took as many bookings as they could and having made the effort to reach the location and organise all the logistics, it is no wonder that they often tried to take off in unsuitable conditions. Every time they failed to take off, it cost them a huge amount of money.

George was getting older; in 1835 he was turning 50. Margaret, just entering her thirties, was becoming the more enthusiastic and energetic half of the partnership. While she had still only achieved fourteen flights, when she went up as a pilot she drew bigger crowds and more money. She was slowly becoming quite knowledgeable and skilled, learning how to control the ballast and, more importantly, how to vent enough gas to ensure a slow descent. She was also learning how to work out drift to land in open spaces, ideally sheltered by trees. By experimentation rather than instruction, she was becoming a real professional, although for the equipment she still relied on her husband, who would organise the logistics and oversee the complicated filling of the balloon.

So when, in August 1836, the Duke of Brunswick showed an interest in being taken for a flight, Margaret rather than George was the choice to fly this important aristocrat. Dressed in her brightly coloured green silk cloak which perfectly hid yet another pregnancy, she set off by trap for the Flora Tea Gardens, just north of London's Hyde Park, for her biggest display yet. George had gone earlier to oversee the filling of the balloon and, when she stepped down from the carriage at the tea gardens, Margaret must have felt she had really arrived. Many of Britain's leading aristocracy were gathered, dressed in gorgeous fashions and strolling around the charming gardens and little stream as they chatted among themselves. Another big moment came when Margaret was introduced to her passenger, His Serene Highness the Duke of Brunswick, a man of great self-importance and flamboyancy. Margaret loved it all, walking among the great and the good as the star of the show. There was a firm south-westerly breeze blowing across London at the time, but the park and launch site were wonderfully sheltered, surrounded by tall trees and some sturdy high buildings.

The launch of the balloon went well. The duke and Margaret looked down and waved at the spectacle of ladies in their lovely hats and smartly dressed gentlemen all staring up as the balloon rose slowly above the gardens. The balloon had been well filled with gas; there was no question of an aborted take-off here. The balloon continued to rise and, catching the wind, it started on an eastward trip. The duke was a demanding passenger and, as they travelled over London, he demanded they go higher and higher. He said he wanted to leave the view of the earth and experience the sky. Margaret, no doubt slightly overawed by her illustrious passenger, duly threw out most of the ballast and the balloon rose to a considerable height, higher than Margaret had ever flown before. After a good flight, Margaret felt it was time to descend, to try to spot where they were and think about landing. She vented some gas but wasn't sure if the balloon had responded; it was hard to judge any rate of descent from so high. So Margaret vented out some more gas. The balloon, initially slow to respond, now entered into a steady descent.

Margaret would have noticed, as they sunk into the farmland below, that not only were they being blown rapidly across the ground by a steady wind, but they were also coming down very fast indeed. However, having thrown out so much ballast to take the duke so high, she had little left to arrest the descent. The ground suddenly started approaching at an enormous speed and then, with a jarring bang, they hit the ground with considerable force. Quite what happened to Margaret is unclear as both she and the duke gave different stories to save face. The duke claimed he was thrown out of the basket by the force of the landing; Margaret's version was that, against instructions, he jumped out of the basket immediately, causing the then lighter balloon to rise again. Either way Margaret was left hanging on to the hoop of the balloon as it rose to about 30ft before she dropped off. While the duke was shaken but unharmed, Margaret had fallen from a considerable height and was lying in the field unconscious while the balloon, now with no load at all, ascended merrily back into the sky.

It was an ignominious end to what should have been a real highlight for Margaret, her planned triumphant return with the duke to meet the applause of the prestigious crowds still milling around the Flora Tea Gardens. Instead, a Mr Moir, the farmer who owned the land, rushed to the scene and carried Margaret back to his home, Converse Farm near Doddinghurst in Essex. A local doctor was soon called and within half an hour Margaret regained consciousness. However, she had bad head and back injuries and lost the baby she was carrying. It had been a nasty accident.

It must have been a very difficult time for Margaret. Despite the kindness of Mr Moir and his family, Margaret must have lain in bed in pain and worried. She had children to look after and an older husband well into middle age who was more of an inventor than a businessman. She had hit on a wonderful way to earn good money herself and even to become famous, yet suddenly she was incapable of doing anything and had no idea whether she would make a full recovery. Margaret, fretting and worrying, stayed at the Essex farm for four weeks until the end of September when, with one eye still closed and unable to walk across a room without assistance, she was taken back to her home in Poland Street, central London.

As Margaret lay recovering at home, surrounded by well wishes and family, her confidence returned. She became hopeful that, by the following year, she would be ready to fly again and bring in more money to help feed the growing family. She probably wouldn't have rested so easily if she had known that the most dramatic years of her flying career were still ahead.

Margaret spent the autumn of 1836 at home gradually getting her strength back. Money was still needed in the large household and George took over the flying again, giving a couple of successful displays, but he had lost his zest as a pilot. As the weather closed in, instead of organising shows, George spent the winter of 1836–7 working on an exciting new project, a proposed British Aeronautic Association which would promote geographic surveys by balloon.

In the meantime, cash was urgently needed for day-to-day living and Margaret became determined to get back into flying. By mid February 1837, the year she turned 33, she had made a good recovery and the weather was kind. She was ready to fly again. The Grahams' balloon was erected at the Yorkshire Stingo in Marylebone, central London. It was a semi-enclosed garden offering good protection for a balloon launch.

It seems minimal pre-advertising was done for this flight, indicating perhaps that Margaret was a little unsure of herself and wanted to get her first flight after the accident over with. It was only six months after the disastrous landing and this time, as she waited for the balloon to fill, Margaret must have been nervous. By 6 p.m. the balloon was ready to fly and Margaret was assisted into the balloon by her husband. She was then joined by a friend, Mr Warwick of the Surrey Zoological Gardens. The flight was short but it went well, ending with a soft, controlled landing, and Margaret started to regain her confidence.

After that, the Grahams were back in force, with the older George, now in his fifties, supervising the arrangements and Margaret doing virtually all the flying. The strong media coverage of her accident and then of her subsequent vigorous dispute with the Duke of Brunswick over the cause of the incident had ensured she was now very well known, so seeing her take off was a big attraction. As always, there were incidents, including an especially nasty accident when her grappling hook caught hold of an iron suspension bridge near Reigate in Surrey, and she was tipped out of the basket from a considerable height. Luckily, this time she landed in a soft field without injury.

Then, in 1838, possibly the grandest opportunity of all arrived. The official coronation of the new queen, Queen Victoria, was planned for Thursday 28 June. This would involve massive celebrations including a big fair in Hyde Park, central London.

Margaret soon obtained authorisation to give an aerial ascent from an adjoining launch point in Green Park. Coronation day dawned fine and clear and it must have been a very excited Graham household that woke up on the Thursday morning and carefully dressed for this splendid occasion. With all arrangements made in very good time, there was no problem gassing up the balloon and the take-off was easy and smooth, cheered on by thousands of onlookers. However, it was a day of very low wind and Margaret, once in the air, became quickly aware that there was no drift to enable her to reach an open area for landing. So, after a short flight, she descended carefully above a street. Venting gas, she then let down some ropes from the balloon and called down to the crowds below to help. Crowd control is always tricky and, on such a beautiful and exciting day, people thronged in enthusiastically to assist. Instead of a gentle pull to guide the balloon basket safely to the ground, a lot of keen helpers grabbed the ropes and pulled vigorously. This jerked the balloon downwards fast, but it was near a building and the netting of the balloon became caught up on the roof of an old house. As the crowd continued to heave, the netting dislodged two heavy stones from the roof which crashed down into the people below. The basket was grabbed and pulled down on to the ground and Margaret got out without a problem, but the envelope of the balloon had been badly torn and worse, two members of the crowd had been injured by the falling stones. One of them, a 26-year-old from Devon, died two weeks later. This was another unfortunate incident that the media played up and it began to strengthen the rumour that Margaret was an accident waiting to happen. There was the inevitable inquest and accusations about bad balloon handling, which Margaret tried to fend off as best she could in court.

After that, the next few years appeared slightly more peaceful. The Grahams continued to fly, usually with Margaret as the pilot, and apart from mishaps here and there, it was a relatively incident-free episode in her ballooning life. Margaret was still the only female aeronaut in Britain and no longer just a gimmick either. She was now a knowledgeable and proficient balloonist and, despite or perhaps because of the accidents, she was still a good crowd-puller.

A new decorated balloon called the *Royal Victoria and Albert* was constructed for the Grahams for the summer of 1850, and Margaret undertook the season in a confident mood. At 45, and after many pregnancies, she had put on some weight, but she still had amazing energy and enthusiasm to keep going. George, though, was approaching 65 and was becoming a far less active partner; he preferred to spend his time on a range of scientific interests. Margaret had now done over fifty ascents in a balloon and was quite happy to take over complete control.

Later that year, there was good news. Details were announced of a planned Great Exhibition to be held the following summer in 1851. It would be centred around a special Crystal Palace to be built in London's Hyde Park. The exhibition quickly became the talk of the town and Margaret recognised this as a huge opportunity. After the sad ending to her coronation display, this could be the really big one. It was the first ever World Fair and it was expected to be the most spectacular event ever, attracting crowds from across the nation and from overseas as well. While Margaret spent the winter looking after her large family, she also spent time booking various displays and, most importantly, working on all the details of a balloon flight at the exhibition.

The exhibition opened in May 1851, and from the very first day it created astonishment and was a huge success. The sensational centrepiece, constructed of cast iron with massive plates of glass, was unlike anything anyone had seen before. The building was 1,851ft long and 128ft high, and housed more than 14,000 exhibitions from around the world. There was now easy access to London by train and this brought in visitors from far and wide and the exhibition, which ran for six months to October 1851, was crowded out every day, attracting a total of around 6 million visitors.

Margaret had arranged with the organisers that she would do her first flight at the exhibition in mid June. She wanted to have a window of good weather before announcing the actual date. Her husband decided for once to join his wife on this prestigious flight. Great care was taken on all aspects and Batty's Hippodrome, an open-air amphitheatre in the adjacent Kensington Gardens, was chosen as the launch site.

Everything was organised in detail and to start with it all went exactly to plan. With a forecast of good weather, the date was decided and the announcements were made. The day dawned fine with gentle winds and, with a small team of helpers, the balloon was set up and filled. When Margaret and her husband stepped into the basket, they felt confident of a gentle flight over the crowds and they fully expected their flight to be recognised as one of the highlights of the exhibition.

As with so many of this determined lady's flights, it didn't quite work out as expected. When the tether ropes were released and the big balloon started to rise, it gently drifted directly into the top of one of the tall flag poles that surrounded the area, ripping a small tear in the fabric of the balloon. This, of course, released some gas, and as the balloon drifted onwards towards the beautiful Crystal Palace, there were fears that the balloon could collide with the top of the building, shattering the glass on to the crowds below. What a time for such an unfortunate incident! Margaret and George desperately jettisoned all their ballast, scattering sand on to the crowds looking up at them, and then they threw out everything else they could find. It was touch and go, but as they drifted on they managed to avoid a collision with the magnificent glass structure by just a few feet. But all was not well and the balloon was not gaining the height required for a good flight. Heading east, they began to lose height again as the gas steadily escaped and, before they knew it, they were skimming just above the buildings in Piccadilly. Then, as they descended even further, the inevitable happened. The Grahams' basket and grappling iron, the lowest points of the balloon, crashed hard into the roof of a four-storey house at 16 Arlington Street, just off Piccadilly. It had been a really violent collision which knocked masonry into the road below, and the Grahams were reported to have been thrown out of the basket on to the roof of the house, where they clung on in shock as they gathered their wits about them.

It had been a bad accident. George, at 66, no longer had the resilience of youth and had suffered a broken collarbone, deep cuts and bruising, and possibly some concussion. He may well have sustained other injuries as well. Margaret, in her late forties, fared better. Carrying a lot more padding than her husband, she sustained less serious injuries although she was still badly bruised and shaken. They were rescued with difficulty and taken into the house where they were attended by a local doctor before the police put them into a cab to take them back home. The balloon was torn and in a real mess. One police constable, who examined the balloon at Vine Street police station, commented that the silk was in a very decayed state. But the balloon was returned to the Grahams and eventually patched up. Unfortunately, the residents of Arlington Street were not impressed, and a substantial claim for damages was sent to the Grahams.

Why the balloon wasn't initially buoyant enough to ascend directly and fast out of the launch area avoiding the tall posts will never be known. Perhaps it was an unexpected gust that bounced the balloon on to one of the flagpoles; perhaps the balloon hadn't been filled very full so that it would drift low enough to be seen clearly by the crowds; perhaps, after much usage, the balloon was getting worn and the fabric porous. Whatever the cause, it was a disaster.

As the Grahams lay recovering in their Walworth home, the media had a field day. Along with official reports came vigorous comments from members of the public concerned with aviation accidents. A Mr Swaine, a regular contributor of angry letters to the newspapers of the day, wanted to know why, while there were laws to prevent men damaging each other on the ground, this adventurous female, through mismanagement of a balloon, was being allowed to continuously knock housetops upon innocent passers-by and to imperil her own life as well as the lives of others.

Margaret might still have been nursing her injuries but nevertheless, even in this Victorian age of gentle manners and fragile femininity, she wasn't having this. She replied robustly and fluently to any criticism including long drawn-out acidic responses to Mr Swaine. The media loved it and their continuing correspondence entertained readers across the nation.

The couple were lucky; they could easily have fallen from the rooftop on to the hard pavement below, but the crash was enough to persuade George that his ballooning days really should be put behind him. While he still liked to call himself an aeronaut, on his daughter's subsequent marriage certificate he changed his occupation to chemist and he clearly had many other interests to concentrate on.

Margaret, though, wanted to keep going. With unmarried children still at home, ballooning, when it worked, was such a good way to make money. With all her experience, she clearly felt she could go on. By the end of August 1851, at 47 years of age, she made her seventieth flight at a charming local fete at Rotherhithe, east London, surrounded by bands, bell ringers, a steam engine, singers and an illuminated railway. She then made another successful flight near Bury St Edmund's in Suffolk which, according to the two passengers she took up with her, offered wonderful vistas from the basket.

That winter, though, her adventurous life began to take its toll and she booked far fewer displays than usual for the following season. In fact, she was only going to take off another eight to ten times in her life, putting on just a handful of flying exhibitions during the next couple of years. There were the normal hiccups associated with this weather-reliant pastime, including a legal claim for a non-show and a display at London's Hoxton where the balloon, before being attached to the basket, escaped during the fuelling process and flew off by itself. In 1853 Margaret undertook a tour of Ireland with all the logistics involved in getting a balloon across the Irish Sea. Along with two very successful flights, she had a slight collision with a roof on one of the flights in Dublin. But the incident was minor and without injuries.

Sadly, in 1856, her eldest daughter died but Margaret also had several grandchildren who appeared close. This must have brought her comfort and happiness as she entered her mid fifties and began to realise that her ballooning days were drawing to a close.

The Grahams may have relinquished their balloon at this time because they now moved to a house in Eastcheap, just east of London Bridge. Three of Margaret's children were still living at home: Jane (22) and Margaret (17), who were both working as needlewomen, plus their son Edward (19) who had enrolled in the Surrey Volunteers. While Margaret was still involved in her family, George was continuing with his lifelong interest in mystical topics and science.

The family then moved to 109 Upper Thames Street, London, nearer the river, and here Margaret spent the last few years of her life. She died in 1864, aged 60, from what was then diagnosed as dropsy but was probably some sort of heart condition.

Margaret had set the scene for women to make a real contribution to flight but in her last few years there was no obvious replacement to carry on the work. None of her children took up ballooning and, while men continued to experiment with a range of ideas, there were few women becoming involved in any way at all. It was not until much nearer the end of the century that British women jumped back into the extraordinary and exciting world of aviation.

4

EMILY DE VOY

1889
THE FIRST FEMALE BRITISH PARACHUTIST

By the mid 1860s ballooning was well underway, but so were a mass of other ideas and experiments as people across the world tried to get into the air. Parachutes were only slowly evolving. Since 1797, when Andre Garnerin made the first descent in a frameless parachute and, in 1804, when Jerome Lalande introduced a vent in the parachute canopy to reduce the violent swinging, there had been no dramatic breakthrough. There were only a handful of fearless enthusiasts who attempted descents by parachute including poor Robert Cocking who fell to his death from a jump from a balloon in 1837 in central London. The following year John Hampton became the official first successful British parachutist when, in 1838, he made a descent at Montpelier Gardens in Cheltenham – and survived!

As the century moved on, more women were beginning to show an interest in aviation and certainly, for a few courageous or sometimes desperate women, it could now offer employment thanks to male balloon owners anxious to add something new to their balloon displays. Women holding flags as they ascended in a basket; women being taken up sitting and waving as they clung on to a trapeze fixed below a tethered captive balloon; balloonists were looking for every gimmick possible to attract crowds and income. While performances still attracted big audiences, not everyone was in favour. Queen Victoria had already written to a show organiser expressing her strong disapproval of young girls risking their lives by giving aerial performances, and this highlighted a growing sentiment among the public.

None of this worried young Londoner Emily de Voy, however, when she decided to be Britain's first ever female skydiver in 1889. By the time she entered the scene, the old cumbersome rigid parachutes had been superseded by new conical parachutes made in lighter weight fabrics. These would blossom out into a full parachute once the fabric caught the air.

There was also a new way to attach this type of parachute to a balloon while it was lifted up to height. It was called a static line and had been developed by American Mr Van Tassell in 1888 just a year before Emily's first jump. A thin break cord, or cotton tape, would tie the top of the parachute to the balloon. This cord easily broke once it had any weight on it. When a parachutist jumped and pulled the parachute down behind them, the static line would snap, freeing the balloon. Then the parachute, being pulled down by the jumper, would catch the air and billow out into its full shape. It was a neat arrangement. Even Van Tassell's young American wife Jenny had given it a test, and it worked.

By the following year, 1889, parachuting had already become quite developed and while Emily De Voy wasn't going to be the first ever female parachutist in the world, she was certainly leading the way in Britain. At 19 years old, she was young and confident but, even so, surely she would have felt just a little apprehensive as she got ready for her first parachute jump in Cheltenham in May of that year. It was not going to be an event for the faint hearted.

But Emily De Voy wasn't a stranger to challenges. Born as Emma Dovey in May 1869 into a poor family in St Pancras, central London, life as she grew up was not much fun. Her parents John and Bridget had married in 1852 and set up home in what was then a very poor area of London. It was adjacent to Agar Town near St Pancras, which was described as one of the most run-down areas in the city, with wretched hovels and roads a complete bog of mud and filth. There was no sewage system and a lot of sickness.

But things were tolerable. Her father John was working as a shoemaker and there was just enough money to keep the family and home together. For some years things were okay until the 1860s when Agar Town was demolished to make way for the ever-expanding railway systems into London's St Pancras and King's Cross stations. This was a common event at this time, and it was estimated that overall railway clearances evicted nearly 60,000 people, mainly from the poorer working classes, to make room for the new train systems.

The Doveys' home and the adjacent shoe shop, which took and sold John's carefully made products, disappeared, and that meant any income disappeared as well. As both money and food ran out, there was no alternative. In 1872, Mrs Dovey and her children, including 3-year-old Emily, were admitted into the St Pancras workhouse.

The whole experience must have been horrifying but for young Emily there was a fraction of light. The year before her birth, the St Pancras Guardians decided to build a new industrial school for pauper children in the parish. They built a splendid new building on 38 acres in what was then open countryside at Leavesden, Hertfordshire. While no one chose to go into a workhouse, at least for Emily it meant a dry bed, food and lessons. As soon as they were old enough, the children were found positions in domestic service and this is what happened to the Dovey girls.

Emily's older sister Matilda linked up with and then married a Mr George Higgins, who had come from a very poor family in Buckinghamshire but was making a good living as a coachman in London. Through his work George met a professional balloonist who was including parachuting displays from a balloon as an extra attraction. George was immediately taken with the idea. He learned all he could before his ballooning friend died in an accident in August 1888 and George decided he could take over.

During regular visits to her sister, Emily showed a serious interest in George's aerial activities and a willingness to be involved. George, 18 years older than Emily, realised, like many before him, that if he included a young woman in his aerial activities, there was potential for much more interest, sponsorship and income.

While his wife Matilda was busy looking after the family, George started training up his young sister-in-law. At the time he was using a parachute built with light canvas attached to flexible wickerwork ribs, although he modified this later. He built a small hanging trapeze at the family home in Clapton, London, and tested Emily's strength. He talked her through how a parachute works and what happens on a flight during the ascent and descent, ensuring she understood all aspects. Emily even did some practice landings, rolling on to her back to distribute the weight away from her feet. At 19 years old, she was up for it all.

George was thorough and also wasn't slow in getting organised. He had by now already done ten jumps, sitting on a trapeze as he ascended under an unmanned balloon and then releasing himself, and he felt he had a good understanding of what made a popular display. He was also an astute businessman and managed to get Kendall and Dent, a firm of watchmakers in Cheapside, London, to pay for a new 23,000 cubic ft, 53ft-high balloon. In addition, he obtained two new parachutes, both about 28ft in diameter and made of silk. For Emily's first jump, he had worked out a plan to put on a spectacular double parachute display with both of them jumping at the same time. This, thought George, should really attract the crowds. What his wife Matilda thought about all this is unrecorded but clearly George was not spending a great deal of time with his family. With young Emily an enthusiastic participant, the date for the first double jump was set for May 1889 at a show in Pittville Park in Cheltenham. A woman parachutist had never been seen in Britain before; it was very big news indeed, and it was at this point that Emily changed her birth name of Emma Dovey to Emily De Voy, more appropriate for the new star attraction. What to wear was the next consideration; the long flowing skirts of the age would not in any way be suitable for a lady parachutist. To solve this problem, Emily dressed in adapted men's clothes – in those strict Victorian days, these alone would have been quite a talking point.

Travelling up to Cheltenham to stay overnight at the Royal Hotel with an older man who was also the husband of your sister would not have been acceptable in normal Victorian circles, but Emily was probably too excited about the whole event to worry too much about these niceties. On Saturday, 4 May 1889, they reached the park early. The display was scheduled for late afternoon but the laborious process of filling the balloon with gas took a long time, so preparations started in the morning.

During the hours while the balloon was being filled, thousands of excited people poured into the park, buzzing with anticipation. Was a woman really going to parachute through the sky and fall to the earth?

Eventually all was ready and the balloon was standing upright, firm and buoyant, while the weather, clear with a soft breeze, was perfect. There was no passenger basket. Instead, there were two seating trapezes hanging below the mouth of the balloon. The top of each parachute had been attached to the side of the balloon with a break tie and, from the bottom of the parachute canopy, long lines ran down which were tied on to a small circular ring. This ring in turn was attached to a simple leather harness-and-belt affair for the parachutist. It was a very basic, uncomplicated system but it worked; George had already jumped successfully. There was no reason why it shouldn't work for Emily.

In front of the enthusiastic crowd and a mass of helpers, Emily and George walked up to the balloon and put on their harnesses. This time it was for real. The noise from the crowd diminished slightly as they watched George carefully doing a final check on Emily's harness and the attachments. As Emily waited, she would have been more than aware that she was the focus of thousands of eyes. It took a great deal of courage and control for her to concentrate.

When all was ready, Emily and George sat themselves carefully on the two swaying trapezes below the balloon. The plan was that they would sit there, holding the sides, while they ascended. When they were at sufficient height, they would push off their trapezes and fall down, pulling the parachutes behind them. There was quite a bit to think about and Emily must have been in a bit of a daze. The buzz of the huge crowd would have reverberated in her ears as she saw the large balloon gently swaying above her and her parachute hanging limply down from the side. It all must have been a surreal moment for this young girl from a workhouse. Even if she had wanted to, by now it was far too late to back out.

George would have given her some final encouragement and also reminders; hang on really firmly to the sides of the trapeze: don't let go until I give the word. It was vital not to slip off the trapeze early at too low a height.

Once everything was ready and Emily and George were safely seated, the order was given to let go and the twenty or thirty members of local army reserves who had been firmly holding the balloon down released their grasp. The balloon, to the cheers of a massive crowd and with Emily experiencing her first ever flight, lifted smoothly up from the ground.

Emily, clutching on very firmly indeed, would have looked down to see her feet dangling above the green park with its throngs of people and sea of upturned faces; people who gradually became smaller and smaller as she ascended into the air. While she had the comfort of knowing George had jumped successfully before, nevertheless the reality of being high above the earth on such a flimsy swinging perch would have hit her. It must have been totally terrifying. She held on very tightly indeed as they climbed higher and higher. With no wind noise, George could talk to her easily, ensuring all was well and pointing out landing places below, but Emily may well have stopped looking down, concentrating all her efforts on the idea of launching herself into space when the time came. It took a little while but eventually the balloon reached around 3,000ft and, with the green fields of the Gloucestershire countryside spread out below her, George told her it was time to go.

This was the moment. Emily was resolute. Stopping herself from thinking too hard, she summoned up her courage and energy and then she let go of the trapeze and pushed forward. Those first few seconds would hardly have registered as she dropped fast down through an empty sky. Then, with a sudden hard jerk on her harness, high above her the parachute caught the air and opened up. Instantly everything stopped, and there she was hanging quietly below a big round parachute. There was some early oscillation, swinging Emily back and forth, but then the motion calmed down and she started descending in a more orderly and gentle fashion.

She had done it! After a mind-numbing flash of sheer terror, suddenly it was all over. There she was safe, hanging below a fully open parachute. The relief must have been totally exhilarating and, for a moment, she would have just hung there amazed at what she had done. The days of anticipation and preparation were over and the silence suddenly engulfed her. She was alone in the sky, floating down gently towards the earth. Her leather strapping held her firmly attached to the ring which was holding the lines of the parachute, and high above that, outlined against the sky, was the sturdy white fabric of the fully open parachute canopy. It had all worked according to plan. Looking around at the distant horizon, the small fields and the crowds in the park, the feeling of excited relief was almost overwhelming. She really had done it!

But then, after only a short time, reality would have stepped in again as she could see the earth coming up fairly steadily. She was heading for a large field near the racecourse and she saw some cattle running away as she approached the area. As the grass got nearer and nearer, she prepared herself for a landing and then, in an unexpected instant, she was down. Of slight stature, Emily had landed softly without any drama. She could almost have stood up. It must have been a totally wonderful moment for this young girl who had had such a challenging start to life. Picking herself up and gathering up the parachute fabric and its lines, she would have been in a state of high excitement as she waited to be collected.

George Higgins had risen a little higher in the balloon before jumping off, and had landed in the orchard of Prestbury Park Farm a little distance away. He came into contact with the lower branches of an apple tree on his landing, but no damage was done. Soon both successful parachutists had been found and were installed in a pony carriage where Emily would have eagerly recounted her experiences as they headed back to big celebrations in Cheltenham. Here, Emily was the major centre of attraction with an applauding crowd all wanting to see her and know more about the only woman in

Britain (and one of just a handful in the world) who had attempted this astonishingly daring feat.

George told the excited crowds that Miss De Voy had ascended to a height of 3,500ft and dropped over 100ft through the air before her parachute started to open. The crowds thronged around to hear more and it was some time before George and Emily could finally get away. They collected the balloon which had deflated soon after George had jumped thanks to a clever little system. A small bag filled with sand was attached to the top of the balloon. As soon as George's weight had gone from the balloon, this small bag then became the heaviest aspect of the balloon and would fall to earth, turning the balloon envelope upside down. With the mouth of the balloon now facing upwards, the gas would escape, the balloon would collapse and it would fall down to the ground. It was a neat and simple arrangement.

Having retrieved their balloon, the couple returned to the Royal Hotel for a celebratory evening. After such a successful event another display was quickly arranged, this time in Manchester, and the booking prompted George to move right out of London. The situation with his wife Matilda in London was probably becoming decidedly tricky as he and Emily became closer. Separation by distance probably seemed a very good idea. George obtained a job as landlord of the Lord Nelson Inn in Monks Coppenhall, now incorporated into central Crewe in Cheshire. It was a good base for his aviation display business as there seemed more scope to book displays across the north of England than the south, where most of the current balloonists operated. It was all organised quickly, and with accommodation available in the pub, Emily moved up happily with him. It is doubtful she received a fond farewell from her sister.

Their first display in the north was at Manchester Racecourse, not too far from their new home. It was scheduled for the end of May 1889, just under three weeks after Emily had made her first successful descent, and the same pattern was followed, with a slow filling of the balloon and an early evening ascent. Again they were lucky with the weather, with few clouds and low winds. Emily would have had a different set of emotions this time: less panic as she had already done a jump, but increased scary awareness of the detail and what was going on. As they rose above Manchester, she would have heard more clearly the fading cheers of the crowd as they ascended and been more conscious of the height and distance down to earth. As the town and then countryside spread out below her, she would without doubt have experienced a serious flutter of nerves as they got higher and higher.

But the routine was the same and, once they reached sufficient height and still within viewing distance of the crowds at the racecourse, Emily launched herself off the trapeze. Again there was a breathtaking moment of fast falling and air rushing past and then the sudden jerk as her fall was arrested by the opening parachute. This time she experienced a really vigorous oscillation, but as the world began to steady she could look around to see where she was heading. The light wind was carrying Emily above the workings of the Manchester Ship Canal, which was under construction. But again all was well, and she cleared it easily to make a gentle landing on a clear grass area.

George, meanwhile, had again risen a little higher before jumping and had caught a slight northerly drift. The crowds on the ground noted he was swinging and kicking under the parachute trying to alter its course but with the light wind he wasn't travelling any distance and he landed right on the edge of the racecourse. Once George had jumped, the balloon turned itself upside down by the weight at the top, lost its gas and lift, and fell to earth, also landing back on the racecourse.

It was a tidy, professional display and again the audience just loved it. George addressed the crowds after they arrived back and the couple were met with prolonged enthusiastic cheering before they finally left the grounds. What with the wages from the pub and income from their dramatic parachuting displays, George and Emily must have been feeling good about life.

With their dramatic double parachuting show, displays were not hard to find. In June the couple put on an excellent show at the Stanley Hospital gala, a fundraiser in the Bootle area of Liverpool. For this show, Emily went higher than usual before jumping and then they were invited to attend the local Westminster Music Hall in nearby Kirkdale. At the end of the show George and Emily were invited on to the stage where the proprietor of the hall, Mr James Kiernan, introduced them to the large audience who responded with a tumultuous welcome. He then presented Emily with a lovely brooch studded with tiny diamonds and a pair of earrings in recognition of the skill and bravery she had displayed. Altogether it had been a really successful trip and after staying in a nearby hotel, they departed, still tired but happy, back down to Crewe.

Emily, as a female parachutist, was becoming quite a celebrity, with reports on her exploits appearing in newspapers up and down the country. People wanted to know more about her, and various newspapers remarked on her gentle, quiet demeanour, her pale but regular features and even the firm set of her jaw. Instead of chasing displays, they began to be inundated with offers. George Higgins, businessman that he was, put up their minimum fee to £200, a huge amount in the 1880s, and still they were turning down requests for displays.

By July they had fine-tuned their tentative double act into a really professional show. The couple would arrive at a showground with various helpers, the balloon would be laid out and the inflation begun. Emily was now helping with all aspects of the operations but, with fast growing confidence, she was also becoming adept at talking to the crowd. She gave lively anecdotes of her parachuting and began describing herself as the only female parachutist in the world. The crowds loved it all. The couple had special matching costumes made out of blue serge with gold lace trimmings which evidently showed off Emily's petite figure to exceptional advantage.

Sometimes, such as for a show they did in July in Leicester, they didn't sit on a trapeze below the balloon. Instead, a small passenger-carrying car would be attached to the balloon and the couple would sit on the side of the basketwork, dangling their legs over, waiting for the moment to jump. This meant that a balloon pilot would have to take them up, but it also meant they could take a fare-paying passenger up as well; someone who was willing to pay extra money to see this brave couple plunge into the air.

It wasn't all smooth sailing. In late August 1889, in Barrow, George decided it was too windy for lightweight Emily to jump. However, with thousands in the showground, he decided to take off to give some sort of show but as the balloon was released, George's trapeze seat caught against some nearby wires, dislodging him from his seat. He fell fast to the ground, pulling the parachute behind him but with no time for it to open. He landed hard, knocking himself unconscious and breaking an ankle.

That meant he was out of action for a few weeks as he recuperated at home. This was not the best timing as it was the peak period for displays in England. Also, they were becoming aware that competition was growing. There was even another woman who had started giving successful parachute displays now, an American. Alma Beaumont, only 22 years old, was the daughter of a well-known American balloonist and, after doing some jumps in America, headed for unknown reasons to England, where she began making descents mainly in the north of the country.

With George recovering from a broken ankle, Emily saw no reason why she couldn't continue with the displays on her own. She had learned so much that summer, and while their double parachute descent had always attracted the crowds, a single parachute descent by a lady on her own would surely also be a big crowd-puller. Emily was determined to bring the attention back from Alma Beaumont, the American interloper.

Even better, why not go for a new height record as well? In early October Emily, after a final check of her parachute and the attachments, took off from the Pleasure Gardens in Preston and rose to an estimated 5,000ft before jumping off into the cool air, dragging the parachute down behind her. The breaktie, which connected the top of the parachute to the balloon, broke easily and after a short fall with the cool wind rushing against her face, Emily felt the customary jerk as the parachute fabric caught the air above her and spread out into its full shape. It was a very successful descent. Just two weeks later, Emily decided there was no reason why she couldn't go even higher.

A display was arranged at Wolverhampton for the end of the month. The weather was beginning to close in; the long calm evenings of summer had disappeared. However, a nearby large high-pressure system ensured one of those beautiful calm early autumn days that can happen in England in late October, with a soft but chilly breeze coming from the south-east. At this time, the town was fast establishing a reputation for being the leading bicycle-making area of the country and, despite the cooler weather, many people pedalled to the park to watch this parachute display by a lady.

George was now fit enough to help Emily with the preparations and, harnessed safely to the ring of her parachute, Emily took off on time, swinging gently below her well-filled gas balloon. The air became chillier as she climbed but at least there was no wind-chill factor, and the balloon moved with the air flow. Hanging on tightly, she climbed higher and higher. Soon she was out of sight from the crowd and they started to disperse. Her hands may well have become a little numb as she hung on firmly as she rose to 7,000ft, 8,000ft and then 9,000ft. Looking down, the town and its surrounding fields were disappearing in an early evening darkening haze and she would have felt very quiet, very alone and rather small as she hung there in silence, lifting further and further into the sky.

In those days, if properly set, aneroid barometers were quite sophisticated, calculating air pressure to indicate height and, after the jump, George reported that an aneroid barometer attached to the balloon showed Emily had risen to 10,000ft. Bearing in mind this was very much showbusiness as well as serious aerial activity, there appears some doubt about this height or indeed whether an aneroid barometer had been used at all. Nevertheless, Emily had definitely reached a considerable height and this was certainly her highest jump yet.

It all went very well. After she launched herself off into the hazy, darkening sky, the parachute spread out fully above her and Emily had a long slow swinging descent down to the earth below. She landed in a field some miles away from the town and a witness described her as alighting from her harness with the utmost ease without any injury whatsoever. Whether the media were getting tired of aviation activities or because of some doubt about the height of the jump, there was less acclaim for this achievement than would have been expected. It warranted just a paragraph or two in the general media. Nevertheless, it was a great finale to what overall had been an amazing season for Emily who, just a year before, had been a poor working girl in London. She had a solid home, a terrific partner and an excellent income; the future was looking very good indeed.

With British weather, shows were put on hold for the winter but, after a few months of just running the pub and arranging forthcoming displays, by early spring 1890 George and Emily were off again. By April, just under a year from her very first jump, Emily had made over fifty parachute descents and now her performances were becoming more routine. The main setback was weather. George started releasing a small gas balloon before they took off so that he could see which way it went, giving him an idea of the speed and direction of the wind at upper levels and what to expect once they had taken off.

There were, of course, the usual adventures and odd mishaps in the course of displays up and down the country, but generally it all went very well. But as the spring weather of 1890 turned to summer, competition was hotting up. Male balloonists had quickly noted the publicity that had been given to Emily and once again started searching for young girls willing to take some risk for the chance of money and fame. Women jumpers suddenly started appearing and also grabbing headlines. In July, young Adelaide Bassett made a successful parachute descent in Bury St Edmunds and Maud Brooks did a good jump at Cleckheaton Agricultural Show in Yorkshire. London parachutist Ida McDonald made the news when her balloon was released and started to lift before she was fully prepared and before the parachute had been connected to the balloon. Even worse, the main attachment for Ida hadn't been fitted properly either, and she was pulled up into the air connected by only one thin rope, pulling her parachute up below her. The balloon rose to over 2,000ft before the rope broke and down Ida fell, doubtless in a high state of anxiety wondering if the limp, upside-down parachute hanging down below her would work. She overtook the parachute as she fell through the air and then, with her weight below and the drag now on its periphery, the parachute partially inflated, allowing her a slow enough descent to the ground to survive with only minor injuries.

For the female jumpers of that summer, though, it was all about partnerships. Emily with George, Maud Brooks under the instruction of a Captain Whelan and Adelaide Bassett supported by a Captain Orton; all the displays involving women were still very much driven by men. This was not because of lack of interest, courage or innovative ideas on behalf of women; instead it was simply a reflection of society and a general lack of opportunity available to women at the time.

Emily and George continued their successful aviation displays through the summer of 1890. During the winter, they ran the pub while planning displays for the following summer.

Unaware that this season would mark the end of Emily's extraordinary career, a large number of shows were booked throughout the summer, starting earlier in the year than usual. One of the first displays of 1891 nearly ended in disaster when Emily landed in the deep waters of the Welsh Harp in north London. Luckily, a nearby boatman rescued her quickly and there was no real damage. But the season went on with generally successful descents and very good money being paid by spectators. Despite the growing competition, Emily was still the most famous parachutist and all went well until August.

On Saturday 15 August 1891, the couple had booked a display in Kirkstall, Leeds. Everything was going as planned and, with both of them safely seated on their trapezes, the balloon was about to be released when Emily noticed a large tear commencing at the mouth of the balloon and extending up about 3ft. She immediately got off her trapeze and called out to everyone. However, at the very same time, George had given the word to let go, and the balloon was released. While Emily remained on the ground, the balloon, with George sitting on his trapeze, started to rise. Because of the tear, gas was pouring out and the balloon lifted slowly, drifting sideways and sluggishly climbing high enough to just clear some telegraph wires. Telegraph wires were by now beginning to criss-cross the country everywhere and were a growing hazard for balloonists. George's legs, dangling down below the trapeze, caught the wires and, while this had happened once before, this time the outcome was truly tragic. Catching his foot on the wire as the balloon dragged him past, George was flipped off his trapeze and fell heavily to the ground, a drop of about 35ft. It had not been high enough for the parachute to open. George hit a hard barricade and then bounced on to the ground as he landed. Despite being reached quickly by the crew of the local infirmary ambulance, he died soon afterwards.

This was a shattering blow for Emily. There was a lot of publicity about the accident, of course, and a public collection was started for her, as many believed her to be George's young widow. However, at the official enquiry into the accident, the court got a shock. George's still legal wife Matilda turned up to tell the court that she was the official marriage partner and mother to their children. How Emily greeted her sister is not clear, but it was unlikely to have been a joyous reunion! Matilda subsequently received some of the donated money and the women once again went their separate ways.

Emily had many supporters, including George's brother Charles, who assisted her during the inquest and subsequent weeks, and she was clearly keen to keep up her parachuting. It had been her life and livelihood, and what else was she to do? Just two weeks after the inquest she did a successful jump at Todmorton, north-west of Manchester, possibly still in a daze but wanting to keep the show on the road. But without George's ability, technical knowledge and enthusiasm, it was hard. The following year Emily changed her name to Emmie, perhaps to help start her new life, and signed up with another leading aeronaut, Richard Baldwin, but the enthusiasm and dedication weren't there and she was really now just a hired parachutist with a great deal of competition from new women on the scene.

After a handful of displays in 1892 and 1893, she began taking bookings organised for her by the famous Spencer ballooning family, but with far less involvement in the displays than she had had in the past. Often, she would simply turn up by train, perhaps give a talk, do the jump and, possibly after a night in a hotel, get back on a train to go home.

By now there were more and more women trying to get their share of the excellent money offered by dramatic parachute displays. Incidents were common and these, together with the media being crowded with international events and developments, meant that the big newsworthy days for Emily were over. Gradually she faded from the public arena and her last event appears to have been in 1895, when she did a spectacular jump in Luton that nearly went very wrong indeed. Soon after she took off, the break tie that connected the top of her parachute to the balloon broke and the parachute fell beneath her as she rose into the sky. She was concerned she could get entangled in the parachute flapping about below so she held on to her trapeze, which she said afterwards was pretty tricky as the parachute was catching the wind and pulling at her vigorously. But she gripped tightly and stayed with the balloon to an immense height to give her as much time as possible to sort out the mess. When eventually her fingers were so cold and numb that she finally had to let go, she fell clean into the fabric of the upside-down billowing parachute below her. Luck was with her though. After vigorously trying to disentangle herself as she and the parachute fell fast down through the air, she finally managed to free herself from the fabric and, still trying to escape the tangled lines, she tumbled below the chute. Eventually the parachute flapped open into a fairly stable shape above her, slowing her descent to a just acceptable level, and she landed hard but safely. Having been picked up, she headed back very late to the gathering who had patiently waited to welcome her, and she gave a professional and unruffled talk. She did, however, say, 'I have never had such an escape and I never want another like it.' She then shook hands and, reportedly in good spirits, hurried off to get her train home.

This incident had taken its toll, though, as this appears to have been her last ever parachute descent. She would have realised how perilous the jump had been plus she had also lost her supportive partner and close associate. It was probably not a hard decision to accept that her jumping days were over.

Emily faded rapidly from the public arena. It seems she may have gone back to domestic service with a family who were involved in the balloon business, at least giving Emily a tenuous link to the days when she was queen of the sky.

5

DOROTHY PILCHER AND ROSE SPENCER

DOROTHY PILCHER, 1897
THE FIRST BRITISH WOMAN TO DO A FIXED-WING GLIDING FLIGHT

In the final years of the nineteenth century, the glory days of ballooning and parachuting were slowing down. While aerial displays still attracted good crowds, the real interest was heading towards the amazing advances being made in the world of heavier-than-air flight.

Knowledge was by now extensive, with substantial understanding of lift and theory. Experiments and trials were going on across the world with fabulous new ideas plus splendid and, in some cases, astonishing machines being built. Curved aerofoil sections, multi-wings and monoplanes; every aspect of basic flight was under examination and re-evaluation. Some achieved a degree of success with even short hops off the ground. Others, such as experiments with incredibly heavy steam-powered planes or projects based on the 'more wings the merrier' theory, offered at least tremendous entertainment.

It would still be a little while before British women really came into their own in aviation, but they were now beginning to seriously nibble around the edges and, across the land, women as well as men would have been watching and talking about the dramatic progress that was being made. But was it Ella or Dorothy Pilcher who was the very first British woman to make a flight in a heavier-than-airmachine?

The Pilchers were everywhere in late Victorian England, one of those huge families which were fairly common in this era. Lots of brothers and sisters all having children who in turn had lots of children; when you were born a Pilcher you were never alone in the world. Ella and Dorothy Pilcher were first cousins once removed and records indicate that it was the younger Dorothy who became the first British woman ever to go gliding and the first woman to be lifted off the ground by a fixed-wing aircraft. But this would never have happened without the help of Ella, who was absolutely key to the groundbreaking development of this early person-carrying gliding vehicle.

Ella, born in 1863, was 4 when her younger brother Percy was born in 1867 and they both had a tricky upbringing. Their father died young and their mother was left with very little money. Soon after she was widowed, Ella and Percy's mother took them to Germany, but more tragedy was just around the corner when she also died, in May 1877. Ella, at 14, and Percy, aged 10, were now parentless, overseas and with very little money – not an auspicious start in life. But thanks to financial support and direction from an older brother and maybe other members of the extensive Pilcher family, the children were brought back to England to stay with relations. Ella finished her schooling while Percy headed for a naval career; he joined the British navy when he was just 13.

After their mother's death Ella may have felt responsible for Percy. She followed his career carefully and, when he left the navy in 1887 to take up an engineering apprenticeship in Glasgow, 24-year-old Ella quickly agreed to join him to help look after the house. They moved south for a spell and then, in 1891, moved back to Glasgow. Percy had been offered the job of assistant to a professor at Glasgow University and Ella was very happy to move up with him, ensuring he had comfortable lodgings and, each evening, a meal on the table to welcome him home.

By then Percy had become obsessed by the idea of flight and his new position gave him time to develop his interest and undertake experiments. Right from the beginning, Ella became fully absorbed in her brother's pursuits, helping not only with looking after the household but also with the sewing and construction involved in first small model versions and then full-sized experimental man-carrying gliders. In the rugged open countryside outside Glasgow, Ella endured many a freezing hour as she helped to put together, balance and then test Percy's early flying machines. Despite the restrictive long skirts of the day, Ella helped carry cumbersome equipment and strode stoically up and down through damp grass on sloping hills as Percy tested his new home-built gliders. She must have loved her younger brother very much.

Percy watched carefully the developments in aviation going on around the world; his knowledge of German would have been useful when he corresponded with and then went over to Germany in 1895 to talk to Otto Lilienthal, who was also helping to lead the world in the development of man-carrying gliders.

Before long Percy was making serious inroads into developing a powered man-carrying aircraft and was fast becoming recognised as a leading expert and pioneer in flight. Ella, so involved in design and construction, would also have been at the forefront of understanding the full theory of flight and the latest exciting breakthroughs. A major problem was to develop an engine that was lightweight but still able to provide adequate power, and then to try to design a wing that would give enough lift to cover the additional weight of this engine. Percy, along with others, quickly found that simply increasing the wing area to give extra lift also added too much extra weight to a machine. Percy corresponded with all the leading names in the world who were also working on similar problems, including the perceived solution of stacking wings above each other to generate more lift. There appeared to be no easy answer. Ella understood the problems and would spend time listening to Percy and sometimes making useful suggestions as well as being responsible for creating and sewing the fabric areas for the planes.

Percy decided to revert to single-winged planes but increase the central upward curve or camber in the wings. This is today an accepted fundamental of flight: a cambered wing means air passes more quickly over the top surface of the wing than below it. This results in lower pressure over the top of the wing than the bottom and this works as a basis for lift. By March 1896, Percy had built a new glider which included deeply cambered wings. He called this the *Hawk*. Again Ella was heavily involved in all aspects of the construction and the testing.

When Percy resigned from Glasgow University in spring 1896, 33-year-old Ella happily moved south with him so that they could base themselves in London. Percy and Ella were now very excited about their breakthrough designs and Percy was becoming well known for his aviation exploits. His futuristic plans for a flying machine with an engine and a screw propeller to push it through the air were attracting a lot of attention.

With Ella constantly at Percy's side, there is a small chance that during their hours of testing, both in Scotland and at other sites including in Kent, she might have stepped into the harness for a short hop in a trial flight off the ground. But there are no records of this and the general consensus is that it was Dorothy Pilcher, Ella's much younger first cousin once removed, who was the very first British woman to fly in a heavier-than-air machine when she stepped into a harness below Percy's glider on a momentous day in Kent.

Dorothy Pilcher was nineteen years younger than Ella and had had a very different upbringing, with a childhood spent in privileged homes supported at times by maids, cooks and even under-footmen. As Dorothy entered her teens, her family had moved to an elegant large house in central London and undoubtably her relations Ella and Percy Pilcher would have been talked about over the dinner table. It is more than likely that on occasions Ella and Percy also called round to give tantalising accounts of their aviation exploits, the flying machines they were developing and their planned trials.

Dorothy grew into a young and lively teenager yearning for adventure, and she would have been enthralled by the stories and experiences of her older Pilcher relations. When Percy, in order to raise interest and additional funding, eventually decided to give his first public demonstration of the *Hawk*, his latest flying machine, enthusiastic Dorothy was not going to miss out.

It was an easy train ride from central London out to Eynsford in Kent, and on Sunday 20 June 1897 Dorothy joined a large group of spectators to watch Percy's latest experiment in man-carrying flying machines. Cousin Ella, as always, was a key player and co-organiser of the event, first acting as an efficient hostess offering tea to all the visitors and then assisting with the setting up of Percy's *Hawk* machine.

The Pilchers' latest machine was constructed mainly in bamboo together with fabric and wires. Its wings were 24.6ft by 18.5ft and it weighed just 50lb. Originally, Percy did away with a vertical rudder on the plane, as he felt it managed well without that extra weight in low wind, but after some early tests he found he would drift sideways fast and on one occasion he was turned upside down when a gust caught a wing tip. So he went back to including a rudder at the back of the plane. He did find, however, that he could steer sideways to a limited extent by moving his body to the side he wanted to turn. He added a sprung wheeled undercarriage which helped the craft land.

In modern aviation, mono-wings, rudders on the tail and so many aspects of flight are as familiar as a cup of coffee, so it can be hard to fully appreciate the breakthroughs that Percy and Ella were making. But every aspect had to be considered at this fledgling state of flight.

Earlier tests had been done by Percy and Ella with the help of a tow rope to pull the glider forward through the air to generate lift. At the back of Percy's mind was always the idea of adding an engine, and this latest test day was simply a step towards this goal.

At Eynsford in Kent, the much revised and adjusted *Hawk* aircraft was duly taken to the top of the nearby hill while the crowd thronged around waiting to see the spectacle. Dorothy was in among the thick of it, a very enthusiastic supporter of this new conception of flight.

The plan was to attach the glider to a tow rope, a thin affair of about 600 yards in length, which was pulled through two blocks around 550 yards away. Ella was supervising the smooth running of this vital tow system from the rope's fixing point and she signalled that there was a slight hold-up getting it all set up.

Whether Dorothy pestered Percy or whether it was a spontaneous, generous offer to his young relation, either way Percy agreed that while they waited for the tow rope to be sorted, Dorothy could have a little 'go'. Percy said he would run the glider down the hill just a little way and the enthusiastic teenager was strapped into the pilot's position under the great wings of the plane. She quickly tied her flowing skirt round her legs with string and standing there underneath the big glider at the top of the steep hill, watched by a large group of eminent scientists as well as others, it could have been a significant moment for the young girl. At the time, however, it is far more likely that Dorothy just viewed the whole thing as a bit of fun. Either way, she did not hesitate and as Percy started running downhill pulling the machine forward, Dorothy took a few small steps and then, very quickly, she was up, soaring above the ground as the hill dropped away below her.

Percy's *Hawk* glider was much more successful than he and Ella could have hoped. As soon as it started forward, it took to the air and glided upward easily and fast. Percy had to let go in a hurry. The plane's lifting capabilities were far greater than anticipated. With Dorothy positioned just below the wings, the British public suddenly experienced the spectacle of a person up in flight. Ella, at the far end of the long tow rope she had been fixing, must have looked up in astonishment, surprised but also thrilled that after so many years of hard work, their latest and most beautiful machine was flying with so little effort. Even better, their calculations of lift had been correct. There was enough capacity to include a person and a lightweight engine into future adaptations of the design. It must have been a moment Ella remembered all her life. Here, at last, was tangible confirmation that her total dedication to her brother's work had all been worthwhile.

It was only a short flight and the aircraft possibly only soared to about 30ft or so off the ground, but for Dorothy it was also a memory of a lifetime. Moving quietly and freely through the air with no big balloon above her, seeing the ground moving past below her –

at that time it was an extraordinary concept and an extraordinary experience. Achieving this level of flight without a tow rope was well beyond anything Percy and Ella had dreamed of.

Unfortunately, towards the bottom of the long hill, and directly in Dorothy's flight path, was a photographer who had set up a high camera to capture any moments of flight. After sailing gracefully through the air, Dorothy and the flying machine started to come down and caught the top of the camera, which was hurled into the ground. Dorothy, losing speed and lift, descended easily back on to the ground and no real damage was done.

Immediately after, the long tow rope was fixed and Percy took the machine back up the hill. In the second flight of the day, Percy strapped himself in and easily soared up to possibly 70ft or more before the tow rope broke. The *Hawk* behaved impeccably as it lost speed, gliding steadily forward and landing just short of 200 yards down the hill. It sounds unbelievable now, but this was one of the longest soaring stable flights ever achieved in a man-carrying aircraft at the time.

The crowd, of course, were hugely enthusiastic; they acknowledged Dorothy, the brave young lady who had flown in the *Hawk*, and gave huge congratulations to Percy for his achievement. But credit should also have gone to Ella, who had put so much work into the development and construction of Percy's inventions. She was a major contributor to the achievements that have made Percy recognised as a leading pioneer in aviation. Possibly, once he had fitted his new engine and all had gone well, Percy's plane might well have beaten the Wright brothers in their conquest of flight six years later.

Sadly, it was not to be. While Dorothy recounted her exciting experience to her friends and relations, Ella continued to support her brother doggedly until the fatal day two years later, in autumn 1899, when, during another demonstration of his *Hawk* glider, he crashed and died. Percy was just 32. This was a shattering blow for the entire Pilcher family. Dorothy had the consolation of a close sister, Maude Violet, with whom she continued to live until her death in her seventies.

Ella, in her grief, was determined that her brother's brilliance would not be forgotten: she wrote to Robert Baden-Powell, who had shown some support for Percy's experiments. Robert was a member of the Aeronautical Society of Great Britain and Ella asked him if she could become a member so that her brother's experiments wouldn't be forgotten. Just a few weeks later she was voted in as an honorary member.

To help get over her grief and years dedicated to supporting her younger brother, Ella decided she needed a major change. Just a few weeks after Percy's death, she left the UK to assist as a civil nurse volunteer in the Boer War, which was then raging in South Africa. It was probably here that she met her future husband, army officer Edward Cecil Tidswell. Edward enjoyed a long and successful career in the army, surviving the First World War, and for a while they were posted to Kumasi in Ghana. This was certainly a big change for Ella; it was a long way from the misty moors of Scotland where she had first helped Percy with his groundbreaking experiences.

Ella and her husband ended up living in Jersey until they died, but it would be nice to think that she kept in touch with Dorothy, and perhaps they even visited each other, sharing their memories of a short but historic moment in the history of British aviation.

ROSE SPENCER, 1902
THE FIRST WOMAN TO FLY A POWERED AIRSHIP

The world's first ever woman to fly a powered air machine was, like so many of the early women in aviation, a very unlikely contender to make history. Rose Isabel Hawkins had no family background in aviation and the fact that she took off, did several circuits at height, and then landed successfully, is quite remarkable. It seems she was also several months pregnant at the time which only adds to the story.

When Rose was born in Islington, London, in 1872, she joined a financially secure although by no means wealthy Victorian family. Her father, from Portsmouth, was a property auctioneer, a solid and acceptable profession in that class-obsessed era. Her mother was an author in a genteel Victorian way, mainly creating and sending poems to the local papers. Living in a comfortable home in Islington with a sensitive mother, an older sister and brother, and four younger siblings, Rose's background gave no clue to her future.

As Rose grew up, the family moved down to Beach Road in Portsmouth, again to an adequate home although without any servants which, in that era, would have helped to denote real middle class. But it was a happy childhood and, just a few streets back from the sea, Rose would have taken part in some enjoyable excursions with her brothers and sisters.

How she became involved in the famous Spencer aviation family is not known; perhaps the families had made contact during their time in Islington. But when Rose met the good-looking and exciting young Stanley Spencer who had some amazing stories to tell, it is no wonder that her head was turned.

Stanley Spencer, Rose's husband-to-be, was born in London in 1868 and was the grandson of Edward Stanley, who had flown balloons as far back as 1836. Stanley's father, Charles Green Spencer, was a gliding pioneer and leading balloon enthusiast who set up C.G. Spencer & Sons, an innovative balloon-manufacturing workshop in London. Stanley's uncles were also involved in ballooning and as he grew up, Stanley's four brothers all became heavily involved with balloons and took to the skies. It was inevitable that, as a member of this famous aeronautical dynasty, Stanley would himself become a professional aeronaut, involved in a range of flying activities and adventures.

The brothers often discussed how to create a practical flying craft with an engine that could carry passengers across the sky rather than the existing balloons of the day which could only go where the winds took them. Stanley was a huge believer in powered flight and had total confidence that air travel would become an accepted form of transport in the future.

As Rose got to know Stanley, she became fascinated by his ideas. They married when Rose was 23 and Stanley 27, and as she walked up the aisle of St Mary's, Islington, in 1895, surrounded by a congregation full of the major names in British aviation, she knew she was entering an exciting new world.

They made their home in Islington in the heart of the Stanley family area and Rose, along with looking after the house, immediately took a keen interest in her husband's work. A couple of years after their marriage they had a son who died at just 5 months old, but two years later a little girl, Gladys, was born.

During this period, Stanley was showing specific interest in weather and, as he entered his thirties, he flew a hydrogen balloon for meteorologist Arthur Berson to discover conditions of the higher atmospheres. They are reported to have reached 27,500ft, a record at the time.

Rose calmly kept house, listening to the stories of her husband's dramatic exploits as she looked after their little girl. One thing the couple would have talked about was the flight of Alberto Santos-Dumont; this famous Brazilian aviator had fitted his new elongated hydrogen airship with a 12hp engine which drove a propeller, and in October 1901 he achieved a world first with a well-steered trip around the Eiffel Tower and back to his starting point. This motivated Rose's husband to pursue even more vigorously his desire for powered flight. Stanley was working on a new airship but was running out of money. It may well have been Rose who suggested they contact Mellin and Company for sponsorship. The company was a successful manufacturer of infant formula and Rose had already lost a son and now, with little Gladys turning 2, Rose was continually looking for the best children's products. It was a great idea. Mellin agreed to become a sponsor, with an initial £1,500 contribution towards the construction costs of a new airship.

While Rose spent most days looking after their daughter, in the evenings she listened attentively to the news and detail of the progress of Stanley's new airship. He was building it in a large shed at Crystal Palace Park in south London and it was going to be a magnificent vehicle. The airship was being created with a bamboo framework covered with a silk envelope. It would be around 75ft long with a capacity of 20,000 cubic ft of hydrogen and powered by a 3.5hp petrol engine. This would drive a carefully constructed wooden propeller mounted in tractor configuration at the front of the airship to pull it along through the air. This, Stanley thought, was better than other airship designs which used a back-mounted propeller. The motor was manipulated through cords attached to a clutch between the propeller and the motor. Another cord was attached to the motor's timing gear to help regulate speed.

Over dinner and then in front of the fire, Rose spent many an evening listening to all the details as an enthusiastic Stanley talked about his day's work. He added a few additional ideas such as a fan pump and valve to replace lost gas with air so the envelope didn't lose shape, and he also added an innovative design that would ensure that if the envelope collapsed, it would form a parachute shape to help lower the pilot down to the ground safely. He added an open bamboo gondola and finally ensured that the name Mellin was clearly showing on the side of the envelope.

In 1902 the airship was ready. While this wasn't the very first attempt to use an engine to power an air machine, nevertheless it was still a pioneering path. It would be another year before the Wright brothers added a propeller and engine to their glider in 1903.

Rose continued to be hugely supportive of her husband's work. Unlike early parachuting and ballooning, with the new airship plus a petrol engine there was a lot of technical information to get on top of. But Rose absorbed it all and was as keen and supportive as ever.

By June 1902, the airship was ready, and Stanley made some small test flights above the large grassed grounds at Crystal Palace, beating his British rivals in mastering powered flight. However, with such a limited engine and very slow changes of direction controlled through the cables in the basket, the flight was never going to be sensational. By the end of the month, Stanley had made some improvements and felt confident enough to give a public display with invited guests. On Saturday 5 July large numbers of troops visiting from the British colonies as well as the invited guests turned up to watch Stanley and the flying machine. Rose was there, of course, and many members of the extensive Spencer family attended.

With the aircraft's propellers revolving at high speed, Stanley made a series of successful flights at heights of up to 250ft. To demonstrate just how safe flight was, at one point Stanley suggested his little niece, Marie Spencer, daughter of his brother Percival Spencer, should come up for a short flight. This was agreed, and despite the extra weight, it all went very well and they went for a short trip up into the air. Stanley was gaining more and more confidence in his airship, taking off and circling around the polo ground before making very gentle descents back down to earth. It was all going very well.

Stanley continued to do test flights with his new machine at Crystal Palace and then, at some point, Rose agreed that she would be willing to fly the airship. She may even have suggested it. Conscious of the baby product advertising on the envelope, it would have seemed appropriate for Rose to be seen to be closely involved. However, agreeing to fly the airship was a bigger decision for Rose than it might first appear. Women had simply not been involved in the rush for powered flight, and no woman in the world had driven a powered aircraft.

Flying in control of an aircraft driven by an engine would be difficult enough; flying in the middle of one of the great cities of the world would make it even more challenging. It was definitely not a simple task of stepping into a basket or harness like all the earlier women who had taken to the air. Rose would have to be in total control, and there was a great deal to master. Rose needed to be aware of how the controls worked, how to climb and also how to descend, what control to pull to turn the airship round and what to do if the engine stopped, a very likely event in those early days. Then, what if the envelope started to leak, or she got blown out of the park? This was a very real risk with the limited steering available on Stanley's machine. There was just so much to get on top of, and so much that could go wrong.

Rose, however, took it all in, and on Tuesday 15 July 1902, on a calm dry morning, she stepped up on to the platform of the airship. The flights on that day hadn't been widely publicised; for Stanley these events were just work in progress. But nevertheless, as always, there were some curious observers, and this time it seems the audience included some high-profile names including Arthur Conan Doyle, creator of Sherlock Holmes, and W.G. Grace, the famous cricketer.

With her husband's assistance, Rose took hold of the controls and he once again checked she understood the system and how the airship operated. Then, with the little engine roaring into life and the propeller starting to whizz around, the tether ropes were released and Rose, dressed elegantly in a charming long skirt, took off.

It was a very gentle take-off and the forward movement was slow but steady. With her young daughter and numerous spectators watching, Rose contained any excitement or fear and gently and calmly manoeuvred the airship, lifting it into the air to a height of around 200ft. Slowly pulling on the cabled controls, she found the airship responded well and she gently circled the park. Gaining confidence, round she went again. She would have felt a little wind on her face, but concentrating carefully, she continued with her flight, resisting any temptation to look around too much at the view or to wave to the crowds on the ground. But she was well aware of her height; 200ft is quite a way up when you are standing in a very small basket. It was a huge responsibility, and any accident or damage to the airship would set her husband and their little family back enormously.

Listening to the engine, Rose carefully handled the controls to keep a level flight and then made gentle steady turns as she slowly flew through the air. Finally, it was time to come down and, slowly adjusting the flight of the big airship, she steadily descended to make a gentle landing. Rose had given an excellent display of very professional flight control.

Reports afterwards say she flew the airship in an easy manner, that she was under perfect control and that she was aloft for nearly half an hour. It wasn't a great height, she didn't go any real distance, but for the first time ever a woman had taken control of a powered aircraft and flown in the sky. It would be nearly another year before 19-year-old American Aida de Acosta piloted Alberto Santos-Dumont's airship for a short flight in Paris, although she is still often acclaimed as the first ever solo woman 'aero-driver' of a powered aircraft in the world.

When the Mellin airship landed, however, there was no dramatic excitement or huge applause when the quiet and self-contained Rose stepped out of the gondola on to the grass. She accepted the congratulations from a small group and then simply gathered up her daughter and headed back home, possibly even to cook the evening meal. Newspapers of the day reported the event, of course, but in a dignified, factual manner. Rose was of a quiet and thoughtful demeanour; she was not after glory or fame like many previous female aeronauts and so she would not have provided exciting copy to the journalists attending the event. Generally, there was more interest in the controls and workings of the airship than in the fact that a woman had flown it.

Interestingly, it also seems Rose was pregnant at the time of her flight, for she gave birth to a daughter, Sylvia, just four months later on 25 November. With the flowing dresses of the time, it is likely that no one but Rose and possibly Stanley knew she had also taken up a passenger.

Stanley Spencer, much buoyed by the success of his airship, continued to improve and develop his idea, and in September that year he took off from Crystal Palace and, at 300ft, flew around the dome of St Paul's Cathedral in the city of London. He was hoping to return to Crystal Palace but the steering on his machine wasn't up to it, and he finally made a gentle landing at Eastcote near Harrow, a three-hour flight of about 30 miles. Rose was there to meet him and she also accompanied him the following month when he took the airship, split into several parts for transport, up to Blackpool for a demonstration at the seaside town.

In June 1905, Rose produced a boy, Edward, and later that year Stanley, desperately short of money, headed off to India on an exciting new project: a series of tethered displays and long-distance balloon trips in connection with a planned visit to the country by the Prince of Wales. Early in 1906, as Stanley returned home on the ship the *City of Benares*, he went down with typhoid fever. He disembarked in Malta but the typhoid had gained too strong a hold and he died on the island at the end of January.

The shock for Rose and her young family can only be imagined. The excitement of being involved in aviation, the support from the man she loved and indeed the income had all disappeared in a flash. It must have been a devastating time, and money quickly ran out. There are reports of the family being in straightened circumstances and even of the elder daughter, Gladys, being placed in an orphanage. By 1910 Rose felt it was all too much of a struggle and in August of that year, together with her young son Edward, she embarked on the SS *Philadelphia* from Southampton for New York. This was a courageous step and is another indication that underneath Rose's quiet and placid character there was a high level of fortitude and grit, a side to her character clearly evident when she took the airship up for a flight.

Happily, America seems to have worked for her. Son Edward and daughters Sylvia and Gladys, who joined her later, all established themselves well, marrying and starting new dynasties in the US. As Rose settled into her new American life, attending her children's weddings and adapting to a different way of speaking and a different way of living, it is doubtful she ever mentioned that she was actually the first woman in the world to pilot a heavier-than-air machine.

6

EDITH COOK

1909
THE FIRST FEMALE BRITISH AIRCRAFT PILOT

It is extraordinary that Edith Cook never got her pilot's licence. After all, she was so determined to fly that she saved enough money, researched flight training and enrolled on an expensive course. Then, at the very end of 1909, she made her way down through France to a flight training school at a time when no other woman in the world had flown a plane and also when a woman travelling on her own across the Continent was very unusual.

On the busy and boisterous little airfield of Pau near the French Pyrenees, Edith mixed with some of the best aviators of the day and received the latest instruction. Reports of her early flying abilities were highly favourable and early comments said Edith had the potential to be a really good pilot.

So what went wrong? Despite Edith spending many weeks training at Pau, she didn't complete that final test that would have been recognised by the Aéro-Club de France, the world's first official organisation to issue aeroplane pilots' licences. If she had done that final check, she may well have beaten Raymonde de Laroche, the world's first female pilot to achieve her licence, granted just a couple of months later in March 1910. Nevertheless, Edith was the first ever

British woman to pilot an aeroplane and also one of only a handful of women in the world to fly at this time. No small achievement for the daughter of a Suffolk confectioner.

Having a dad who made sweets must have been a perfect scenario for a young lively girl. At home in Ipswich, little Edith was probably a tad spoiled; it was her dad's second marriage after his first wife died, and Edith's mum came to marriage and motherhood late in life. She was 42 when she gave birth to Edith in 1878, and she had another child, a little boy Bertie, two years later. They were well-loved children in what appears to have been a happy home.

It was a good time to be a confectioner. Milk chocolate had come into the market just a few years earlier, creating a fast-expanding demand; there were also fruit pastilles, pear drops, humbugs and other exciting new delights and cake ideas being introduced to a population loving the availability of such sweet treats. It is easy to imagine two little children popping into the workshop and pestering an indulgent older father for samples from the latest batch. Central Ipswich was also a great place to grow up. Based around a prosperous dock and a strong manufacturing base, with good shops, a railway and the recently formed Ipswich Town football club, the town was full of life and excitement.

Nothing in Edith's upbringing suggested groundbreaking adventure but, at some point, something fired her imagination and she started becoming interested in the aerial activities of the day. This may have been started by balloon ascents. On Saturday 2 June 1888, when Edith was 9, a huge scarlet and yellow balloon, *Eclipse*, ascended from the middle of Ipswich in front of big crowds. It seems more than likely that Mr and Mrs Cook took their two energetic young offspring to this event. Smartly dressed, the family would have joined the huge crowds thronging down the streets and chatting excitedly about the big beautiful balloon.

Just over a year later, in September 1889, experienced aeronaut Professor Fleet gave a balloon and parachute display a few miles north of Ipswich at Harleston. Edith had just turned 11 and would not have had any idea that this man, in just a few years' time, would set her on an extraordinary path to establish her name in British aviation history.

During the 1890s, as Edith entered her teens, displays involving parachutists were becoming far more numerous. Balloon and parachute displays were booked for fetes and events throughout the summer months and there were a handful of courageous young ladies who were employed as parachutists to add extra drama to some of the shows. They would sit prettily in their harnesses below the balloon and often wave flags or hankies as they were drawn aloft before descending by parachute. Of course there were several tragic accidents, but there were also many very successful descents by women, including some around Edith's home region in Suffolk by a well-known lady parachutist, Maud Brooks.

Whatever it was, something gave Edith an idea: if these young women could go up in the air, why couldn't she? It shows a remarkable determination and initiative on her part that she decided to follow up the idea. How she got in contact with Professor Fleet is not known. Professor Fleet was neither a professor nor a captain, as he sometimes theatrically called himself, but he was an experienced balloonist and parachutist, who put on displays all round the country, including East Anglia. Edith may have approached him at a show, or perhaps she had made enquiries through other show operators. Either way, in the summer of 1897, when Edith was 19, she told Professor Fleet she wanted to do a parachute jump.

Professor Fleet was good looking with a charismatic personality. Married and living in Harrow, north London, he was a natural showman and had developed a profitable little business doing dramatic jumps from a balloon. He would have noted that some rival aeronauts had joined up with lady parachutists, which brought in more bookings, so when Edith showed a willingness to take to the air, he was more than pleased. After their first meeting, he noted she was small but sturdy which would work well for parachuting, plus she was vivacious and very cheerful which would appeal to the crowds. It was the combination he wanted, and he agreed she could do a jump.

Whether Edith initially told her parents what she was up to is not known, but it is unlikely they would have approved. This sort of dramatic showmanship was not considered a good career for a well-brought-up girl, to say nothing of the dangers of going up in the sky.

Nevertheless, in early spring 1898, she went down to Professor Fleet to give it a try. He, with a wife and two young children to support, had a constant lack of funds and had turned towards hot air rather than costly gas to inflate his balloon. It was far cheaper to light a fire and channel the hot air into the mouth of the balloon to give it lift than pay for gas. He demonstrated this to Edith, and then went through the training with her.

This didn't amount to a lot; Professor Fleet was a practical man and thought the best way to learn was by experience. However, he took the time to talk through the basics of his system with Edith. Instead of using a break tie, the top of the parachute was connected to the bottom of the balloon with a connecting pin. The jumper was dangled below the parachute in a sling style harness and, once an adequate height had been reached, the parachutist would pull the release cord. This travelled up and removed the connecting pin, releasing the parachute from the balloon. Air would catch into the mouth of the descending stream of parachute fabric and quickly inflate it. A final idea was a sandbag attached to the top of the balloon. This idea had been used for some years and worked well. After the parachutist and his (or her) weight on the balloon had gone, the sandbag would then fall down, turning the balloon over. This would release all the hot air so the balloon deflated and would fall quickly to the ground. It was a tidy and simple arrangement and ideal for a one-person show. A final thing that Edith was told about was landing. Keeping her knees bent and rolling on to her back could be useful to lessen the shock to the legs.

Edith listened carefully and appeared to take it all in her stride. Her first jumps were at Professor Fleet's favourite ground of Wembley Park near his home. That very first time must have caused some butterflies, surely. As soon as the balloon was let go and started to lift, Edith, on her first ever flight, was completely on her own. As she rose higher and higher, she knew it was vital not to pull the cord and release the connecting pin too early. That first descent, summing up the courage to pull firmly on the cord, that immediate breathtaking moment of dropping down through the air, the relief watching the parachute billowing out above her and then the safe landing and realisation she had done it, must have given her a rush of emotions.

After her first success, Edith wanted to do more jumps and was pleased when Professor Fleet offered her good money to jump on displays. It was certainly a lot more than she could earn elsewhere.

One early jump resulted in a tree landing on Willesden Green followed by a fall into the roadway below. Edith suffered a few bruises but was generally uninjured and clearly not put off at all. Being an astute professional, Professor Fleet had already suggested she use the name Viola and quickly started advertising her as Viola, the World-Renowned Lady Parachutist. That was the way to bring in crowds and from her very early jumps, Edith was on show.

Unlike most of the other female parachutists of the time, Edith showed a real interest in the technical aspects of parachuting and ballooning. She watched carefully as her mentor prepared the balloon, digging a trench in the ground and covering it with iron sheeting, then placing earth on top to make it airtight. The two ends of the trench were left open. At one end was a good quantity of wood and straw, while at the other a small chimney was fixed. With the help of supporting poles and a pulley, the mouth of the balloon was hoisted up and positioned over the chimney. Then, at the other end of the tunnel, the fire was lit and the hot air and smoke would channel through the tunnel to the other end where it rose up into the balloon.

There was always a crowd of willing helpers available at any show and these were brought in to assist, including holding the balloon down by ropes until it was ready to be released. It usually took only around half an hour to an hour to fill the balloon with enough hot smoky air to give it buoyancy.

Edith soon got used to strapping herself into her harness and standing there while Professor Fleet checked all the attachments. When the order was given to let go, the balloon would rise quickly and, all being well, off it would sail up into the sky, pulling the parachute and parachutist up behind it.

For the next couple of years Edith joined Professor Fleet in many displays all over the country. Professor Fleet was not shy in publicising his show with exaggerated embellishments, but this was common at the time and certainly brought in the crowds – and the money. Around £2 or so was a general going rate paid to the handful of female parachutists in this era. When you compare that with the salary of, say, a typical waitress in those days, maybe around 1*s* 3*d* a day, and take into account there were 20 shillings to each pound, it was clearly very good money. At some events two displays on the same day were booked, making it a very profitable day's work indeed for the parachutist as well as the balloon owner and organiser.

Even better, shows away often paid for excellent hotel accommodation and feted the parachutists as real stars, giving them dinners and applauding them with flowery speeches. Compared with home life in Ipswich, for Edith there were huge advantages and attractions in being a female parachutist.

As the new century moved on, Viola, as Edith was now generally called, was becoming recognised as a proficient and courageous female display parachutist. Professor Fleet sometimes advertised her as Viola Fleet, adding extra importance to his name.

At the time, there were a few key aeronauts such as the Spencer family and Auguste Gaudron who dominated the display scene across the UK and sometimes also used women for their events. Edith was happy to take any booking she could get and by 1903 she was also doing displays for the Spencers and for Auguste Gaudron when they needed an extra woman. By that summer, five years after she had started, Edith had done 100 jumps, and was also using the name Viola Spencer at some shows, simply to imply close links with this highly regarded family of aeronauts. Up and down the country, on buses, trains, pony traps and even in the odd early motor car, Edith would travel and do a display for whoever wanted to book a female parachutist.

Edith experienced jumping from both hot-air and gas balloons, going up sitting on the side of passenger-carrying baskets or doing solo ascents with the parachute fixed to the balloon. At some point she also used the name Kavanagh, although there seems no family connection to the surname. At various times she jumped as Viola Kavanagh, Viola Spencer Kavanagh and once as Elsa Spencer. Occasionally she worked with other female jumpers to make a double spectacle. Fellow lady parachutist Dolly Shepherd, eight years younger, became a close associate, if not a friend, and they worked in pairs several times, including doing a double jump from the same basket on at least one occasion.

It was all an extreme form of showbusiness but it brought in very good money and a level of fame. Compared with the alternatives for a working girl in the Edwardian era and despite the risks, it is fully understandable why Edith and her colleagues continued with their parachuting careers for several years. Many shows were at weekends, giving Edith time off in the week. Sometimes she would go home and help out at her father's confectionery business. It was said she worked in a quiet unassuming manner and was very popular with all who knew her. Her father, though, could never really support his daughter's risky activities.

As the Edwardian years moved on, there was more and more talk of heavier-than-air flight, and while shows with balloons and parachutists were still pulling crowds, they were beginning to lose some of their fascination. By 1908, Edith had done nearly 300 displays and she may have begun to tire of it. Each jump required quite a bit of effort and there was always a risk element. A show she did in Derbyshire in that year was nearly her last; her detachment pin jammed and she couldn't release herself from the gas balloon. She had a very cold and frightening ascent, hanging firmly on to her harness and travelling to a great height until the balloon started cooling and descended again, finally settling her back on to solid ground at about 10 p.m.

Edith, with her connections to the Spencer family, would have heard about Percy Spencer's visit to Le Mans in France in September 1908. Percy witnessed three flight trials by Wilbur Wright in his Wright Model A aircraft powered by a 35hp engine, and came back bursting with enthusiasm for the potential of heavier-than-air flight. This was followed by Samuel Cody's groundbreaking flight the following month when, in a small biplane with a 50hp engine and horizontal control surfaces mounted in front of the wings, he made the first recognised powered and sustained flight in Britain.

With so many balloon ascents and so many parachute descents under her belt, the thought occurred to Edith that perhaps flight could be the next step. No other woman in Britain or the world had flown one of the fledgling aircraft; this could be a unique opportunity.

Saving as much money as possible, in 1909 Edith made up her mind; she wanted to learn to fly. For an Edwardian lady of 31, in an era when big hats, long skirts and traditional female roles were still generally the norm, Edith was showing enormous independence.

She continued with her parachute descents but her thoughts were now strongly directed towards powered flight. Louis Bleriot made history in July that year when he became the first to fly across the Channel. Along with many of the aviation enthusiasts of the day, Edith may have visited Selfridges store in central London to stare in admiration at Bleriot's monoplane, on show there after the dramatic Channel crossing. The delicate little plane, with its gently shaped wings, elevators and rudder, with its part box type fuselage made in ash and its flimsy-looking cross-wire bracing, was definitely a thing of beauty. With the engine mounted in the front and its big pram wheels for take-off, it also offered a fascinating glimpse into a new future.

The cross-Channel flight gave extra impetus to Edith's desire to fly and it also heralded a sudden surge of enthusiasm in aviation across the UK. However, learning to fly was no simple matter as there were no proper training facilities in the country at that time.

In France, things had progressed a little faster. Five years after the Wright brothers had made their first successful heavier-than-air powered flight in North Carolina, Wilbur Wright visited France. He settled on Le Mans, in central France, as the base for the first European demonstrations. Using his 1905 Flyer monoplane, he gracefully made some sweeping circuits around the racecourse, demonstrating clearly how rudder and wing warping could be incorporated to help control flight and turns. The spectators had expected just a few short hops and, on seeing this prolonged flying, they became wild with enthusiasm. However, the weather meant there were many delays on subsequent flights and it was suggested to Wilbur Wright that Pau, a town near the Pyrenees in southern France, offered a much more suitable climate for flying. Wilbur went down to Pau and, along with giving further demonstrations, started a flying school there. When Wilbur moved on from Pau, the school continued to operate. Bleriot had visited Pau to see the Wrights' flights and, in November 1909, he too opened his own flight school just outside the town. Pau had quickly become a recognised leading centre of aviation.

Edith decided that not only did she want to fly, she also wanted to learn with the best. She counted her money, wrote letters, and finally she enrolled at the Bleriot flying school in Pau. By this time both her parents had died, but she must have mentioned it to her colleagues and friends. Most would have been totally bemused by what she was up to; it is very unlikely that many of them had even seen a plane.

Edith had never been overseas, yet in late December 1909, in midwinter, off she set on the steam trains and ferries of the day, changing trains in Paris and, with her luggage, finally arriving at Pau in the south of France, a busy town of around 35,000 people. It seems likely she headed for the Hotel de Londres, a popular accommodation centre for trainee pilots. After signing in and sorting out her room, she had to complete the final leg of this journey, which was a 5-mile trip down to the airfield. It was common for would-be pilots to hire a bike to cycle from the hotel, but there were pony and traps and carriages, plus an increasing number of motor cars were appearing in the town. It must have been an exciting moment, after so much thought and planning, when Edith finally arrived at Pau airfield.

In more recent years, Pau would turn into a modern airport, with a control tower, passenger terminal, hangars and a large car park. It wasn't quite the same when Edith arrived. The airfield was a large, unfenced and treeless flat area of grass almost a mile square known as Pont Long. There were a few hangars plus one small building converted to a rudimentary café area. Despite the lack of facilities, Pau had quickly developed into a hive of activity. Demand for flying lessons had grown very quickly, and when Edith arrived there were already many lessons taking place. Even in those early days, Bleriot had more students than he could cope with and had put together a team of dedicated aviators to help handle this side of the business for him. When Edith turned up, it is doubtful she would have been fussed over as a female. In that era, the instructors would have generally preferred to concentrate on teaching wealthy young men with a passion for flight and also with the potential to buy a plane rather than a woman who, they may well have thought, wouldn't understand the theory, who probably wouldn't want to get oily or covered in grease and who probably would get scared as soon as she took control.

There were a few Englishmen at the school, including charismatic British-born Claude Grahame-White. Claude had arrived at Pau the previous month and was already well on his way to mastering basic flight in Bleriot's Type XI monoplane. Of a similar age to Edith, he had been involved in engineering and motor cars before he turned his energetic enthusiasm to aviation and he was happy to swap notes and information with this unusual young woman who also wanted to learn to fly. Despite the numerous young men and handful of women who visited the airfield every day, Edith didn't make any close attachments; her interests were firmly directed towards the new tremendously exciting aspect of powered flight.

It seems probable that Edith's early introduction to an aeroplane was supervised by Bleriot's right-hand man, the experienced French balloonist and aviator Alfred Leblanc. He had a slightly cynical attitude to would-be pilots, saying that 90 per cent of his students should never have attempted to leave the ground; 8 per cent would make fairly safe flyers under normal conditions and the remaining 2 per cent were born flyers. Nevertheless, he was extremely knowledgeable and generally a good instructor.

The training planes used at the Bleriot school were of course Bleriots. After numerous experimental models, and great assistance from a talented Frenchman Raymond Saulnier, Bleriot had come up with the XI, a single-engine monoplane built from ash wood with a streamlined fuselage and wire cross-bracing. The undercarriage consisted of two main bicycle-style wheels and a smaller tail wheel. With wing warping for lateral control, joystick control with a foot-operated rudder bar plus a three-cylinder, 25hp air-cooled Anzani engine, it was a remarkable plane for the time and orders for the Bleriot XI were growing fast. Along with various versions of the Bleriot XI, Edith would also become aware of the other popular aeroplanes being designed at that time, including the Farmans and Voisins. It really was a time of fast development, tremendous innovation and stunning progress, and Pau was at the forefront of it all.

Edith joined the stream of would-be pilots and started her course in late December 1909. Bleriot was not there; earlier that month he had been flying over Istanbul and met with an accident when a sudden gust of wind had turned him over. He sustained broken ribs and some other injuries and was in hospital for three weeks. But the school, with Bleriot's carefully assembled team, continued, and training took place every day when possible.

Wind was a particular problem, especially for students, and many a day Edith would have to sit it out with fellow trainee pilots, watching the elite group of more experienced aviators taking off and landing in front of an attentive audience. Planes were also limited, and quite often pilots spent the day sitting on the grass waiting for a slot. Even more frustrating, Edith would have quickly realised that people like Claude Grahame-White, who had already bought a Bleriot plane, were being given priority over a student who was just paying for instruction.

But despite all this, Edith started being introduced to heavier-than-air flight. After the simplicity of ballooning and parachuting, initially it may have all been a little overwhelming. There was a lot to take in, including the theory of flight and basic ground instruction on engines and controls. The machine itself needed to be understood. Prepping an Anzani engine involved opening valves for oil and fuel flow; pre-flight checks included checking dozens of wires and fittings, plus ensuring the wood and fabric and complicated landing gear were all in good order. But it was a heady atmosphere dedicated to all things aeronautical and there were always fellow enthusiasts ready to go through aspects with her. Gradually Edith managed to get on top of it all.

However, when the time finally came for Edith to climb up and sit in the pilot's seat, there was another problem. Edith was short, and she found she couldn't reach the foot bar. Special blocks had to be fitted before she could begin to start practising control of the machine on the ground, an aspect required before she would finally be allowed to fly. In those days, the term 'grass cutters' was jokingly used by a lot of the students at the school to cover the week or two they had to practise taxiing up and down and turning on the grass before they were allowed to try a take-off.

Finally, on 4 January 1910, the time had come and Edith was considered able enough to do a solo flight. She was by now familiar with climbing up into the fragile wood-and-fabric aeroplane, she was getting used to the burring engine noise and the propeller whirring away in front of her, and she was getting more and more used to the feel and controls of the little aeroplane. But, nevertheless, that first flight was a big step forward. To start with, the students simply lifted up into the air in a straight line and then landed the plane again. The field at Pau was wonderfully long and flat, allowing a substantial margin for error for the students, although even this didn't stop some of them careering into a boundary tree or having other mishaps.

But Edith managed it all quietly and efficiently. With the engine roaring, she held the flimsy wood-and-fabric plane straight as she sped over the grass and gained enough speed. Then, the moment had finally come. Pulling gently back on the control stick, she eased the machine off the ground. She would have felt the sudden smoothness as the wheels left the slightly bumpy surface and she would have been aware of the wind in her face as she sped up above the ground. Concentrating intently on all she had been taught, she held the plane at a low height in a straight direction before gently descending back on to the grass. That first flight may not have been quite as scary as her first-ever parachute descent, but Edith was ten years older now and there was a lot more to think about. There were also, as always at Pau, many spectators on the ground. Edith must have been a little nervous, but she made no mistakes. It all went very well and was an excellent achievement.

On the same day that Edith lifted off the ground for the very first time as a solo pilot of an aircraft, Claude Grahame-White received his official French licence from the French Aero Club. He was number 30 to achieve this honour; he also became the sixth person to receive an official British Aviator Certificate after the Royal Aero Club started issuing official licences in March that year.

Claude Grahame-White had always been business-minded and had for some time been keen not just on flying but also on setting up his own operations. He asked Louis Bleriot if he could rent a hangar at the Pau airfield to set up his own school. Initially Bleriot was not at all keen on the idea, but there were more than enough would-be pilots for both of them, and finally he agreed as long as Claude concentrated on training mainly British pilots.

The deal was done and Claude quickly set up his own flying school at Pau. Edith chose to go with him, moving across the airfield to his new school. It was extraordinary that Claude accepted the idea. He had already firmly stated his opposition towards women learning to fly, saying that women were not temperamentally suited to handle the controls of an aeroplane. It says a lot of Edith's capabilities and attitude that Claude was happy to include her in a group of six students who joined his school early in 1910. At this time Edith, for some reason, had changed her name again from Miss Kavanagh-Spencer to Miss Campbell.

She remained at Claude's school for a couple of months, continuing her training and gradually gaining experience on the Bleriot monoplane, taking off, circling the airfield and landing. It was an interesting time for Edith. She was mixing with aristocrats and people of considerable wealth from all over Europe and this may have led to some doubt: was she doing the right thing? Edith was aware that the costs were beginning to add up. The original flight course alone would have been more than £100, plus there was the hotel and of course everyday living expenses. However, she would also have been encouraged by news about a number of Frenchwomen learning to fly, including Elise Raymonde de Laroche, a plumber's daughter from Paris, who became the first woman in the world to gain an official pilot's licence in March 1910.

So Edith steadily persevered, taking to the air when she could, dressed in her linen overall and additional clothes to help keep warm. Her longest flight is reported to have been around 3 miles. This makes it even more surprising that she did not take her official French licence. Perhaps she felt she still needed to polish her skills, perhaps the cost put her off, or perhaps she thought she would wait until she could obtain her English licence when she got back home.

Things changed when, in early spring 1910, Claude Grahame-White told her he had decided to close his school and move back to the UK. He was too ambitious and energetic to remain in a quiet region in the south of France. He returned to England in time to take part in the London-to-Manchester air race. This had been set up by the *Daily Mail* newspaper, which offered a massive £10,000 prize for the first pilot to fly the 185 miles between the two cities with no more than two stops and the journey completed in less than twenty-four hours.

Grahame-White was competing against Frenchman Louis Paulhan. After setting off on 23 April and making good initial headway, engine problems and then high winds delayed his flight, and finally he had to concede the race to Paulhan.

Edith also returned to England in April that year. After months of having been totally immersed in aviation, she was very enthusiastic about the exciting developments taking place and also keen on progressing as one of the few females in the world involved in flying. At the time, she said her aim was to take part in some of the flying events being planned in the UK, and some reports suggested she was in the process of ordering a British-made aircraft although, with new Bleriot XIs selling for around £400 and other planes costing around the same or more, it seems doubtful she herself had enough money to afford this. She may well have been hoping to attract some sponsorship or another means to help fund a plane.

Whatever her plans, money was still needed for her to continue these expensive flying activities and she quickly went back to her old career of parachuting to earn some speedy cash while she got herself organised. Her brother had taken over the family interests in the confectionery business in Ipswich, and Edith based herself back in St Nicholas Street in the town, just a short distance from where she grew up.

At a display in Halifax, in May 1910, she mentioned that she was the only woman in the world flying monoplanes and also stated that while she still enjoyed parachuting, flying now was her main interest and she had an aim to fly across the English or Irish Channel. For a woman to have done this in 1910 would have been remarkable and a huge first for Edith.

In early July Captain Gaudron, who was still running numerous balloon and parachute displays across the country, contacted Edith to ask if she could stand in for another female parachutist, Dolly Shepherd. A parachute descent had been booked for 9 July at the Lillywhite Sports Ground in Foleshill, Coventry, and Dolly couldn't make it. Edith, in her willing manner, was more than happy to oblige; after all, every extra jump she did meant more money for flying. It was windy, but nothing too extreme. After a normal ascent Edith released the parachute and started a descent. All went well and she was hoping to land in the Coventry Cricket Ground. However, it wasn't to be and instead the wind took her over to the Market Hall Buildings in West Orchard, now a shopping centre. In those days it was a narrow thoroughfare and her feet struck a roof of the Centaur Cycle Works. She held on there for a moment but then the wind dragged her parachute sideways and pulled her off the roof. She fell unsupported through some telephone wires on to the hard roadway below, a drop of around 40ft.

Some policemen were quickly on the scene to give first aid, and among a growing crowd of onlookers, Edith was lifted into a motor-car and taken to the Coventry and Warwickshire Hospital. She had a badly fractured pelvis, a fractured left elbow and other injuries. By the following Wednesday Edith was fully conscious and taking nourishment, and Sidney Spencer, a member of the Spencer family, visited her. Unfortunately, she then took a turn for the worse and died the following day, Thursday, 14 July 1910, aged 31.

The outcome of the inquest was one of accidental death, but there was agreement that parachute exhibitions were dangerous and the coroner added that it was time this thing was stopped.

Edith had had the business sense to leave a will, not at all a common thing to do among young single girls in Edwardian Britain. She left £30, a good sum but not nearly enough to fulfil her dream of becoming the proud owner of her very own plane. Her early dedication to aviation might have come from a keenness to experience a more profitable and exciting life than Ipswich could offer at that time, but she persevered to become a knowledgeable and accomplished aviator. Despite her life being cut short, Edith deserves full recognition as Britain's first ever female pilot.

7

LILIAN BLAND

1910
THE FIRST BRITISH WOMAN TO DESIGN AND BUILD A VIABLE AEROPLANE

In the winter of 1909–10, as Edith Cook was taking flying lessons in the south of France, another British woman was going a step further. Forsaking the traditional feminine dress and behaviour of the day, one groundbreaking woman was working quietly in the family workshed at the back of the house, measuring up wood from spruce, ash and elm trees with the aim of making her own flying machine.

The truly extraordinary thing is that, surrounded by her carefully prepared notebooks and technical drawings, plus a range of tools and equipment, she not only created a plane that worked but, without any pilot training, she flew it successfully.

Lilian Bland was a female pioneer, and not just in aviation. She started breaking out of the traditional female roles way back in her childhood and, when she took up riding astride a horse instead of using a sidesaddle, wearing breeches instead of a skirt, smoking and even earning a living from photography, she created a lot of talk and not a little astonishment among many sectors of the population.

It wasn't meant to be like that. Lilian, born in 1878, had been brought up beautifully in a very traditional Victorian family. Both her grandfathers were men of the church and with her father a successful and talented artist, a lot of care had been taken by Mr and Mrs Bland to instil in their three children all the genteel values of the day. The eldest child, Eva, was nine years older than little Lilian, and big brother Robert was six years older, so while Lilian didn't have close siblings as playmates, nevertheless, as she grew up, she was ensconced in a warm and loving family.

The family home was ideal: not overly ostentatious but big enough for comfort and excitement. Situated just to the east of Maidstone in Kent, Willington House in Willington Street was a solid two-storey building adjacent to the 180 acres of what is now Mote Park. In those days Mote Park was a private property comprising the most beautiful gardens with exotic plants and a stunning lake. Lilian's father, John Bland, was a sensitive soul; among his art he included soft and gentle landscapes and his appreciation of the beauty of the local countryside would have helped to mould the young Bland children as they grew up. One can imagine him taking the youngsters for a local walk, pointing out aspects of interest, perhaps even visiting the big lake in Mote Park with its glorious trees and plants.

Mum Emily, pretty and feminine, ran the home carefully with adequate paid help to ensure she too had time for the children. All round it was a gentle, charming household backed by the financial support from John Bland's illustrious and aristocratic Anglo-Irish ancestry which can be traced back to the sixteenth century and before. Sometimes, in the family home in Kent, there may have been talk of some of the more memorable ancestors, perhaps about namesake John Bland, a rector in Kent who was tried in Canterbury for heresy against the Catholic tradition and was burned at the stake in 1555, or Sir Thomas Bland, who was made a baronet in 1642 by King Charles I for his active zeal and devotion to the royal cause. Learning about history which involved family members must have made lessons more interesting for young Lilian and also instilled a confidence in her which served very well when, as she entered adulthood, she dared to be different.

With adequate funds available and staff looking after the house, as they grew up John Bland took his offspring on many trips to the Continent. While he visited favourite locations for inspiration for a new picture, the children were exposed to a wealth of new sights and experiences. Switzerland, Italy, France: Lilian was taken all over Europe. Escaping from lessons taught by a governess in the schoolroom at home, these trips must have provided very exciting interludes in Lilian's childhood.

But still there was nothing to show or even encourage the truly independent spirit that was soon to develop. For a short time, when she was around 12, Lilian went off to a small school for gentlewomen situated by the sea at Margate in Kent, but then she was back at home. As she entered her late teens, to finish her education Lilian spent short spells abroad, studying art in Paris and music in Rome. It may well have been during one of these trips that she started to become interested in photography and also to move away from the conventional English way of life for well-to-do young ladies of the time.

In 1900, when Lilian was 22, there was a dramatic change. Her mother Emily became very ill and moved to live in the south of France near the Mediterranean in the hope that sea air and a warmer climate would help. Lilian's sister went with her. Lilian's brother was already away following a military career and Lilian's father, left alone at home with a daughter, decided he would move back to the area where he had been brought up and live with his widowed sister in Northern Ireland. It made sense for them to join forces so his sister could run the household while he could continue with his art. Lilian moved to Northern Ireland along with her father.

Tobarcooran House in Carnmoney, just north of Belfast, was a beautiful, detached property with grounds, and not long after she arrived, Lilian was up at the top of the nearby Carnmoney Hill admiring the view down to the water and watching the birds. She loved taking pictures of them in flight, and soon Lilian set up a dark room in a well-appointed workshed at the back of the house to help further her interest in photography.

There were many members of the large Bland family around to introduce her to the leisure activities of the area and before long Lilian was beginning to make a name for herself, not just as a photographer of ability but also as a daring horse rider. As both activities flourished, Lilian moved fast into adulthood, the adulthood of her choosing. She was far away from any guiding influence from her mother or older sister. Her father, now aged 72, and her 68-year-old aunt were at a loss about how to cope with the modern ideas of younger generations. This all left Lilian reasonably free to fully develop not only her interests in life but also her independent spirit.

Along with riding and photography, Lilian also took up fishing and shooting but her interests weren't just in country pursuits. As early as 1903 she cycled to the local station and took a train down to Athy, south of Dublin, to see the Gordon Bennet car race. She went down with a female friend and said it was the race that gave her the idea of trying to sell some of her photographs.

Back home, riding remained a huge interest; it offered a perfect challenge for her energy and physical skills but also an excellent subject for photography. As she reached her mid twenties, Lilian was starting to sell some of her photographs to newspapers and magazines. This was no passing whim of a well-brought-up lady filling her time. Lilian really studied photography and had a deep knowledge of the latest cameras and developments of the day. She also rode for two years for a training stables, exercising horses, schooling and breaking in hunters and qualifying thoroughbreds for hunt races. Her energy and ability were extraordinary and she hunted regularly across Ireland and occasionally joined well-known hunts in England as well.

Her father and her aunt were supportive, but only to a certain extent. When Lilian had begun riding astride a horse instead of riding sidesaddle, they had been firm in their disapproval. When Lilian took to wearing breeches instead of a long skirt and then took up smoking, there were some serious discussions in the family home at Tobarcooran. Lilian, however, was growing into a very determined young woman and was no longer going to be told how to behave in proper society. Also, these aspects of her behaviour were somewhat mitigated by her growing success in selling her photographs to magazines and newspapers. With the relationship between art and photography, Lilian's father must underneath have been very proud of his unusual daughter as she managed to sell more and more of her photographs, mainly featuring horses but also other subjects such as bird life.

Lilian's mother died in France in 1906 without recovering her health and sadly did not live to see Lilian's photography really take off. Her shots were beginning to appear in many leading magazines on the Continent as well as in the UK. Lilian also began to write articles about riding and about photography in general, and these were also very well received.

Her wide area of interests continued; she helped to set up the Antrim Rifle Club and, visiting friends in Scotland's west coast, she took time away to study and photograph coastal birds. Some of her bird pictures from this trip were shown at the Royal London's Photographical Society exhibition.

In 1908, as Lilian turned 30, the postman delivered to the Bland home a postcard from Paris that instantly caught Lilian's imagination. The card was from her uncle Robert and showed a Bleriot monoplane. So soon after her careful study of the flights of the birds in Scotland, this proved fascinating, and in true Lilian style, she decided to find out all about it. She investigated the latest ideas in aviation from any books or magazine articles she could find. She gathered all the information she could to understand the basics of flight; of the importance of a curved shape on the top of the wing to create lift; the best way to connect and control elevators; and the best position for an engine. She studied every little detail she could find.

In October 1909, three months after Bleriot had crossed the Channel, Lilian took the ferry from Belfast to attend Blackpool Aviation Week. This was the first official air show recognised by the Aero Club of Great Britain and it must have been hugely exciting for Lilian. She watched, fascinated, as planes such as a Roe triplane failed to take off and a Farman, a Voisin and the delicate Antoinette all took to the air. The crowds were immense and the enthusiasm and excitement tangible. Lilian was instantly drawn into this new, wonderful world of flight. What potential, what opportunities. She took out her notebook and started jotting down in meticulous detail all the information she could find. She visited every flying machine at the show and commented that she wasn't impressed with the English machines, noting they were too small and fitted with motorbike engines. Overall, she was surprised how small the planes were but also how they were all really quite similar in many respects. She watched carefully how early aviator Louis Paulhan flew a Farman machine around the course and how his plane seemed to drift around a corner tail first. She examined the Gnome engine and decided this French-made seven-cylinder revolutionary rotary engine was by far the best. Plans, measurements, construction methods, supply lists, sketches: Lilian was relentless in seeking out information, and her notes from the meeting were extensive.

Back home and looking through her notes, Lilian saw no reason why she couldn't create her own flying machine. Relegating her photographic equipment to one section of the workshop at the back of the house, she put all her notes in order and got going. Her first attempt was to create a model biplane glider with a wingspan of around 6ft. Cutting, fastening, fixing: Lilian's workshop was a buzz of activity as she put her wooden model plane together. It was simply a test for her main full-sized project, but nevertheless the little wooden and fabric winged plane, with its carefully angled struts, was made with a great deal of precision and care. When Lilian took it out into the garden and towed it along like a glider, the little frame easily lifted up into the air and flew well.

Lilian was now ready to build a proper flying machine. Her father and aunt must have been somewhat bemused as every day, after breakfast, Lilian put on her overalls and hurried out to the workshed. Their knowledge of what she was doing would have been minimal and her father was not particularly enthusiastic about the concept at all. These were still Edwardian times and it must have been difficult for him to have such a headstrong daughter who was rebelling against the accepted standards for a well-brought-up gentlewoman. After all, Lilian was the granddaughter of a respected local curate who was also a Justice of the Peace.

But nothing was going to deter Lilian from her plane. Day after day she was in the workshed cutting and sawing and hammering and sewing. Throughout the winter she obtained supplies of spruce, ash, elm and bamboo and cut and shaped them to her plan. She bought some unbleached calico and painted on a homemade mixture of gelatine and formalin to make the fabric weatherproof. She was confident, but not arrogant, and willing to ask and consider suggestions from local friends who were practically minded, albeit with no knowledge whatsoever of flight. In December 1909, she was contemplating using skids on her plane for a sliding take-off and she was still not sure of the merits of ash against spruce. She once filled the house's bathroom with steam so she could fly small aerofoils across the room to check for lift. Her father and aunt yet again must have raised their eyebrows at what young Lilian was up to.

Christmas and the New Year came and went and still Lilian spent her free time down in the workshed. She contacted a company called Samuel Girvan in Ballyclare, a town just north of Tobarcooran, for some special metal parts. Slowly, bit by bit, Lilian's plane took shape. Early in 1910 various sections of the plane were ready. It was to be a biplane, with a wingspan of 27ft 7in, and this was too big for the work shed. So the various sections of the plane had to be transported over to the coach house of her home where there was a large open space ideal for the plane's assembly. She dutifully carried all the parts across and then worked hard to complete the construction of her precious plane.

It must have been a wonderful moment when the last section was finally attached and Lilian could stand back and look at it. It was a real tribute to her painstaking calculations and careful measurements and constructions that the results were so satisfactory. From its cleverly attached rear rudder to its beautiful, rounded wings and the myriad of criss-crossing struts and wires, it was indeed a work of art. Hopefully, Lilian's father gave at least some praise for the beauty of the machine, even if he was unsupportive of its purpose.

Lilian decided to call her little aircraft the *Mayfly*, joking at the time that it may fly, it may not!

The time had come to try it out. A couple of local men helped Lilian carry her precious plane over to the open spaces below nearby Carnmoney Hill. Carefully setting the plane so it faced directly into the wind, they attached tow ropes and then gave the plane a tug. As they strode over the meadow, pulling the plane behind them, the

Mayfly responded quickly, lifting smoothly and easily off the ground. One can imagine Lilian's sheer delight as she saw all her hard work come into effect. Her little plane flew!

A few days later, when the wind was 18mph, the plane was reassembled and taken out for another test flight. Towed forward on its skids, it quickly soared up to 20ft and flew well for a short time, albeit breaking both skids on a far steeper landing than planned. Lilian carefully made more notes which included ideas to change the elevators and strengthen the skids.

A lot more testing was needed and luckily Lilian found an enthusiastic supporter in Joe Blain, a 32-year-old local man who helped with the gardens at Tobarcooran. A couple of members of the local Royal Irish Constabulary were also called in to give a hand and once again the little *Mayfly* plane was carried to the small field at Carnmoney for testing. Soon it became impractical to bring the plane back to the house each evening and a nearby shed was organised for storage.

Testing, adjusting and more testing went on throughout the early months of 1910 and soon Lilian felt confident that *Mayfly* was as good as she could make it. She had used a range of different woods in her final design, finally deciding on ash for the wing spars and skids, spruce for the ribs and the struts, and bamboo for the supports for the elevator and tail surfaces. The engine mounting was planned to be made in elm. The wings were laced to the structure so they could be tightened if necessary. The whole plane weighed just on 200lb. Now, after so many months of hard work, the time had come to add an engine and see if her *Mayfly* would really fly.

Edwin Alliott Verdon Roe was a pioneering British aviator and had built a full-sized biplane which he tested successfully at Brooklands in Surrey in 1908. He founded the A.V. Roe Aircraft Company (later known as Avro), based in Manchester, at the beginning of 1910. Lilian wrote to him about an engine. While she had liked the French Gnome engine, she had to be practical and find an engine she could acquire without too many problems or too much cost. She received a very positive response from A.V. Roe, saying they were happy to help all they could. In July, she hopped on the ferry over to Manchester to collect a 20hp two-cylinder engine and also a propeller the company had made for her. By now Lilian's father and aunt had not only given up on being surprised but had begun to change tactics and were slowly becoming interested in Lilian's amazing construction. Was it really going to fly? When Lilian arrived home with her unusual purchases, this time no eyebrows were raised.

The engine and propeller were fitted successfully and then Lilian undertook a few final tasks to complete her little plane. She constructed a seat with leftovers from a carpet in the house and she appropriated her long-suffering aunt's ear trumpet to decant petrol. It was all coming together and on a final testing, the engine ran well. In early August 1910, *Mayfly* was ready for its maiden flight.

This time Lilian didn't want to risk the small field she had been using at Carnmoney. She contacted Lord O'Neill, whose 800-acre estate included a suitably flat deer park that was reasonably clear of trees, fencing and other obstacles. This was about 16 miles away, south-east of Randalstown. Lord O'Neill, no doubt a little surprised by the request, readily agreed to help out and let Lilian use his land for *Mayfly*'s initial flight.

A shed for the plane was erected at the new site and small wheels were attached to the plane's skids so that it could be towed to the new location. Lilian then supervised the transfer of this extraordinary craft along the roads of Northern Ireland, much to the surprise of several local people on the route.

Just as all was set, the weather closed in. Lilian and Joe, the gardener, cycled over several times to the estate to fine-tune the machine and finally, as the skies cleared and the wind dropped, it was time to give it a go. With her hair neatly tied back and wearing her sturdy overalls, Lilian climbed up into her homemade plane and the engine was started. The little *Mayfly* started edging forward. On its shuddering struts, it moved across the grass faster and faster and then up it went. The *Mayfly* could fly! As Lilian controlled the throttle in her right hand, the plane lurched on at a low height before it descended gently back to earth.

It was the start Lilian had hoped for and over the next few weeks she made constant adjustments to her plane and many trial flights.

Managing to edge higher, she increased the flight distances to a quarter of a mile and further. The plane may sound fairly unimpressive now but, until the previous autumn, no woman had ever flown. This time it was in a homemade plane, a really astonishing feat. Only one other woman, American Emma Lilian Todd, had designed a serviceable aircraft, but this had only made a short hop and was unable to sustain flight at all. There is little doubt that Lilian Bland was the very first woman in the world to design and build an aircraft that managed to fly through the air.

Lilian went on experimenting and improving her plane through the worsening weather of autumn 1910. Her take-off field was not rolled or naturally smooth, and ridges and furrows would sometimes have to be dealt with during take-off and landing. Lilian commented that she treated these as she did on a hunt, taking them at a slant. She flew greater distances and went higher, continually making adjustments and notes about improvements for her little machine.

While money was plentiful, it was not unlimited in the Bland household and Lilian's father began to show some concern about the expenditure. To help out, Lilian decided she could start a business selling biplanes. She decided on some new design ideas for a *Mayfly* Mark II and started work on a quarter-scale model of the new plane. She also designed and put an advert in *Flight* magazine, a new publication for aviation enthusiasts. Lilian's advert offered an improved *Mayfly*-type biplane, standard or racing, from £250 without an engine.

There was, however, no rush of would-be buyers. This was understandable; aviation was now beginning to move forward fast. By 1911 there was a wealth of fabulous new aircraft available, not only from the traditional and hugely respected French aviation experts but also from newly established British companies. The British and Colonial Aeroplane Company had started on its long line of Bristol type aircraft; A.V. Roe Company was gearing up production; the Howard Wright 1910 biplane was attracting attention after being flown by Thomas Sopwith on a record-breaking distance flight; the Short brothers had started making the first of their long line of machines.

With so much going on, who was going to rush to buy an unproven plane from a lady in Northern Ireland? It wasn't to be, and Lilian's father provided the final nail in the coffin for her aviation career. He was becoming increasingly frightened about the safety of his daughter as she flipped around in the air and to distract her, he offered to buy her a brand new motor car, a Model T Ford.

This caught Lilian's imagination. She probably began to realise that, despite her efforts, aviation developments and events in mainland England were overtaking her and it would be very hard indeed to keep up. A car could offer untold possibilities and excitement. Also, she was very fond of her soft and gentle father who had so consistently given her money to help cover her various exploits.

The deal was done; the plane was stored and then finally given away to a local gliding club. Lilian, in her true style of breaking boundaries, not only enthusiastically started driving all over the place but also set up an agency in Belfast to sell Ford motor cars. Something, though, was missing from her life and she was ready for a new adventure. As she turned 33, Lilian got together romantically with her somewhat wayward cousin, Lieutenant Charles Loftus Bland, who had had a chequered career which included time with the army in China and working as a gold prospector in California, where he had been caught up in the devastating San Francisco earthquake in 1906.

The couple married secretly in Tonbridge, Kent, not far from Lilian's childhood home, and they moved to Canada to set up a farm in a remote area on north Vancouver Island. It was a tough life in a fairly primitive homestead involving lots of hard physical work but this suited Lilian. In 1913, when she was 35, she had a daughter, Patricia, but as the years went by the marriage got into difficulties. After Patricia died at the age of 16 from an infection after a tetanus injection, life became a challenge for Lilian. Just a few years later, now well into her fifties, she decided to move back to England alone.

Lilian first moved in with her brother in Kent and worked locally as a landscape gardener while taking up painting. Her nature hadn't changed and she hit her new interests with full energy and innovation, returning to a slightly avant-garde lifestyle. As she approached her late seventies, Lilian moved down to Sennen in west Cornwall, where she continued with her painting and became recognised across the region for the beautiful gardens she created. Few, if any, local people were aware of her extraordinary background in aviation. Lilian lived in Cornwall for the rest of her life, until she died aged 92 in 1971.

8

HILDA HEWLETT

1911
THE FIRST BRITISH WOMAN TO RECEIVE AN OFFICIAL PILOT'S LICENCE, THE FIRST TO RUN A FLYING SCHOOL AND THE FIRST TO RUN AN AIRCRAFT FACTORY

By 1911, even the most cynical must have realised that the new-fangled craze of flying was here to stay. In the eight years since the Wright brothers had made their first tentative hops off the ground, aviation had changed beyond recognition. Now planes were developing fast, and the pilots along with them. It was time for a woman to be officially recognised as a fully qualified and capable pilot.

The Royal Aero Club of the United Kingdom was set up in 1901. Thanks to the influence of aviation enthusiast Vera Butler, who had helped encourage the formation of the club after a balloon flight, it was open to women right from the start. From 1910, it started issuing Aviators' Certificates for the rapidly increasing number of aeroplane flyers who were taking to the air. There were various requirements, including a distance flight and an altitude flight, and by the end of August 1911 nearly 120 pilots had demonstrated their skills and been awarded a certificate. They were all men.

When Hilda Hewlett joined this elite group, being awarded Aviator's Certificate Number 122 in September 1911, she was the first British woman ever to receive a pilot's licence. This meant she had already secured a place in the record books and she really didn't need to go on to be the first British woman to form a flying school and the first woman to start an aircraft manufacturing business as well.

Even more surprising, Hilda only took up flying when she was in her late forties; she was nearly 40 even when the Wright brothers got off the ground. When she was born in London, in February 1864, the only way up was by stairs or possibly in a balloon. Achieving her official pilot's licence in 1911 was thus a stunning achievement for Hilda, especially as before she could take up flying, she first had to break free from a fanatical, domineering mother and an ill-matched, dreamy poet and writer of a husband.

This was not easy, especially in the late Victorian era. Hilda's mother had married a Church of England vicar and took her religious beliefs to the extreme. Prayers, learning scriptures by heart, sins, repentance: Hilda's entire childhood was dominated by her mother's rigid beliefs in sin, confession and remorse. Her father, a much milder soul, was totally immersed in his flock and may well have been unaware of the strictures placed on his children in the family home in south London.

This rigid upbringing was especially difficult for young Hilda who, along with being lively and good natured, also had a stubborn side and showed a strong independence from an early age. After mainly being educated at home with a governess, she was enrolled at the South Kensington Art School, which she quite enjoyed. Then, when she was 19, her parents took her to Egypt.

This was unexpected; the trip was planned because Hilda's father was in poor health and it had been suggested three months in a warm climate would help. It was a great bonus for Hilda and she loved every minute of it. The heat, the brightness and the bustle of Alexandria in the 1880s overwhelmed her. Listening to the fascinating language of Arabic, seeing the Eastern art and eating different foods, Hilda was enchanted and excited by almost everything she saw. Her mother, true to nature, tried to keep Hilda under control, and even on the trip sat her down to preach about original sin and repentance. One can imagine young Hilda sitting in the heat, dressed in her pretty, long white cotton skirt, and looking around at the colourful, fascinating surroundings and intriguing locals as her mother droned on. This trip may have helped Hilda finally break free. Coming home after a fabulous three months in the sun, Hilda was ready to escape.

She managed to persuade her parents that nursing was a suitable next step and, under her mother's still careful supervision, Hilda spent some time in a hospital in Berlin. It was hard work but she did well, also learning German. Once back home, as a dutiful young daughter she accompanied her mother and other family members to various social events.

It was at one of these events that she met Maurice Hewlett. Maurice was from a reasonably prosperous family, tall, pleasant-looking, naturally quiet but very educated and extremely well read. He loved the classics, especially Plato and Homer. They met a couple more times and then Maurice proposed. After a few days thinking it through, Hilda telegrammed back her response. The answer was yes. Her mother was furious; she had been unaware of the proposal and was not happy. At one point during the engagement, Hilda's mother secretly wrote to Maurice saying the engagement was off.

Hilda was having none of that. At 23, it really was time to break free. She wrote to Maurice saying they needed to marry immediately and she then showed her mother the letter. There was nothing more her mother could do and Hilda married Maurice early in 1888, just before she turned 24.

Maurice had a steady job in antiquarian law and the couple moved into a nice flat in Bayswater, just to the north-west of Hyde Park in London. Hilda settled into the role of dutiful wife well but she found she had a lot to learn about her new husband, including his preoccupation with writing and his idea that he would really like to be a poet and an author. The household, though, was a happy one. With Maurice out at work and Hilda sorting out the home and beginning to socialise with her own friends, everything was working well. In 1891, three years after they were married, Hilda gave birth to a son; four years later she had a daughter.

Then, in 1898, things changed dramatically. Along with many other poems and stories, Maurice had written a historical romance called

The Forest Lovers. To the surprise of even the publishers, the book was a wild success and suddenly the Hewletts had serious money.

Their household and home life changed tremendously. Maurice gave up his job to become a full-time writer and they rented a new substantial family house in Maida Vale, London, plus later a country retreat west of Salisbury. Life had suddenly become very good indeed. With five servants, with Maurice writing and the two children busy being educated, Hilda had time and the money to enjoy more social outings and further her own interests.

The Hewletts then invested in a car and a chauffeur, and Hilda was especially fascinated by the machine. She learned to drive and took it all very seriously, working with their chauffeur on the mechanical aspects of the car and learning all she could. She found she really enjoyed driving and the independence it gave. She began to make longer journeys, driving on her own all over the place, visiting friends and going on trips. After a lifetime of quiet duty and correct behaviour, suddenly Hilda really did have freedom.

Meeting and talking to others, Hilda soon acquired some motoring friends who appreciated not only her enthusiasm and growing skill controlling a motor car, but also her knowledge about how it worked. This was a hugely exciting time in motoring, with club days, hill climbs and trials taking place across the country. Hilda invested in her own tri-car and started attending motoring meetings and even entered some events.

Really, the outcome was inevitable. While the Hewletts loved their children, the couple were moving into very different, separate lives. Maurice was immersed in his career as a writer of note; Hilda just loved the freedom and speed that had suddenly opened up to her and she was making new friends who shared her interest and knowledge. There was one other factor that was adjusting their relationship: Hilda's younger sister Gay, with a deep love of art and beauty, was establishing a close rapport with Maurice, a relationship that was gradually intruding into his emotions. Nevertheless, things might have jogged on if charismatic Frenchman Gustave Blondeau had not appeared on the scene.

Gustave was an engineer working for a car engine company in north France. Thoughtful and talented, he had developed his own two-stroke engine and during his involvement with cars he had become friends with Henri Farman. Farman was already recognised as a leading motor racer but was fast turning his attention to aviation. In 1907, Farman bought an early French Voisin biplane, setting numerous records, and in 1909 he planned to attend the groundbreaking Blackpool International Aviation Week in the north of England.

Seeing Farman's enthusiasm about the Blackpool aviation event, Gustave decided he also wanted to attend. He came over to the UK early and seems to have met Hilda at a motoring event. Gustave, with his moustache and beret, created a striking appearance and with his passion for motor cars and now aeroplanes, he would have been an interesting person to chat to. Speaking very little English, it was thanks to Hilda's limited knowledge of French that any communication was possible at all. They both agreed flight was hugely exciting and the Blackpool aviation meeting was well worth attending.

The week-long meeting at Blackpool involved some atrocious weather but also some outstanding flying, and both Hilda and Gustave were swept away by the magic of heavier-than-air flight. Gustave instantly decided his future would be in aviation; Hilda instantly decided she just had to have an aeroplane.

When Hilda got home bubbling with excitement after the event and full of ideas about learning to fly, her husband decided things had gone far enough. Even for a liberal author, the money, the machine, the danger, the whole idea of his wife taking up flying was absolutely ridiculous. Hilda was no youngster either, she was 45 with a family. What on earth was she thinking of? He kindly offered to buy her a larger car instead and once again Hilda became the dutiful housewife, embarking on a busy round of dinners and teas, theatre outings and other social distractions. But she couldn't forget the amazing world of flight.

Hilda and Gustave Blondeau were keeping in touch through letters, sharing news about new planes and flights, and at one point

Gustave confirmed his intention to get flying as soon as he could afford it. Did he see Hilda, nearly ten years older and clearly part of a wealthy family, as a possible benefactor, or did he keep in touch through pure friendship?

Either way, Hilda finally made up her mind. She simply had to get into aviation and, through attraction or convenience, she decided to ask Gustave for help. She wrote to him and asked if he would be interested in joining her in making a start in aviation if she bought an aeroplane. What an offer!

The answer of course was yes, but then came the problem. How could Hilda find the money, plus how would she explain this to her husband and friends? Even for someone with Hilda's determination, this was a tricky time. Dressing carefully, she must have been slightly nervous when she set off to attend a secret meeting she had arranged with the family lawyers to request a loan. The discussions weren't easy, but Hilda was very determined and also happy to sign that she would pay back the money in a few years. She managed to win them over and just enough money for a loan was found. She contacted Gustave Blondeau excitedly and was in full agreement that a French Farman aircraft was the best plane to buy, especially because the Farman Aviation Works would also offer free flying lessons to any purchaser of one of their planes. While Gustave went ahead in France with ordering the aircraft, Hilda then had to confront Maurice.

Perhaps it wasn't such a blow after all. Maurice was very taken with Hilda's younger sister Gay and this might afford them more time together. Also, Hilda wasn't seeking divorce; Maurice believed her when she explained she was just desperate to fly. Hilda agreed to go to Farman's base in France under the name of Mrs Grace Bird, no doubt to help stop any scandal, and the deal was done.

In January 1910, the same time that Britain's first female pilot Edith Cook was learning to fly further south in Pau, Hilda travelled through Paris and on to the Farman centre just over 100 miles to the east of the capital in Camp de Mourmelon.

It was an inauspicious arrival. Delighted to meet up with Gustave again, after booking into a hotel she then met Henri Farman who gave her bad news. First, their aeroplane was nowhere near ready, and secondly, only one pupil per machine ordered could be given free flying lessons. This needed a bit of thought but again Gustave came out a winner. It was agreed, with his superior engineering knowledge, that it made sense for him to undertake lessons first.

But until their plane was ready, neither of them would get up in the air. This must have been a strange time for Hilda; she wasn't the usual type of person hanging around an airfield. Somewhat older than most of the other enthusiasts, the middle-aged English lady at the French flying school must have caused considerable comment. The area itself wasn't a sunny upland conducive to dreams of flight either. In the middle of a cold winter, the airfield was bleak and often muddy and windy; the buildings were shabby, the facilities minimal. Hilda did have the comfort of her hotel, 2 miles away, but even that didn't serve hot food. Clothing, without any of the modern insulating materials and styles available, wasn't easy either, but Hilda had come prepared. She had invested in the heavyweight leather, natural wools and cottons of the day and also in some very wide knee-length culottes which, with woollen stockings and sturdy flat heeled shoes, certainly helped to keep out the cold.

While there was a delay on her plane and no flying for Hilda, there was a lot to enjoy during her days and weeks on the airfield. Surrounded by similar aviation enthusiasts and with growing fluency in French, she could chat away to everyone, learning so much while she watched various new pilots and their flimsy machines trying to get into the air. All aspects of flight began to intrigue and captivate Hilda. Farman offered Gustave and Hilda the use of a space in one of his construction shops to base themselves; they could study flight there and also help with aspects of the build of their very own plane. Nevertheless, it was all a phenomenal contrast to Hilda's comfortable lifestyle in Britain. It was a tribute to her determination and possible obstinacy that she remained. Another attraction may have been Gustave; after all they were by now spending pretty well all their time together.

But as the days and weeks went by, still Hilda's plane was not ready. The Farman workshops were incredibly busy with orders and Hilda's plane was just one in a long line. Other pilots and planes came and went, or more than occasionally succumbed to various crashes and disasters; but for Hilda and Gustave there was no flying. It was a hugely frustrating time. At last, in April, three months after they arrived, both Hilda and Gustave finally managed to get up into the air. A friendly Ukrainian, who had just taken delivery of his brand new Farman plane, kindly offered to take Hilda up for a flight. Suddenly, after so long, Hilda was going to experience the reality of flying in a beautiful aeroplane. With her strong interest in the engine and controls, she watched every aspect carefully as they taxied along and then took off. It was all she hoped for with a smooth engine purring away, the earth gently falling away below her and the wind whistling against the fabric and through the struts and wires.

They didn't go very high at all, but it was enough. Gliding back to earth, the flight reassured a very excited Hilda that she had made the right decision. All the discomfort, the expense, the challenges: everything had been more than worthwhile. Sitting in a heavier-than-air machine as it sped off the ground and flew through the air was simply the most amazing experience.

Towards the end of April, Gustave also managed to get into the air and was taken up quite a few times until he was feeling confident enough to go solo, but they needed their plane. It was all getting a little too frustrating. They hadn't unlimited money and it was proving expensive living at Mourmelon.

Finally, in May, their plane was ready. What an exciting moment that must have been. After so much effort, expense and waiting, at last the plane they had ordered all those months ago was finished. It was a beautiful Farman biplane and after so many weeks of watching and waiting, Hilda knew every part of it intimately. The ash airframe, the ribs, the spars, the fabric-covered wings and tail surfaces and the excellent Gnome engine; Hilda was totally thrilled that at last her very own plane was now a reality. She called it *Blue Bird*.

It must have been another fabulous moment when Gustave finally got in the little seat with his feet on the rudder bar and the control stick in front of him and started to move forward. As he soared into the air, Hilda watched closely how her little plane performed, carefully taking notes. Hilda tried out her new plane taxiing across the ground, enjoying every minute as she fine-tuned her knowledge of how the Gnome engine and the plane operated. She now felt she was ready to have some flying lessons and really learn how to fly properly, but it made sense for Gustave to maximise the free training at the Farman school and obtain his official licence before he started teaching her.

Not long after delivery of her new plane, there was a surprise for Hilda. Her husband Maurice turned up at the airfield with Hilda's younger sister. In recent months, Maurice and Gay had become closer still in their joy and appreciation of the artistic, and they were on an educational trip around the Continent.

It must have been a strange meeting of husband and wife and their two still just possibly platonic partners. There seems to have been no real ill-will, however, and Maurice even went up for a flight, albeit not with Gustave. They didn't stay at the airfield long. Gustave kept flying under the direction of the instructors at the airfield, and finally he achieved his Aéro-Club de France Aviator's Certificate Number 101 on 10 June 1910.

Once Gustave had his pilot's certificate, he and Hilda were free to consider the future. Hilda now wanted to try to start making money from her big investment; the money she had obtained to buy the plane was only a loan and needed repaying. There would also have been a more urgent necessity to obtain funds to cover their everyday costs as her marriage, and Maurice's level of financial support, were slowly petering out. Hilda wondered if Gustave, along with teaching her, might be willing to teach others too. There was no shortage of would-be pilots. If they used their plane to set up a small flying school, they might be able to make some useful money. She discussed the idea with Gustave and they both agreed it was a possible idea, something that could work.

Blue Bird was packed up into crates and the couple returned to England. Hilda visited her home, saw her much-loved children, and explained her idea of setting up a flying school to recoup the money. For this she needed to be based by an airfield. Husband Maurice was becoming resigned to his determined wife, so there was little to be said. Hilda and Gustave decided to base themselves at the Brooklands Club in Surrey; along with its famous motor course, it also offered hangars to rent and was even starting to hold flying events to help draw in spectators.

They rented Hangar No. 32, unpacked, reassembled *Blue Bird* and started to fly. Now at last the scene was set for Hilda to learn. However, in those early days of aviation, it soon became clear there were also many other people really keen to learn to fly, so the couple agreed that Gustave would start taking students immediately to help bring in some much-needed money. Hilda registered their fledgling business as the Hewlett and Blondeau Aviation School – her name first, of course. After all, she had initiated the whole thing and had paid for and fully owned the aeroplane.

Gustave turned out to be a meticulous and patient instructor. Their first student was a Frenchman, Maurice Ducrocq, and their second was Sandhurst-educated Englishman Richard Snowden-Smith. They achieved British pilots' licences numbers 23 and 29 respectively.

By early 1911 Hilda was fully absorbed in their new school of aviation. Gustave was still doing all the instruction and flying but Hilda was assisting with practically everything else. She didn't have anywhere near Gustave's depth of technical knowledge, but she did know a great deal. They made a good team and the students kept coming. She wasn't getting much flying done – she had managed to fit in just a few tentative attempts at controlling the plane on the ground – but she was certainly very busy.

Steadily, their flying school was building a reputation for being very safe and very thorough. Nevertheless, every so often the plane was out of action for servicing or repairs and there was always a risk that one of their students could really damage or even destroy their little plane. They decided they needed a back-up plane. Gustave had an idea for a lighter plane with reduced wings and it became clear that the cheapest way would be for them to build it themselves. Drawing on his wide knowledge and experience of engines and flight, Gustave drew up and finalised his design. It wasn't radically different from *Blue Bird*, but it was lighter, and Gustave hoped it would also have slightly improved control. It was time to start the build.

Gustave was a meticulous craftsman but they took on an additional carpenter and an assistant to help complete the aircraft. They bought an oxy-acetylene welding torch, one of the first in the country, and made some extra money from hiring it out to others at Brooklands. With financial assistance from one of their ex-students and imported parts including their favourite Gnome engine from France, the plane took shape. Hilda not only sewed together all the fabric covering for the wings but also fitted it to the frame and then carefully treated it all with varnish to make it watertight. She was definitely hands-on in building this exciting new machine and endured many cold damp hours in their hangar at Brooklands. However, she and Gustave had also rented some basic accommodation in nearby York Road in Byfleet for a warm base to retire to.

It must have been a nervous moment when their homemade plane was finally completed, checked, and then rolled out for its maiden flight very early one misty spring morning in 1911. Hilda got into the pilot's seat to warm up the Gnome engine and then stepped out, handing over to Gustave to take off. The flight was a tremendous success and all they had hoped for, with light controls and excellent handling. While it could only manage a maximum of around 50mph, this was more than acceptable at the time.

The whole enterprise was going well, and a steady stream of would-be pilots were applying for training, eager to pay the £75 at a school that was increasingly receiving excellent reports. But still Hilda wasn't flying. After such a long involvement in aeroplanes, perhaps the excitement was wearing off, or perhaps she found the logistics and business aspects of it all so absorbing that finally taking control of a plane had become less important to her. In the many months of taking passengers it was odd that a little time hadn't been put aside to let her at last fulfil her original dream.

By midsummer, with excellent weather, the decision was made that, finally, Hilda should learn to fly. Gustave, now an experienced and very capable instructor, helped her gain experience, often with flights as early as 4 a.m. to take advantage of the calm still weather of early morning before the winds picked up. Hilda had lived with aeroplanes for over eighteen months; she had been on quite a few flights as a passenger and fully understood not only all aspects of flight and controls, but also how the engine worked. There couldn't have been a better-prepared student. By mid July Hilda was becoming a capable pilot. She could take off easily and felt the plane handled beautifully; she could climb and descend and had mastered making gentle turns with minimal pressure on the controls. After a few more flights she felt she was ready. She notified the Royal Aero Club and a date was fixed for her to take her test at Brooklands.

Early on the morning of 18 August 1911, at the age of 47, Hilda got into the new home-built plane. Carefully controlling the throttle, she lifted off smoothly and easily, completed five figures-of-eight, landed within 50 yards of a designated landing point and then completed a further five figures-of-eight including climbing to a height of 160ft before making a smooth touchdown and rolling to a halt. It was a neat, professional display of well-controlled flight. Stepping out of the plane, she was loudly cheered by a growing crowd of ex-students, Brooklands colleagues and friends. Hilda had passed the test! She had become the very first British woman to earn an official pilot's licence, Royal Aero Club licence No. 122, the first British woman to do a right-handed turn and the first British woman to reach a height of over 100ft.

Today this may not sound particularly impressive, but in those days, in the wonderful wood-and-fabric planes, with their precariously open pilot's seating and basic controls, it really was an exciting achievement. No British woman before had passed the Royal Aero Club flight test.

It was a fine accomplishment and only enhanced the flying school's reputation. After obtaining her licence, Hilda took the plane up on short flights more regularly and proved to be a very efficient and competent pilot. She even entered a quick get-off competition at Brooklands, beating recognised pilots such as Thomas Sopwith, Henry Petre and Edward Fisher. This gave her another record: the first woman to win an open aviation competition. Hilda, however, had found that she enjoyed running a successful business as much as she enjoyed being in the air, and she flew occasionally rather than regularly.

Her qualification as a pilot lifted Hilda's reputation with her family, who were becoming far more supportive now she had achieved real success. Her husband Maurice and other friends visited Brooklands and everything seemed rather cordial. Their two children also visited the school and, just three months after she gained her official licence, Hilda taught her son to fly. At the same time, in November 1911, Britain's second female pilot, Cheridah de Beauvoir Stocks, achieved her official licence at the Hendon flying school run by Claude Grahame-White.

While her achievements gave Hilda some fleeting fame, financially it didn't make much difference. While they still had a good stream of pupils, what with maintaining the planes, renting the hangar and their little house and all the other day-to-day expenses, money still remained tight. Also, their two little planes were fast being superseded by new designs and developments put together by groups with far better financial backing. Official interest was now increasing in aviation; the British War Office had bought a de Havilland No. 2 biplane and the Army Air Battalion had received four Bristol Boxkites from the British and Colonial Aeroplane Company. There was growing competition from facilities able to offer excellent new-style aeroplanes and full flight training.

It was really thanks to their very first pupil, Maurice, that the next stage of Hilda's aviation career took place. Ducrocq had excellent connections with the French Aéroplanes Hanriot et Cie company. In the spring of 1912, the Hewlett and Blondeau Aviation School was asked if it could take a contract to make three Hanriot aeroplanes. These were two-seater slender wooden French monoplanes. Hilda was enthusiastic. There was still money to be paid back on her loan, and making aeroplanes offered excellent profit potential. They had already proven they could make a good aircraft.

There was another factor. Hilda was seriously concerned, almost annoyed, that Britain was behind other countries in the world of aviation. She had been preaching for some time that flying would revolutionise war, and now she felt strongly that Britain's supremacy of the sea would be useless unless the air above the ships and around the coast could also be defended.

An opportunity to start manufacturing aircraft could be something really worthwhile. Admittedly the first contract was for French aircraft, and indeed her partner Gustave was French. But right from the beginning Hilda realised this could just be a start of something really good for her country. Enthusiastically, the Hewlett and Blondeau Aviation School accepted the contract. Suddenly, from a friendly little organisation showing excited students how to fly, Hewlett and Blondeau were to become professional aeroplane manufacturers.

It was immediately clear that the current hangar at Brooklands simply would not work. It was small; it had no power or water; there were minimal facilities. After training a total of thirteen pupils at their school, it was time to move on. It was decided new premises and also a new name were needed for this grand step forward. With Hilda's energy, both were soon resolved. The new name, Omnia Works, was more than appropriate, a name not – as generally thought – chosen from Latin but much more likely from the Egyptian origins meaning 'a wish'. Perhaps Hilda had come across this on her visit to Egypt all those years before.

Finance was also organised, in part thanks to Hilda's husband. She was still visiting her married home on occasions and Maurice was becoming increasingly proud of what his errant wife was achieving. It appears he was now willing to put some money forward to help the new venture. This, along with early money from the contract, enabled Hilda to rent a new site in Vardens Road in Battersea, just south of the Thames in London. The premises were ideal: a small open space that had been an old roller-skating rink and then used by a car company. Gustave, armed with all the design and manufacturing specifications from Hanriot, worked out with typical precision the full plans for the materials and equipment needed and how the manufacturing process would work. Hilda, with her enthusiasm and drive, organised everything else.

Starting a new aeroplane factory was going to throw up many problems. There were parts and stock to purchase and right from the start Hilda did all she could to ensure all their supplies were made in Britain. Aircraft at the Omnia Works were going to be British made! Then Hilda had a set-to with two union officials who came to call about payment to their carpenters, with the result that she instead advertised in the north of England and Scotland for apprentices who were not union members. There were numerous letters to be written and accounts to be paid, and Hilda was not a natural correspondent or record keeper. But it all got going and the machines started to be built.

Day after day the Omnia Works were full of activity, with men working on the wooden structures of the planes on one side of the floor and metal workers on the other side. While Gustave supervised all the manufacture, Hilda was often at her sewing machine making the fabric wings for the planes. Even running such an enterprise didn't stop Hilda being hands-on and, as with the first plane they had made, she did all the fabric work which included not only sewing, but also the stretching, fitting and doping required to make the wings operational.

Hilda was in the works at 8 a.m. every day, and to make things a bit easier she rented a flat a couple of miles away in the Prince of Wales Mansions just south of Battersea Park. This was a huge step up in accommodation for them both and much more suited to Hilda's background.

As the Hanriot aeroplanes started to take shape, Hilda also spent time looking for additional contracts for the workforce they were employing. While she had been doing a few pleasure flights and had even taken part in a flying meeting held at Hendon in summer 1912, really her flying days were coming to an end. The Omnia Works were full on, but it was all enormously satisfying.

Another order came in, for a Cauldron biplane, and then finally, after a lot of very determined effort, they received an order from the Royal Aircraft Factory at Farnborough for two BE2c biplanes designed for reconnaissance work.

At one point the couple decided a holiday was a necessity. They had been working so hard and a break was becoming essential. Hilda, Gustave and both of Hilda's children plus Hilda's big dog all hopped into Hilda's car and went for a short camping trip to St Leonard's

Forest near Horsham in Sussex. But then it was back to work. The couple took a small stand at the Exhibition of Aeroplanes and Aero Engines at London's Olympia in both 1913 and in 1914, where they offered aeroplanes built from customers' designs plus engine plates, housings, fuselages, rudders, seats and all accessories. They also offered oxy-acetylene welding as a speciality. They were happy to take on any aviation-related work and the business flourished. In spring 1914, just a couple of months after Hilda's 50th birthday, their business became a fully registered limited company with Hilda, Gustave and Hilda's husband Maurice holding the main shares.

As the company expanded, the premises in central London were no longer ideal and Hilda and Gustave found some affordable land in Leagrave, north-west of Luton in Bedfordshire. It was near a railway station so parts could easily be delivered and crated plane sections sent off. Hilda showed her determination again as she grappled with all the organisation involved in building an efficient aircraft factory.

And then the First World War was declared. Hilda had always shown deep-rooted patriotism and, with her new factory up and running, she was now determined to do her bit. A well-planned meeting at the Admiralty secured a massive breakthrough, a contract for eighteen more aircraft. This was a fantastic order for Hilda's company, but there was no time for celebration; this was now war work and needed to be done for the country as well as for profit.

Hilda was working non-stop to manage the dramatically expanding workloads; at one point the factory was employing hundreds of workers and she organised a canteen. In 1915, things changed again after Hilda's company was declared a Controlled Establishment under the auspices of the Ministry of Munitions. This meant that the government could now inspect and control certain aspects of the factory and Hilda was not pleased. Work went on at a new level of intensity, with major new contracts coming in, but now a new manager, a Mr Ashley Pope, was organising things and, for Hilda, it was never the same. One of their biggest orders was for Armstrong Whitworth FK3s, two-seater general biplanes, but as they lifted their production levels, supplies started to become difficult and

Hilda found herself immersed in paperwork and calls trying to keep up. Even worse, difficult and bullying government supervisors with minimal aviation knowledge started examining their work. This infuriated Hilda.

The entrepreneurial spirit that had drawn Gustave and Hilda together years before was now missing. They were now making hundreds of aircraft, but it was all becoming simply hard work. As the war dragged on, Hilda's youthful spirit and vigour were beginning to diminish. Now in her mid fifties, as the war drew to a conclusion, so did her desire to do her bit for the country. She had lost direction.

Overall, the company had manufactured more than 800 military aircraft and employed nearly 700 people but now, as the war ended, military orders stopped coming in. The couple thought about turning the factory into one making agricultural equipment. Like many companies after the war, though, they found the demand wasn't there. The couple had ploughed all their money back into the company and the workforce. There was no high level of savings to fall back on. In October 1920, the company went into liquidation.

The early 1920s also marked a quiet goodbye to both the key men in Hilda's life. Maurice died in 1923 and Gustave moved away, becoming close to his former secretary at the factory. He continued to live near her in Bedfordshire until his death at the age of 94. It was time for a new start for Hilda who, with time on her hands, had started to travel a little, visiting friends overseas as far afield as New Zealand.

Her daughter, Barbara, always known as Pia, had remained close to her mother despite the break-up of her parents' marriage, and at the end of the war Pia had married. Her new husband had been in the army during the war and wanted to make a new start; they all agreed New Zealand was the place to go.

With all her affairs settled, in 1926 Hilda went out to Tauranga in New Zealand to start a new life. At 62, her drive had not diminished and after settling in New Zealand she purchased, together with a business partner, Southern Cross Airways with its one plane. Unfortunately that didn't work, but she was very involved in the establishment of the Tauranga Aero and Gliding Club and was elected the club's inaugural president in 1933. To complete the family setting, Hilda's son joined them later and subsequently became the club's third president.

It was a happy ending for Hilda, who had devoted her life in various ways to the exciting concept of aviation. When she died in 1943, aged 79, she would have been very aware of the Hurricanes, the Spitfires and all the amazing new aircraft that were being developed. Hopefully, she was also proud of the contributions she had made in the very early days of the aviation industry.

9

SYLVA BOYDEN

1919
THE FIRST BRITISH WOMAN TO USE A PACKED PARACHUTE AND THE FIRST TO PARACHUTE FROM AN AIRCRAFT

For the first time, 20-year-old Sylva Boyden was really frightened. There was no sudden reason for this. The 0/400 Handley Page converted bomber aircraft was flying steadily at 1,200ft, its powerful Rolls-Royce engines purring away smoothly. For spring 1919, the weather was good and there was a clear open area far below in the centre of Alexandra Park in Manchester.

But as the air rushed passed and the pilot indicated that it was time to jump, suddenly the park seemed a very, very long way down. Sylva's parachute was safely stowed in its special container on the fuselage and she was tightly fitted into her harness, but nevertheless she hesitated and almost froze. Colleagues on the plane started talking and encouraging her; after all this was a well-publicised important jump, a special stunt organised by the *Daily Mail* newspaper. Sylva had jumped from the plane before; she had full confidence in the parachute system; her previous landings had been fine. What was the problem? The pilot circled around the airfield again. Having got this far, it really was too late to back out.

With a final push of encouragement from the pilot and one of the men on board, Sylva finally plucked up her courage and off she went, diving headfirst from the back of the plane into the clear air far above the crowds in the park so far below. Suddenly the noise and bustle in the aeroplane were gone. She fell down fast through the rushing air and quickly felt the pull as her harness was jerked up from the shoulders. Above her, a large round red and white canopy was billowing out into its full shape and the world was coming back to normal. Swinging a little as the canopy oscillated back and forth, she descended gently on to the grass in the park and into the awaiting acclaim and publicity.

What a relief that must have been for Sylva. If she hadn't jumped, she would have let down the organisers, the expectant crowd, the manufacturers of the parachute and, worst of all, she would have let down Major Orde-Lees.

Thomas Orde-Lees was not a man to cross. He had served in the Royal Marines, had seen action in the Boxer Rebellion in China in 1900 and he was a survivor of Shackleton's Antarctic expedition. More recently he had joined the Royal Flying Corps, the air arm of the British army, and had become keen on parachutes. He was an early enthusiast about installing parachutes on planes to save the lives of airmen and in 1917, just two years before Sylva did her first jump, he had done a spectacular jump off Tower Bridge in London to show how the parachute could save a life, even at a low level. The parachute opened just in time to give him a reasonably gentle splashdown.

It was Orde-Lees who got Sylva interested in parachutes. Sylva had been born in 1899 as Grace Ellen Pothecary, and during her early childhood, first in Lambeth and then in Twickenham in south-west London, finances were very tight. Her father was a carpenter, and even when the First World War started and he joined up to serve on a paddle minesweeper, talk at home would have been about the war effort, not about developments in aviation.

For Grace, though, as she grew through her teens, wartime London was an exciting place. With so many men away at war, there were lots of new opportunities for women. At one point Grace decided to take on a new name to create a better image for herself, selecting her grandmother's surname and a first name she liked. From then on

Grace became Sylva Boyden. Maybe this helped; sometime in 1918 she caught the eye of Major Orde-Lees. The general story she told was that she met him at her job in a military establishment, and that could well be so; many women were employed in a range of official organisations during the First World War. However, another report of their first meeting seems more likely. This indicates that Sylva approached Orde-Lees when he was supervising a parachute drop in Richmond Park in south London and asked if she could get involved.

Either way, they got talking. Attractive, bubbly Sylva was only 19 years old while Orde-Lees was in his forties, with a lifetime of experience behind him. When Orde-Lees started to explain his determination to make parachutes available to save the lives of British airmen, Sylva was immediately interested. He may have glossed over the aspect of commission that he would receive from parachute sales; for Sylva it was a clear-cut matter. If parachutes worked so well, why on earth weren't they already compulsory equipment in aeroplanes? She learned about Orde-Lees's special enthusiasm for the British-designed 'Guardian Angel' parachute and listened attentively as he explained how it worked.

At this point, it is doubtful she really took in all the advantages of the new design that Orde-Lees was going on about, how the parachute was folded neatly into a small container so that it could be safely attached to an aircraft in flight, and how the parachutist would fall from the plane and then pull the parachute out behind. There was no risk of the parachute becoming entangled; the mouth of the canopy was held open by a little ring to ensure it inflated quickly. It was perfect for brave pilots to have in their aircraft as a way of escape in emergencies.

If all this detail was a bit over her head, Sylva still thought it all sounded wonderful. At some point she mentioned she would be more than happy to give the Guardian Angel parachute a try.

Early in December 1918, Orde-Lees contacted Everard Calthrop, designer of the Guardian Angel parachute, saying he had a friend, a girl, who was keen to make a jump. Both Orde-Lees and Calthrop were anxious to publicise the benefits of the Guardian Angel parachute and both quickly saw the possible benefits of having a young girl demonstrate the equipment. Calthrop responded saying that if the girl had the requisite nerve and was really keen, then he would be happy to arrange for her to jump on the next testing day he was organising. These jumps were being done from cheaper balloons rather than using aircraft. Sylva definitely had the nerve and if anything, her initial idea of doing a jump had only strengthened. After all, she would not be the first woman to jump from a balloon. What fun it could be.

The trials had been taking part in Richmond Park on the outskirts of London. With its wide open spaces, it was an ideal location for parachute testing. For the next trials, in February 1919, several drops had been planned to test two different types of parachutes, a Mears parachute and Calthrop's Guardian Angel.

The winter of 1918–19 was one of the coldest for a while, with widespread snowfalls and very chilly conditions. Luckily, however, Friday 28 February dawned calm and still. Ready for adventure, Sylva, well prepared with protective clothing and a fur-lined flying helmet, accompanied Major Orde-Lees to Richmond Park.

The jumps were planned to be from a stationary balloon tethered at about 800ft and, after jumping off through the door in the basket, the parachutist would fall for around four seconds until the canopy opened. Orde-Lees had a job to do, watching and reporting back to an official committee on the descents but for Sylva, all her thoughts were on her planned jump. Her harness was fitted and the parachute, carefully packed into a conical container, was secured on the outside of the basket. She got in and up they went. It was a quiet ascent, and once the balloon reached the required height, she would have been aware of the silence and the proximity of the ground below. 800ft isn't very high and she would have been able to see all the activity in the park beneath her quite clearly. The thought of launching herself out into the air was totally terrifying, but Sylva was determined to do the jump. Once the instructor in the balloon was happy, he gave Sylva the indication to go and that was it. Sylva did not hesitate, and jumped out into the air. No problems at all. As she fell earthwards, the line firmly pulled the parachute out of its container and it quickly blossomed above her.

In no time at all, after a gentle, steady descent, Sylva was back on the grass of Richmond Park. It had all worked as expected and she was definitely up for more. Orde-Lees felt having Sylva involved was a huge benefit for emphasising the safety of the Guardian Angel, and soon more jumps were arranged.

By now, at last, there was growing official interest in parachutes from both the government and the military. Another trial was arranged to be carried out at the end of March 1919, this time in the presence of American, Canadian and Japanese as well as English officers. It was the ideal event to promote the British Guardian Angel parachute and Sylva agreed to carry out three descents. She was as enthusiastic as ever, saying she didn't feel nervous at all. Each jump went well; Sylva came down lightly, bending her knees as Orde-Lees has instructed her for a gentle landing. She commented at the time that there was no greater shock on landing than jumping from a mantelpiece.

Calthrop and Orde-Lees were by now becoming anxious for the success of the parachute, both to save lives and also to make money. A great deal had been invested in the development of the parachute, and sales needed to be made soon to keep Calthrop's business afloat. They were also aware that other parachute makers were bringing out new designs, so there was now an urgency to get sales going. Orde-Lees looked at obtaining sponsorship to cover further development and displays of the parachute, including in the US, and he also arranged some more demonstration jumps for the following month. This time, however, he planned the jumps would be from an aeroplane, and they would include Sylva. No woman in Britain had ever jumped from an aeroplane before; in fact it would very nearly be a world first. American Tiny Broadwick had been the very first woman to jump from an aeroplane when she took part in her family's aviation exhibition in Los Angeles in 1913. So Orde-Lees felt confident that if Sylva would do it, there would be really good additional publicity for the Guardian Angel. When the idea was put to her, Sylva showed no hesitation in agreeing to jump from an aeroplane instead of a balloon. She had full confidence in the parachute system and she was still keen to help save lives by proving that parachutes could work.

Sylva's parachute descent was arranged to be from a Handley Page Type 0 aircraft. This was a biplane bomber that had been used on the Continent during the war, mainly for the strategic bombing of key targets such as industry and transport. It was first built in Cricklewood in north London and at the time was the largest aircraft ever built in the UK. After the First World War, the planes started being converted to fly passengers and also to carry freight.

On Easter Monday, 21 April 1919, Handley Page had planned a special open day at their airfield in Cricklewood where the public could see the planes fly and even go for a thirty-minute joy flight. A good crowd was expected, and so it was arranged for Sylva to do a jump on that day, offering excellent exposure for the Guardian Angel parachute.

Sylva was still as confident and as enthusiastic as ever. Orde-Lees explained everything carefully. The exit would be different from jumping from a balloon, of course. This time Sylva would have to contend with the noise together with the very strong wind of the slipstream as she stood up and then climbed out of the plane. The best way to exit was to dive out strongly into the air headfirst to make sure she made a good clearance from the airframe. As she fell, her weight would pull the parachute out from the container fixed to the plane. Then the parachute would open as normal and she would descend gently down to earth. That was the theory. Sylva had never been up in an aeroplane, but it all sounded feasible.

Easter weekend 1919 was a time of celebration for the country. The war was over and there was hope that even the dreadful Spanish Flu pandemic, which had killed so many people, was now on the wane. People thronged out to places of interest and recreation to enjoy themselves. The weather was still a trifle cold, but bright sunshine occasionally broke through the cloud and there was only a light wind.

On Easter Monday, the crowds turned up in their thousands to see the events at Cricklewood. Sylva was ready to play her part. Dressed in sturdy boots, trousers and a thick sweater plus large gauntlet gloves and a flying hat, she was well protected and, with the harness tightly fitted, all was ready. It was to be a double descent. Also getting into the plane was Professor William Newell, an experienced parachutist.

If Sylva's confidence needed boosting, he would have been the man to do it; he had been jumping from balloons for decades and, in 1914, had been the first in England to jump from an aeroplane.

Sylva clambered on board and sat down in the open passenger compartment just back from the double wings of the large biplane. She was extremely careful not to interfere with the line that reached from her harness over to the bottom of the parachute which was firmly packed in its container on the outside of the plane. She sat there without moving as Orde-Lees checked it all and then she fixed the straps of her flying helmet tightly below her chin. It was all such a new experience and nerves were beginning to kick in. After all, she had never even been in an aeroplane before, let alone jumped out over the side of one. The crowd began to quieten as the large biplane started its powerful engines. Suddenly the noise became louder and the big rattling bomber started slowly rolling forward. Faster and faster it went across the ground, vibrating and bouncing and reaching a rush of speed that had Sylva hanging on tightly. Then it gently lifted off the ground.

Seeing the people and hangars becoming smaller and smaller, Sylva stopped looking out and concentrated on her role. It wasn't really that different from a balloon jump, she told herself. All she had to do was jump off.

The plane climbed higher and higher until it had reached over 1,200ft and then started heading straight across the centre of the airfield for the jump. The crowds of people below all strained their necks staring upwards, waiting for the tiny figures to appear. In the plane, what with the noise from the engines and the slipstream, it was not easy to talk. Sylva had sat there quietly as they climbed to height. Now, as the time approached to jump, she mentally prepared herself, going through the bits and pieces Orde-Lees had told her. Then the pilot gave the signal and it was time. First to go was Professor Newell. Suddenly, he was gone. It was time for Sylva to go. She did not hesitate. Pushing her way up against the noisy, blasting slipstream and holding on tightly, she positioned herself and then, summing up all her courage, she dived forward off the side of the plane out into the air. She fell fast and, pulling the parachute down behind her, the canopy opened. The deafening noise, the violent rush of air, the sudden surge of activity – it all disappeared instantly. A quick fall through the air and then, in just a few seconds, she was hanging quietly below her parachute, floating down gently and silently to the crowds below. She made a light and easy landing near to Professor Newell and the crowds went mad with tremendous cheers and applause. Being one of the stars of such a big show was a new experience for Sylva. Any tension was over. She was the first British woman ever to parachute from an aeroplane. Filled with relief, she was more than happy to talk to the newspaper reporters who rushed up to get impressions of the jump. Buoyant and confident, she gave excellent quotes on how safe it all was, something that was reported all around the country.

Major Orde-Lees was delighted: another excellent display of the safety of the Guardian Angel parachute system to attract new buyers, and lots of extra publicity because a girl had done the jump. Everard Calthrop was equally pleased. He, together with Orde-Lees's help, now had high hopes of selling the parachute to the military both in Britain and also in America and Canada, and they felt confident this latest public success would help. Further jumps now needed to be organised to consolidate the Guardian Angel's superiority over other parachutes.

One aspect of the new Handley Page planes was that they had been converted not only to carry passengers but also to deliver limited freight and newspapers. Newspapers provided a cargo that demanded fast delivery and Handley Page and the *Daily Mail* got together to organise a special stunt. They would fly across the country dropping bundles of newspapers in various towns. The *Daily Mail* loved the idea of beating competitors by distributing their newspapers first; Handley Page were keen to publicise their new civilian services.

Orde-Lees got himself the job of ensuring the bundles of papers were dropped at the best points for each town, and he also arranged for Sylva Boyden to go along to do various jumps along the route. This would give publicity to the Guardian Angel parachute as well. Sylva thought it a splendid idea, plus she would be paid well for her efforts. Packing her little bag for the trip, Sylva still had total confidence in Orde-Lees; she trusted him and she trusted the parachute. It would be an exciting few days away.

On 1 May the converted Handley Page bomber D8350 took off from Cricklewood Aerodrome, piloted by Lt Col William Sholto Douglas, holder of commercial licence number 4. He took off with eleven passengers including Orde-Lees and Sylva Boyden, plus bundles of newspapers.

There was a strong headwind and the flight up to Manchester took over three hours. For Sylva, sitting there on her first proper aeroplane trip, it must have been the biggest adventure. As she was growing up, she never could have dreamed that one day she would be sitting in an aeroplane looking down as the green pleasant fields of England passed steadily by below her. But it wouldn't have been all pleasure. At the back of her mind was the fact that when they arrived overhead in Manchester, she was to jump out over Alexandra Park Aerodrome as extra publicity for the event. All went well, though, and at the moment she was told to leave, she battled through the slipstream and dived into the air. The parachute opened faultlessly above her and she landed easily on the aerodrome.

The following day bad weather closed in but on the day after, the plane took off and made a number of successful drops of bundles of *Daily Mail* newspapers. Orde-Lees supervised the drops on to selected golf courses and on returning to Manchester, once again Sylva Boyden was due to jump down into Alexandra Park Aerodrome. This time, however, suddenly Sylva became nervous. She had only done a handful of jumps and perhaps the reality of what she was doing finally hit her. Looking down over the side of the aircraft, despite wearing her harness and having the parachute safely installed in the container ready to be pulled out, she didn't want to go. She just couldn't do it. The pilot flew across the airfield and then circled round again. This time the people on board came to her rescue and offered support and reassurance. Finally, she plucked up the courage and, after a final push of encouragement, off she went, safely landing under her parachute on the airfield below.

On landing, Sylva was back to her normal self and was happy to continue on the promotional tour. Things didn't always go smoothly. These were still very early days of flying plus British weather was rarely ideal for parachuting. A week later, on 10 May 1919, Sylva was due to jump at Didsbury, 4 miles south of Manchester. It was a little windy and under the parachute Sylva was blown well off target. She must have had a nervous few moments descending as she wondered whether her landing would be on one of the high rooftops belonging to the many houses below her. In fact, she only narrowly missed a railway bridge before luckily landing on a ploughed field at the junction of two roads. Showing good presence of mind, she immediately pressed the quick-release button that was a feature of the Guardian Angel system so that she did not get dragged along by the wind, and all was well.

That was a new experience for Sylva and brought home firmly that things could – and did – go wrong. But she had reacted well and overall it was still a positive display for the Guardian Angel system. The mayor of Manchester and other dignitaries of the town had been for a flight in the plane, *Daily Mail* newspapers had been dropped successfully at various locations, and despite the small hiccup of Sylva missing a target, the whole trip was going very well for everyone. Then, two days later, there was a definite hitch.

On 12 May the plane took off again from Manchester with some more newspapers to deliver to various locations further north. Orde-Lees was on board to supervise the drops and Sylva was also on the plane. After a successful drop of newspapers at Carlisle, on the way back there were some engine problems and the pilot put down in a field to repair a small fault. However, while the pilot had managed to land successfully, the field was just a little tight for take-off. With the repairs done, as the plane lifted off the ground, it caught the top of a hedge causing it to nosedive hard into the next field. Orde-Lees was thrown clear and managed to escape with bad bruising. Sylva was thrown forward, injuring her face and cracking a tooth. The two other passengers escaped with minor injuries but the pilot was badly hurt, with a broken rib and a crushed lung. The pilot was taken to hospital where he eventually recovered and Orde-Lees and Sylva were also checked over in hospital before being released. This was a major setback to the newspaper-dropping stunt and also to Sylva. It adds even more to her resilient character that she was happy to resume parachuting once she recovered. After all, it was the plane, not the parachute, that had let her down.

While Orde-Lees and Sylva had been working closely together for some months now, Orde-Lees took great pains to introduce her as his secretary. They were doing pretty well everything together; parachuting was not a nine-to-five job and the trip to Manchester involved staying in the town. Clearly Orde-Lees was anxious to ensure there was no open indication of impropriety.

It didn't take too long for Sylva to recover from the accident. Her natural confidence had been boosted by her success at parachuting and, having turned 20, she was excited about the future. Adding to this was the fact that Orde-Lees had now organised a promotional trip to America. To America! As her mouth mended, Sylva got ready for the most amazing trip of her life so far. She had never been abroad, never even thought about it. Now here she was, about to board a beautiful ocean crossing ship to head for New York. Sylva had only done her first jump a few months before; things were moving very fast.

Orde-Lees had arranged everything. They were to travel on the SS *Australind*, leaving London for New York on 24 May. Sylva knew she was on the edge of being out of her depth. Orde-Lees was widely travelled and experienced; all she had done was a trip to Manchester. First she had to obtain a passport. Passports had only recently been introduced and were made up of just one page of paper, folded up and held together with a cardboard cover. They were, nevertheless, official documents. Sylva had to revert to her true legal name, Grace Ellen Pothecary, for the journey. It also meant she finally had to explain to her family what she was really up to; she was still considered a minor in the face of the law and she needed their approval for her passport. Her parents were now based in Southampton and while, at first, she had been reluctant to tell them about her parachuting, after all the publicity and photographs it had been hard to keep the news quiet.

However, while travelling around giving shows across the UK was one thing, travelling overseas in the company of a much older gentleman was something else. There seemed no real family objections though; after all, Sylva was doing something she loved and she was earning good money too. Finally, Sylva had to sort out what clothes to take. Orde-Lees arranged for a khaki uniform for her to wear to add a more professional look.

Just twelve days after the plane crash, Sylva was aboard the SS *Australind* waving goodbye to England. It wasn't a cruise ship; it carried just a few passengers along with cargo and it had no luxurious comforts. But it was well appointed, with good meals, and Sylva could sit comfortably on the deck watching the great ocean swells roll under the boat as she dreamed about the future. She would certainly have been on deck as the ship approached New York. With its early skyscrapers and the Statue of Liberty perched as now in the harbour entrance, it made a dramatic and truly memorable sight.

Sylva was travelling to America at an interesting time. It was just two weeks before British aviators John Alcock and Arthur Brown were to make their momentous first non-stop flight across the Atlantic and also at a time when women were very much in the news; votes for women were just about to be approved by the American Congress.

Orde-Lees had arranged the trip to demonstrate the Guardian Angel parachute to American military and postal officials in a very real hope of obtaining some substantial orders. Sylva was going on the trip to jump, helping to endorse the parachute's safety, and a couple of other assistants had joined the team including Lieutenant R.A. Caudwell, an ex-Royal Flying Corps colleague of Orde-Lees. After arriving in the US, the little group spent the first few weeks travelling around to various airfields successfully demonstrating the parachute. Sylva had to jump from a number of different types of aircraft but found it all quite straightforward. All she had to do was dive clear away from the aeroplane and the parachute opening system was the same. Both Orde-Lees and Sylva did several jumps and it all went very well. There seemed to be a good overall response to the Guardian Angel parachute. One important event arranged on the trip was a jump planned at the beginning of July at College Park Airfield just north-east of Washington DC. A large gathering of American army, navy and aerial mail officials had gathered for the occasion. All were now considering looking at the official purchase of parachutes; the orders could be huge.

The jumps went well but Orde-Lees and his team were not the only ones after this big potential market. American inventor Lawrence Sperry was also demonstrating a new lightweight parachute and there was competition from other parachute designers including Leslie Irvin. Irvin had made news when, three months earlier, in April 1919, he made the first freefall descent with a manually operated ripcord parachute; he wore the packed parachute on his back and opened it by pulling a ripcord after he had fallen well below the plane. This was a dramatic breakthrough in parachuting but didn't receive immediate acceptance; there were still many doubters who felt the equipment wasn't strong enough and also that there was serious risk to the health of a person falling through the air before opening a parachute. It didn't help either that Leslie Irvin broke his ankle on landing.

The next venue for Orde-Lees and Sylva was McCook Field, near Dayton, Ohio. It was decided, for this display, that Lieutenant Caudwell would also do a jump. He had done one descent before and was totally confident in the Guardian Angel. This time the team was demonstrating the parachute from a DH.9 biplane. Orde-Lees was the first to jump and had an unfortunate landing in the nearby Miami River although he was successfully retrieved. Sylva jumped next, clambering up over the high side of the plane and making an energetic jump out into the air. Her parachute opened quickly and all went well. Then Lieutenant Caudwell jumped. As he left the plane, his attachment line to the parachute in the container caught and snagged firmly on part of the plane. The line tightened and then snapped before it could pull out the parachute, and Lieutenant Caudwell fell to his death.

It was a shocking, dramatic and tragic event, and the end to what had been proving to be a very successful tour. It was also the end of any hope that the Americans would adopt the Guardian Angel parachute. Sylva had witnessed her first parachute death at close hand and it must have been a very sobering experience. Returning quietly to England, it was a flat finish to a year that had started out with unbelievable excitement.

While Sylva took stock of what had happened, Everard Calthrop needed to continue publicising and selling his new parachute design, and a woman who worked in his office volunteered to help. Nellie Gibson did some very successful jumps from an aeroplane that autumn and was even used in an advertisement that Calthrop put together.

By spring 1920 Sylva had regained her enthusiasm about parachuting and was happy to start jumping again. She loved the fun of it all, and it paid well, plus she felt it was for a worthy cause. She believed that every jump she made contributed another chapter to the gospel of making life-saving parachutes compulsory on aeroplanes. Turning 21, she had also grown up considerably, changing from her youthful girlish character to quite a sophisticated young woman. Her general knowledge, enhanced by her close association with Orde-Lees plus her own personal experiences of travel and aviation, had turned a young enthusiastic girl into a knowledgeable and interesting expert in her area.

Orde-Lees had done a lot to help Sylva get into parachuting, and they were still close, but his main preoccupation remained to promote British parachutes and no doubt earn good commission from Calthrop. In spring of 1920, Orde-Lees went back to the US to do a parachute descent into New York Harbour, landing by the Statue of Liberty, and in late May he left for Sweden as part of a planned overseas selling and demonstration trip which took in several countries across the Continent.

Sylva was happy to continue demonstrating the parachute for Calthrop; she was enjoying an extraordinary life with a level of public acclaim and good money. A big opportunity came when it was suggested she jump at the major Hendon Air Pageant planned for early July. Interest in aviation at this time was immense and this show was planned to be a spectacular event showing off all the latest planes and aerial manoeuvres of the day.

The day dawned with favourable weather, and crowds flocked to the show in their thousands. From her early jumps in the Handley Page aircraft a year before, Sylva was now experienced and knew exactly what to expect. Once the plane reached height and turned in for a straight run over the airfield, Sylva stood up from her seat near the back of the aircraft. Standing there, holding on firmly, she watched the pilot carefully for the signal. Then, against the roaring blast from the slipstream, she dived out and fell fast down below the plane. Quickly the line connected from her harness dragged the parachute from its container and, as the air rushed into its mouth, it opened firmly. It was another smooth descent and, as she looked down on the massive crowd below, she must have known this would be yet another memory she would keep all her life. She landed right in the centre of the airfield and was soon escorted to the VIP enclosure where, amid congratulations and smoking a cigarette, she explained about her jump and continued with her enthusiasm that parachutes should be carried by all aircrew.

Orde-Lees was still demonstrating the parachute on the Continent and, a few weeks later, it was arranged for Sylva to join him to do a demonstration jump near Falsterbo in the south of Sweden. This time she landed in water but was quickly pulled out and, as the first ever female jumper in the country, was a big success. A few weeks later she was in Denmark where organisers were astounded when she agreed to jump in exceptionally windy conditions. But she was prepared to go ahead, saying she didn't want to let down the thousands of spectators who had come to watch. She hit the ground very hard, but luckily it was a soft, marshy area. Quickly pressing the release system so she wasn't dragged, she survived unscathed.

The following year, in 1921, Sylva continued to demonstrate the Guardian Angel, but Calthrop was beginning to struggle financially. He had spent an enormous amount trying to develop and sell his parachute, but he had still not achieved any substantial sales. There was some hopeful news, though. In May that year Air Ministry officials finally agreed it would be a good idea to introduce parachutes for airmen, but there appeared to be no rush. They stated that parachutes should only be introduced when the devices had reached a stage of development to warrant the expenditure.

It was a frustrating time, but Sylva continued to demonstrate the parachute, jumping from aeroplanes in England and on the Continent. In August 1921, in Annecy in France, she landed in a tree but was rescued unscathed by a ladder. Just a few weeks later Professor Newell, who was a keen supporter of the Guardian Angel, had a problem when he was using the parachute at a show in Denmark. On leaving the plane he somehow became hooked up. The pilot, with great presence of mind, headed out to sea for a softer landing, but Newell fell from 600ft and died on impact.

It was a blow for the Calthrop team, including Sylva, who knew Professor Newell well and had jumped with him on several occasions. More bad news came in the way of increasing advances that were being made in Irvin's innovative ripcord system parachute. After trying for so long, it seemed that the cumbersome Guardian Angel system was slowly being left behind.

Orde-Lees had done all he could to try to sell the parachute but realised the writing was on the wall. He said goodbye to Calthrop, Sylva and the rest of the team and decided to head off to Japan, initially taking a role in parachute training over there. He clearly found the country agreeable as he stayed for years, even marrying a local Japanese woman before finally moving to New Zealand.

During the next couple of years, opportunities to do jumps to promote the Guardian Angel faded steadily and Sylva adapted to doing more mundane office work for Calthrop. No big orders for the parachute came in and the ultimate blow came in January 1925, when the decision was finally made that the Royal Air Force should use parachutes for their airmen – but not the British Guardian Angel. Instead, it was agreed the American Irvin chute, with its now improved ripcord system, was the best design. It was a deeply bitter blow and the end of so much hard work and so many dreams. Everard Calthrop died just two years later, still desperately disappointed that, after his groundbreaking ideas and so much effort, it had all come to so little.

Sylva, meanwhile, in her naturally buoyant manner, flourished. Back in Southampton, she started to train as a nurse and in 1927 she married a local musician, albeit under a fictitious surname. She then lived for a while with a civil aviation manager in Surrey, not far from Croydon Airport, and a few years later married Michael Marley, a guardsman in the 1st Parachute Regiment. She didn't use her proper name for her marriages or even her adopted name, Sylva Boyden, which was strange really as she had a great deal to be proud of. Under the name of Grace Ellen Marley, she finally returned to Southampton where she settled for a quiet life, and only in her later years did she once again begin to receive a little recognition for being the first British woman to jump out of an aeroplane.

In June 1851 Margaret Graham crashed into the roof of a house in London's Piccadilly; just one of many incidents that occurred during her long flying career. (Granger Archive / Alamy)

In the years following Emily de Voy's first parachute descent in May 1889, various methods were used to help lift female jumpers up into the sky. (KGPA Ltd / Alamy)

Ella Pilcher (left) played a major role in the design and construction of her brother Percy Pilcher's new flying machines. (Royal Aeronautical Society (National Aerospace Library) / Mary Evans)

It seems likely that it was Dorothy Pilcher who, in 1897, was the first woman to get off the ground in a fixed-wing gliding machine. (The Bookworm Collection / Alamy)

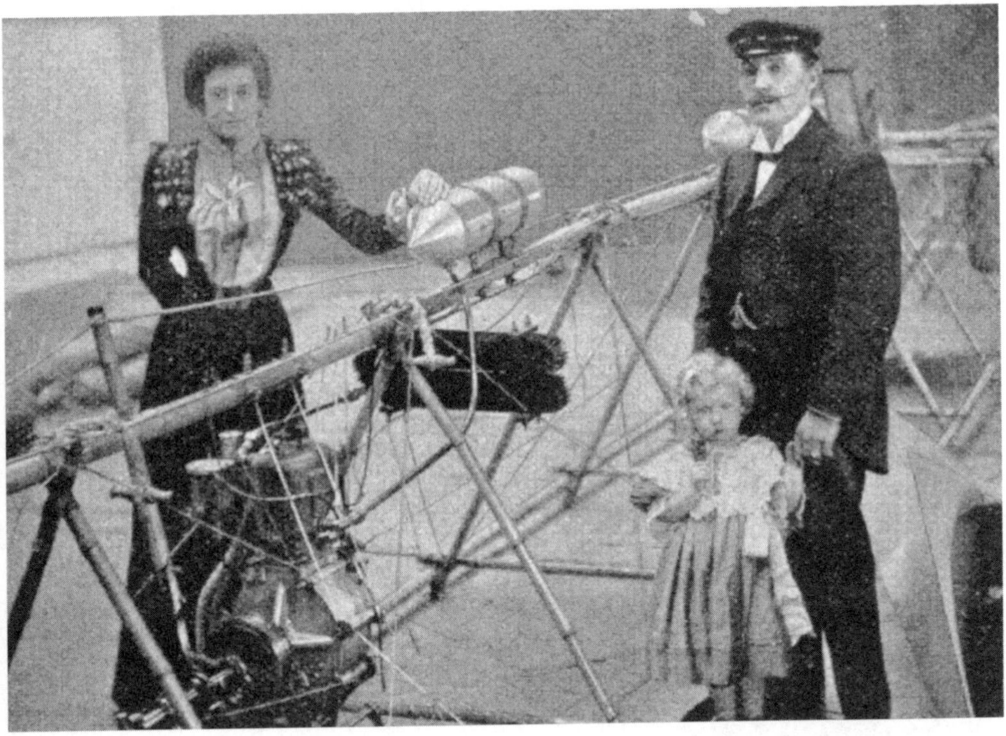

Rose and Stanley Spencer with their daughter. In July 1902, Rose became the first woman in the world to fly a powered air machine.

In 1902, Rose Spencer flew above Crystal Palace in south London for around half an hour before making a perfect landing. (earlyaeroplanes.com / blimpinfo.com)

In the early Edwardian years, top female parachutists including Dolly Shepherd and Britain's first female pilot Edith Cook all did displays with Captain Gaudron and his balloon. (Crowood Press)

Edith Cook travelled to the Bleriot Flying School in the south of France to learn to fly, going solo in January 1910.

Lilian Bland called the plane she had built the *Mayfly*, joking that it may fly, it may not! (*Flight* magazine)

Hilda Hewlett was a loving wife and mother until, well into her forties, she suddenly decided to drop everything and learn to fly, becoming the first British woman to obtain a pilot's licence in August 1911. (From Gail Hewlett, *Old Bird: The Irrepressible Mrs Hewlett*)

Hilda Hewlett established a flying school at Brooklands and then went on to set up a major aircraft manufacturing business. (From Gail Hewlett, *Old Bird: The Irrepressible Mrs Hewlett*)

Hilda Hewlett flying at Brooklands in Surrey. (From Gail Hewlett, *Old Bird: The Irrepressible Mrs Hewlett*)

In 1919, Sylva Boyden did her first jumps from a balloon over London's Richmond Park. (Agence Rol / National Library of France)

Sylva Boyden was the first British woman to use a folded parachute pack and jump from a plane. (Pionnair-GE.com)

In 1919 Sylva Boyden made her first jump from an aircraft above a huge crowd at Handley Page's Cricklewood Aerodrome. (Spaarnestad Photo Collection / Het Leven / Mary Evans)

Lady Mary Heath was given a momentous welcome when she arrived back in London in May 1928. (United Archives)

Lady Mary Heath flying her violet-coloured Avro Avian biplane. She shipped it out to Cape Town for her momentous flight across Africa to London in 1928.

Lady Mary Bailey went one better than Lady Mary Heath when, in 1928, she flew to Cape Town down the east African route and then headed back to London up the more remote western route.

In 1785, Letitia Sage became the first British woman to fly when she ascended in a beautiful silk balloon from London's St George's Fields. (Art Collection 2 / Alamy)

Letitia Sage. (Science Museum / Science and Society Picture Library)

In 1824, young Jane Stocks survived a horrific balloon crash which was reported with various embellishments in newspapers and magazines right across Europe. (Pictorial Press Ltd / Alamy)

In 1825 Jane Stocks joined Charles Green for a peaceful flight over the English countryside. (Royal Aeronautical Society (National Aerospace Library) / Mary Evans)

In spring 1837, feisty Margaret Graham had recovered from a dramatic crash and was ready to start flying again. (Cuming Collection, Southwark Heritage Centre, Southwark Council)

MRS. GRAHAM'S
FIRST ASCENT
SINCE HER ACCIDENT!!

Surrey Zoological Gardens,

The Season at these Gardens will commence on
THURSDAY, 27th of APRIL, 1837,
Being the Celebration of the Birth-Day of
Her Most Gracious Majesty,
Patroness of the Gardens, with a
GRAND
AEROSTATIC FETE,
WHEN
Mrs. GRAHAM,
THE ONLY FEMALE AERONAUT IN EUROPE,
WILL MAKE HER FIRST
BALLOON ASCENT
(Since her most unfortunate Voyage with the
DUKE OF BRUNSWICK,)
FROM THE BEAUTIFUL SHEET of WATER,
WHICH ORNAMENTS THESE GROUNDS.

THE SPLENDID BAND OF THE
ROYAL SCOTS FUSILEER GUARDS
Will perform the most popular airs from "Beniowsky," "Fair Rosamond," "Devil on Two Sticks," &c., in the
NEW GRAND TEMPLE OF THE LAKE!!

ADMITTANCE ONE SHILLING.

OPEN FROM TWELVE TILL DUSK.

King, Printer, College Hill, City.

In 1910 Lilian Bland shocked her relations when she retreated to the garden shed and built her own plane. (Antrim and Newtownabbey Borough Council)

In late 1909, Edith Cook headed to Bleriot's flight school in France and, learning on a Bleriot XI aeroplane, she became one of the first women in the world to fly. (David Oxborn / Alamy)

In 1910, Hilda Hewlett ordered a Farman aeroplane to start her long career in aviation. (Hugh Evelyn Prints)

Farman aeroplane. (Keith Webber Jr / Alamy)

In 1919, when Sylva Boyden heard how the Guardian Angel parachute had already opened successfully in a jump off London's Tower Bridge, she was happy to give it a try. (Royal Aeronautical Society (National Aerospace Library) / Mary Evans)

In 1929, on the huge Graf Zeppelin airship, Britain's Grace Drummond-Hay become the first woman to go round the world by air. (Picture of the airship Wernher Krutein / © Photovault.com. Picture of Grace Drummond-Hay Illustrated London News / Mary Evans)

LADY DRUMMOND-HAY

Gliding really took off in the 1930s. Joan Meakin was the first woman to fly a glider across the English Channel; Naomi Heron-Maxwell was the first British woman to gain the prestigious Silver C award. (Avpics / Alamy)

Britain's first woman to fly a jet, Veronica Volkersz, started her flying with the Civil Air Guard. (Lordprice Collection / Alamy)

In 1963, Diana Barnato took off in this English Electric Lightning to become the fastest woman in the world and the first British woman to go through the sound barrier. (Air Britain Images/ Russ Smith / Mary Evans)

Kate Board, Britain's first commercial airship pilot. (Sueddeutsche Zeitung / Alamy)

Helen Sharman spent a week on the Mir space station, becoming Britain's first astronaut. (Hum Images / Alamy Stock Photo)

Helen Sharman after successfully coming back to earth. (ITAR-TASS News Agency / Alamy)

Mary Bailey had to land in some remote areas on her long-distance flights across Africa in 1928. (Jane Falloon / Lilliput Press)

Winifred Spooner (left) was one of the most successful female pilots of the late 1920s. Here she is talking to the Secretary of State for Air, Lord Thomson, after making a successful test flight using a new fuel at London's Stag Lane Aerodrome in 1929. (Royal Aeronautical Society (National Aerospace Library) / Mary Evans)

Planes at Heston Airport, getting ready for the 1930 prestigious King's Cup Air Race. No one thought a woman would win! (Peter Butt Aviation Collection / Mary Evans)

Winifred Brown, winner of the famous King's Cup Air Race. (Royal Aeronautical Society – National Aerospace Library / Mary Evans)

When Amy Johnson announced she would fly to Australia, her longest flight had been 150 miles and she didn't even own an aeroplane! (Chronicle / Alamy)

In her little de Havilland DH.60 Gipsy Moth, Amy Johnson survived numerous adventures before finally arriving in Brisbane in 1930. (Historic Collection / Alamy)

Record-breaking glider pilots Joan Meakin (left) and Naomi Heron-Maxwell both joined Alan Cobham's famous Air Circus.

Naomi Heron-Maxwell demonstrated freefall and gave parachuting displays in the early 1930s before turning to gliding.

Joan Meakin and Naomi Heron-Maxwell both visited leading German gliding site Wasserkuppe in 1930.

In the 1930s, Pauline Gower (left) and Dorothy Spicer ran a display and passenger-carrying business. Pauline was instrumental in ensuring women were accepted into the wartime Air Transport Auxilliary. (Royal Aeronautical Society (National Aerospace Library) / Mary Evans Picture Library)

In the early 1940s, as the Second World War progressed, British women in the Air Transport Auxiliary were joined by women from many other countries. Flying a huge range of aircraft from Spitfires, Hurricanes and Wellingtons to Tempests and Lancaster bombers without radios or navigation aids, they contributed enormously to the war effort. (De Luan / Alamy)

Diana Barnato, the first British woman to go through the sound barrier. (Grub Street Publishing / Diana Barnarto Walker)

10

LADY MARY HEATH AND LADY MARY BAILEY

1928
THE FIRST WOMEN TO SET LONG-DISTANCE RECORDS IN AFRICA

Two Lady Marys, meeting in the swelteringly hot, sandy and remote Sudanese town of Khartoum in 1928, was not a likely event. However, what made this meeting even more extraordinary was that Lady Mary Heath had flown in a little open-cockpit Mark III Avian biplane north, up from Cape Town, and Lady Mary Bailey had flown in her little open-cockpit Cirrus Moth biplane south, down from London.

Few pilots were flying in Africa at this time; certainly no woman had flown over virtually any of the route. The meeting in the middle of Africa must have been wonderful to witness. Lady Mary, I presume!

The two Lady Marys both had Irish connections. Mary Heath was very much Irish before marrying an Englishman and adopting England as her home for much of her adult life. Mary Bailey was born and spent most of her life in England, although, through her father, she had also lived for some time in Northern Ireland. Both were huge achievers in aviation. The 1914–18 conflict had made it very difficult for women to advance as pilots and the two Marys had to wait until well after the end of the First World War before they could make their mark. When they did, though, it was dramatic.

While the war had not helped the progress of female pilots, it had been very beneficial for aircraft development. Huge financial support had been given to aircraft designers and manufacturers in an effort to give Britain air supremacy. Before the war started, Hilda Hewlett had gained her licence on a flimsy wood-and-fabric aeroplane when speeds of 50mph were considered normal. Just a few years later, after the end of the war, speeds of more than 140mph were common. Flying opportunities for women, though, were still few and far between. After the war ended, while some female parachutists and balloonists were still involved in barnstorming displays, very few women had the opportunity to fly powered aeroplanes.

Mary Heath, who had reached Khartoum first for the momentous African meeting, had gained her certificate, number 7975, in November 1925, the ninth woman in Britain to achieve this. Just over a year later, in January 1927, Mary Bailey was the twelfth woman in the country when she qualified for certificate number 8067. They had both learned to fly at the London Stag Lane Aeroplane Club on DH Moth two-seater wooden biplanes fitted with 60hp Cirrus engines. The two ladies were lively, brave, outspoken and exceptional pilots, determined to break barriers and also break records.

Despite their shared Irish connections, they had come from very different backgrounds. It would be hard, in fact, to find anyone with a background similar to that of Mary Heath. She started her extraordinary life in 1896, in Limerick, as Sophie Mary Pierce-Evans. Her father, an erratic and tempestuous farmer, bludgeoned her mother to death when Sophie was just 1 year old. He was sentenced to a home for the insane, and baby Sophie was quickly transferred to her grandfather's house in nearby Newcastle West and was then mainly brought up by two maiden aunts. Strong willed from the start, there was local talk as to whether little Sophie had inherited her father's mad genes. Certainly, a very independent streak started to emerge strongly as she grew up.

With various relations covering the costs, Sophie progressed to boarding school in Dublin and then on to the town's Royal

College of Science to take various science-based courses. She was bright and proved to be a very able scholar. She was also becoming a very good sportswoman. Growing fast to just under 6ft tall, she towered over most others and could use her great height to good advantage at hockey, tennis and other sports. She soon became part of various teams.

As she reached her late teens, Sophie steadily developed into a strong, formidable woman with definite opinions that she was happy to voice. Perhaps because of her background, she had also developed a burning ambition to do well in life. In the summer of 1916, when she was 19 and still at college in Dublin, she met 41-year-old army captain William Eliott-Lynn. Whether it was for love, an eagerness for a new adventure, or just the thought of being supported by someone with a regular income, Sophie made a decision. The couple were married in Dublin in November 2016, two weeks after Sophie's 20th birthday.

Captain Eliott-Lynn had probably little idea of what he had taken on and the marriage never settled down. After just a few months, Sophie volunteered her services to the war effort and joined the Women's Auxiliary Army Corps, working as a driver. She was away for two years. After the war, when Captain Eliott-Lynn sailed off to start a new life in Africa in April 1920, Sophie stayed on in Dublin to finish her college course and then ended up in London. She now began taking her athletics seriously and while she did make it out to Africa a few times to see her husband, athletics began to dominate her life. She put her mind to training hard and, with her energy and long legs, she was scoring wins in high jump as well as in the javelin and shot. This led to her being selected for top teams, and at the World Championships in England in 1923 Sophie broke the women's world high-jump record and also the British javelin record. Never one to hold back, she also became a strong vocal advocate for women in sport, joining committees and writing papers to get her voice heard.

Then, in spring 1925, Sophie spotted another area that excited her: aviation. She attended the launch of the London Aeroplane Club at Stag Lane in north London and was taken up for a flight in a de Havilland Moth. On landing, Sophie announced that the flight had been beautifully steady and her ambition now was to qualify as a pilot and own an aeroplane.

She may have said this on the spur of the moment, knowing it would grab good news coverage, which she loved. But Sophie was as good as her word and in August 1925 she signed up for lessons. Showing early skill and an easy grasp of the theory of flight, she was a quick learner. Always full of confidence, she clambered into the little two-seater plywood and fabric DH Moth biplane and, thanks to her instructor, quickly got the hang of co-ordinating her feet to adjust the rudder along with careful hand movements on the joystick.

Sophie instantly loved every aspect of flying. She was attracted by the challenge of trying to develop into a competent pilot, and she was also delighted at the opportunity to belong to the small and exclusive group of pilots and flying enthusiasts at Stag Lane. She became almost a permanent fixture at the club, booking lessons as often as possible. She went solo in October and a few weeks later was ready to take her test. On 4 November 1925, Sophie was granted her pilot's licence.

For Sophie, that was just the beginning. Now devoting herself to aviation with the same intensity that she had shown to athletics, she got involved in club activities and also in supporting flying for women. In March 1926, despite constant money problems and reluctance from her husband to continue financing her extravagant lifestyle, she bought one of the aeroplanes based at Stag Lane, a de Havilland Moth G-EBKT. Owning her own plane meant she could now lift her flying to another level. Competitions, fun flights, aviation events: Sophie was packing in the flying hours and quickly establishing a reputation as a highly capable pilot.

Records were a good way to achieve the fame and acclaim Sophie so loved, and both height and distance records were soon on her busy agenda. Things were not so good for her husband, though. He was now in his fifties, and the African venture had failed; he had returned to London, short of money and finding it difficult to get a reasonable job. His very estranged wife Sophie was totally absorbed with her own life and flying. In May 1927, Major William Eliott-Lynn was found drowned in the Thames.

This opened up a new opportunity for Sophie. Along with her non-stop flying, she was lucky enough, if that is quite the right term, to speedily find another husband, a man wealthy enough to cover all her flying and social expenditure. Sir James Heath was 75, a bit of an age gap when compared with Sophie's 29, but he had lots of money. He had been a former MP for Staffordshire and made his wealth in a local colliery; in recent years he had been spending time in South Africa, where he had business interests. They were married in October 1927, less than six months after the death of Sophie's first husband. With Sir James Heath as a husband, Sophie could now relish in the title of 'Lady', and from now on was always known as Lady Mary Heath.

Now Mary Heath had all the backing she needed for her ambitions. She sailed with her new husband to Cape Town in November that year, accompanied on board, to the surprise of many of the passengers, by her brand-new Mark 111 Avro Avian aeroplane.

She had a secret plan. Other women were now beginning to get their licences and be applauded for their achievements. Mary had come up with an idea that should put her right back in the limelight – a flight from Cape Town to London. A flying route to South Africa had been one of the first long-distance trips to be talked about and, in 1920, the *Times* newspaper offered a prize of £10,000 for the first pilot to fly from London to Cape Town. After some accidents, this was finally completed in spring 1920. But, by 1927, no woman had achieved the route either way. If Mary could do it, this would be a sensational first.

It took a lot of planning and much credit must be given to Mary for continuing with her idea when she fully realised the extent of the challenge she was about to undertake, including a complete lack of good maps. In her favour, though, was the fact that she had spent some – albeit limited – time in East Africa visiting her first husband, so she had some knowledge about the continent.

Mary Heath spent the end of 1927 and early 1928 in Cape Town absorbed in detailed planning. Finally, in February 1928, it was time to set off. Excitement was mounting as she told the media her plans and talked to various groups about the expected excitements ahead. She packed the aircraft with extras including a spare wheel, shock absorbers and sandbags, but she also included other items she considered absolute essentials for the long flight. These included a silk evening dress, a fur coat, six pairs of silk stockings, black satin shoes and even a tennis racket and tennis shoes. In 1928, many countries in Africa had close administrative and trading associations with Britain; Mary was hoping that at some places she would receive a good welcome and social invitations.

It is not clear when she heard that fellow female pilot Lady Mary Bailey was planning to fly the route to Africa from the opposite direction. Mary Heath would not have welcomed the news. However, her own journey would end in London rather than Cape Town, which would give her an edge for media coverage. Mary Heath persuaded herself and anyone she spoke to that it was the route from Cape Town *to* London that was important.

Finally, all was ready. Mary Heath set off from Cape Town on 5 January 1928 in her heavily laden little open-cockpit G-EBUG Avro Avian biplane. The plane carried enough fuel for over ten hours' flying at around 80mph, all being well. The first sector of her long flight was planned just as far as Johannesburg via Port Elizabeth and Durban, and en route she intended to give talks on aviation and joyrides to make some money. She was also expecting to attend various functions given in her honour; after all, she was the first female pilot South Africa had seen.

The first few legs went well and were very enjoyable. Mary Heath was only flying a few hours each day and was feted everywhere she landed. After Johannesburg, she headed off to Pretoria for some last-minute adjustments to her plane and then, in late February, her trip north really began. The first leg was difficult, and after six hours' flying Mary was feeling very ill. She realised she couldn't go on. She managed to put the plane down near a remote village 10 miles short of the planned stop at Bulawayo and had to recuperate for some days before heading off again. But as she recovered, her strong determination also returned. She was going to fly all the way to England, come what may. Initially following a railway line, she headed north, flying over the spectacular Victoria Falls before reaching open landscapes covered with wonderful African wildlife, local villages and European farms. At times weather was a problem and she had to land, sometimes simply on a convenient flat spot, and wait it out as heavy rainstorms went through.

At the same time that Mary Heath was attempting to fly up across Africa, another small plane was also flying the same route. Dick Bentley was already an established long-distance pilot and was flying his wife back to England as part of their honeymoon. Knowing another plane was flying roughly the same route at the same time may have made Mary feel safer in some of the remoter stretches of country, but she was also likely to have been aware that this could also detract from her own solo achievements.

It took Mary a full week of flying with various overnight stops to cover the 2,000 miles from Pretoria to a very welcome stop in Tabora, Tanzania. This was a place she knew from when she had visited the region on one of her brief trips out to see her first husband. She had some friends there, and it was a refreshing and relaxing stopover. But she didn't linger, and after a comfortable night in a soft bed, the next day she clambered back into her small plane and off she went again. At one point she descended to watch a herd of giraffes before gaining height again and zooming north to Mwanza, a port on the shore of Lake Victoria. Here Mary found some more old friends and took time off to go on a safari. A good natural shot, she managed to kill a buffalo. On 14 March she set off for Nairobi, where the long-distance flying began to take its toll.

While there were good welcomes and help at her planned stopovers, the flight so far had been no simple task for Mary. Flying for hours on end over sometimes very remote landscapes demanded not only courage but also concentration. Add to that the resilience needed against the continuous buffeting slipstream in her open cockpit and the physical demands of controlling the plane at all times, and it was no wonder that, by the time Mary reached the Kenyan capital, she was beginning to feel jaded. She was also irritated that when she arrived in Nairobi, she found there had been little publicity about her amazing trip.

Nevertheless, her enthusiasm for the flight remained. She organised a few repairs to her little plane, added a few items, and after a week of recuperation, set off again on 22 March 1928. The next 270-mile leg to Kisumu was tricky as the high Kijabe escarpment blocked her route. After trying to get over it unsuccessfully, including throwing out some of her heavier items such as her tennis racket to make the plane lighter, Mary managed to make a detour and successfully pick up her route north again. This sector of the flight also gave Mary a nice record; she became the first woman ever to fly solo across the Equator. Pilot Dick Bentley, who was flying the same route as Mary, caught her up at Jinja airfield in Uganda and here he became really useful. The future route north through southern Sudan crossed the Sudd, a treacherous swamp land. Local tribes were not friendly; only recently a British District Commissioner had been murdered. According to the authorities, allowing a woman to fly the route alone was simply not possible. Mary was not going to be beaten. She offered Dick Bentley £5 an hour to fly alongside her across the Sudd and, when this deal was confirmed, the authorities relented. Mary could continue north.

Refreshed after a couple of days staying in the comfortable home of the British governor of Uganda, Mary was keen to get going again and set off north, this time with Dick Bentley not far behind. She had complete confidence in her little plane and, sitting there with warm air buffeting her face and amongst wispy white clouds as her companions, Mary was by now quite relaxed; she sat for hours in her little cockpit. Occasionally she went down to look at wildlife, becoming disappointed that white rhinos looked a grey colour but excited at seeing large herds of elephant. At one point small black flying beetles landed all over her cockpit which she swept away vigorously. On she went to reach Mongalla on the Nile.

After a stop, it was time to head north across the Sudd. This was the part of the trip that made Mary nervous, knowing what was below if anything happened to her sturdy little engine. Reassuring, however, was the fact that Dick Bentley, as promised, was now flying by her side. Flying steadily north, it didn't take long to cross the dangerous swamp lands and then Mary's usual boisterous confidence returned. When both planes landed at Malakal, north of the Sudd, she found Dick Bentley wasn't in a rush to leave. Mary decided to push on. Taking off in the heat of the day, she found that the air was now becoming very turbulent and was continually buffeting the plane. Mary had to work hard to keep the little aircraft from being blown around too much and to keep it heading steadily in the right direction to cover the 485 miles north to Khartoum. Navigation was a lot easier now, with the Nile sparkling below to show the way but, nevertheless, it was all becoming exhausting. It had been a long, hot, gruelling day. When she saw the aerodrome of Kosti coming up below her, she decided to put down rather than complete the final 186 miles to Khartoum. She made a hard landing in the hot air, just avoiding a couple of camels on the airstrip, but there was no damage to the plane. A relieved Mary clambered out into the soft tropical air and, after being met by a surprised District Commissioner, spent a comfortable night at his nearby house.

Despite its remote location, Mary Heath may have heard here that rival pilot Mary Bailey was not far from Khartoum because she decided to leave early the next morning. She took off again in blazing heat and sandy air, flying steadily north for two and half hours before she finally spotted the cleared, flat area of Khartoum Aerodrome dazzling in the distance near the junction of the Blue and White Nile. It was 31 March, eighty-five days since she had left Cape Town. She had flown a distance well over 3,500 miles. Landing gently, she was given a wonderful welcome by the British community based in this distant outpost. She learned quickly that Mary Bailey was believed to be en route but had not arrived. Mary Heath had reached Khartoum first. She spent the afternoon relaxing and after a visit to the local swimming baths and a comfortable bed for the night, Mary Heath was totally refreshed, up and ready to face the next day.

★★★

When Mary Bailey, with her calmer character, heard the news of Mary Heath's planned flight up across Africa, she didn't stop to consider who should complete the African route first. Mary Bailey was totally immersed in planning her own flight from London to Cape Town and, with her husband's generous support and financial backing, she was not so concerned with fame and glory. She came from the sort of background that Mary Heath envied. Mary Bailey, or Mary Westenra as she was originally, was born in 1890 into an aristocratic family with property in London but also with a huge castle in Monaghan, Northern Ireland, where she was mainly brought up. With staff, grounds and gamekeepers, Mary Bailey had a very privileged childhood. From an early age, like many well-brought-up girls on country estates, she developed a love of hunting, with all its speed, excitement and challenges. She also enjoyed the social events, the balls, parties and receptions, including being a debutante with a formal 'coming out' at Buckingham Palace. It was all a fairly typical upbringing for girls at her level of society in the late Edwardian era, and Mary took to it energetically and happily.

At 21, young, pretty and full of life, it is easy to see how she attracted the attention of Sir Abe Bailey, a hugely successful 47-year-old businessman with a large house in Sussex and substantial investments in South Africa. He, in turn, would have been an interesting catch. Any young girl would have been fascinated not only by his wealth but also by his stories about his background in South Africa, and how he was £4,000 in debt before finding gold in the Witwatersrand gold fields near Johannesburg. After subsequently speculating in property, Abe Bailey had become a very wealthy, very respected businessman.

In August 1911, the couple had a short engagement and a full society wedding in a fashionable church just off Sloane Square in London. Then, at the end of September, the happy Sir Abe and Lady Bailey sailed off for South Africa. During the next nine years the couple split their time between South Africa and another home of Abe's in central London. Money was never a problem and Mary had all the help she needed when children started to arrive; she had four by 1920. In her role as elegant hostess and mother, Mary coped admirably but frustrations began to show quite early on. Her husband was more and more absorbed in his business and now had become involved in political ventures as well; the children had nannies and nursemaids and then went off to school. Mary joined the Women's Army Auxiliary Corps as a driver to help out during the First World War, but then it was back into the role of managing the house and being a society hostess. As she entered her thirties, Mary increasingly felt there was no real purpose to her life, dutiful as she was.

Then Mary heard about the new London Aeroplane Club, not far from their home. In 1926 her husband Abe was very involved in helping the then Chancellor of the Exchequer, Winston Churchill, negotiate terms to end the Great Strike which was paralysing Britain. While he was so absorbed, Mary decided to visit the club to see what was going on and, to her surprise, she found something that was not only interesting but that really fascinated her: flying. Watching the little planes bump along the ground and then take off into the air was amazing. She met Mary Heath at the club, six years younger and not a woman she necessarily took to personally, but she couldn't help but be impressed by Mary Heath's flying abilities and also her sheer enthusiasm for women to fly.

Mary Bailey was a little tentative at first and quietly booked some lessons without telling Abe. She had concerns that she might not be able to do it. How wrong she was! As soon as Mary Bailey got into a plane, she felt it was a natural home. She was taken for training flights with the club's instructors and also on a couple of occasions with Mary Heath. In those days, two women in the air together was certainly an unusual event. Mary Bailey calmly and seriously absorbed all the knowledge she could and by January 1927 she gained her pilot's licence.

Abe, tolerant of his wife's hobbies, agreed that if she needed a plane of her own she could have one, and just a month later Mary was the proud owner of one of the popular de Havilland Moth DH.60s, with registration number G-EBPU. Now she had wings! Mary was going to take full advantage of this amazing fun and freedom and just a few days later she flew her aeroplane up to Norwich to take part in an aerial rally. From then on, Mary flew at every opportunity. In April there was a slight halt when she had a bad accident. In front of the plane, she started to swing the propeller to start up the engine and accidently slipped on the wet grass. She wasn't the first to do this but she was lucky. She had a deep cut on her forehead which took quite a while to heal, but other than that she was fine.

Back in her little plane, there was no stopping Mary Bailey, and she was attending as many events as she could find. That spring, with her flying skills improving week by week, she attended a Ladies' Race, competing against Mary Heath and another female pilot. Mary Heath showed her immense talent by putting her plane into very tight, fast controlled turns to win. Mary Bailey came third, accepting gracefully that Mary Heath was a better, far more experienced pilot. In June that year Mary Heath was going for a height record, and kindly asked Mary Bailey to accompany her. They reached 16,000ft. A month later Mary Bailey decided she could do even better. She went up to over 17,000ft to get the record instead. The competition between two very different but highly talented lady pilots had begun.

Later that month Mary Bailey achieved her own win at the Birmingham Air Pageant, beating not only some very determined male pilots but also Mary Heath, who came second. A few weeks later, in August, Mary Bailey decided to fly to Ireland and become the first woman to fly solo across the Irish Sea.

At the end of 1927 there was a huge endorsement of Mary Bailey's ability. In the same year that she had gained her licence and at a time when there was keen competition from Mary Heath and a handful of other female pilots, Mary Bailey was awarded the inaugural Harmon Trophy for Aviatrix of the Year, a significant achievement. The men's version of the award, the Harmon Aviator Trophy, was given to Charles Lindberg after his epic flight from New York to Paris. The news of Mary Bailey's award did not enthuse Lady Mary Heath, but she politely commented that it was well earned.

Without doubt, in just a few months Mary Bailey had progressed from a tentative student to one of the best female pilots around. However, she still spent much of her time with her family, organising the lives of her young children and still being a social hostess for her husband. As the short days of winter 1927 reduced flying activity in Britain, Mary made as extraordinary decision. Her husband had to go out to South Africa to attend to business matters; Mary decided she would fly out to see him.

It wasn't as crazy a decision as many of Mary's friends thought. By this time Mary was a very competent pilot and she had learned a bit about mechanics during her stint as a driver in the war. She was aware it would be a challenging trip. Geoffrey de Havilland at Stag Lane helped advise her, even to the extent of selling her a 80hp DH Cirrus Moth, registration EBSF, which he felt would be more suitable for the trip. An extra fuel tank was fitted into the front cockpit and others came forward to help Mary get ready.

During her preparations, Mary Bailey became aware that rival Mary Heath was about to take off from Cape Town to fly across Africa. Mary Bailey's reaction was to carefully emphasise it was not a contest. She stated firmly that there was no competition, all she wanted was to have a change of scenery and to show that it was easy for women to make long journeys by air.

During Christmas 1927 and early 1928, Mary Bailey was at her London home, very busy planning and sorting out all the preparations. She was encountering many of the same problems that Mary Heath had found during her similar preparations in Cape Town. Maps were difficult to come by; where were the main British posts across Africa and where were the best locations to touch down to refuel? The fear of a forced landing in jungle or remote area had encouraged both ladies to revise their knowledge of basic repairs and check what supplies they could fit into their little biplanes. There was a great deal to think about.

By March, Mary Bailey was ready. She had done her final inspections on her new plane to check all was prepared for her long flight down to Cape Town, simply to see her husband, as she put it. There was some general concern that this charming, well-brought-up lady didn't really know what she was getting herself into; one comment suggested Mary was sublimely unaware of the dangers ahead. But Mary was calm and quite content. There were lots of places to stop en route.

On Friday, 9 March 1928, as Mary Heath sorted out preparations to leave Abercorn (Mbala) in Zambia to continue her journey north, Mary Bailey was at Stag Lane in London. Dressed in heavy flying boots and a thick protective leather coat, she carefully completed a final check on her provisions and her plane, and then she quietly and gently took off. She didn't go very far, just a quick hop down to Croydon where there was a good crowd as well as family, friends and supporters to officially wave her off.

After this brief stop for a formal goodbye, Mary Bailey started the trip in earnest. Taking off in her heavily laden little plane, she touched down briefly in Lympne airfield in Kent and then headed out over the Channel, sitting resolutely in the rear cockpit as she flew south. She had initially hoped to make Lyon her first stop, but almost immediately she spotted a problem with the compass and so instead she put down in Sacy le Petit, half an hour's flying time north of Paris. She adjusted her compass and stayed overnight. The next day she took off early, but now there was thick fog, so after a very short flight, she decided to put down in Paris instead. While her navigation was now spot on, it was not an auspicious start. When she left Paris the next day the weather was still bad for flying, this time with very strong winds, but Mary decided to struggle on. Well protected in her thick coat and leather helmet against the constant cold slipstream, she flew steadily south to finally arrive at Lyon four and a half hours later. After a short touchdown, despite the challenging weather, she checked her maps and took off again, heading now for Marseilles and a very well-earned rest.

It had been a very long, very exhausting day, and when Mary finally landed in the southern French town, this could have been the time she decided to give up on the idea. She was now 38 and the first sector down to the Mediterranean had been a real struggle, physically uncomfortable and mentally draining. Things really hadn't gone very well. But the next day, suddenly the weather had changed, with no wind and a clear blue sky. The encouragement of a very supportive French media helped to restore her confidence. Mary clambered into her little plane and off she went, rolling right down the runway because of the additional weight of her extra fuel tank before lifting off into a cloudless sky.

Now Mary could relax a little. Heading steadily over the sparkling blue sea towards north Italy, flying was once more a pleasure. She made a series of short hops, touching down at Pisa, Rome and Naples where she took time off to visit the sights. Back over water she headed via Sicily to Malta where she received a wonderful welcome from the British contingent there. En route from there to the north African coast, the dire warnings back in London that Mary didn't really understand what she was doing nearly came good. Dazed by the constant bright sun on the glaring blue sea and the endless blue sky, Mary lost track of both her height and her route and she meandered well off course. Suddenly she became aware she was flying in a bit of a dream. Turning the plane and concentrating on her compass and height, she got back on track to the north African coast and then to Libya, landing safely at Tripoli a week after leaving London.

From then on Mary Bailey returned to form, becoming the superb pilot that the public knew. There were no more lapses of concentration. Mary flew steadily across to Cairo and then down to Luxor where she stopped off to see the Valley of the Kings. Navigation in Egypt was wonderfully easy; all she had to do was follow the sparkling Nile south, with its long ribbons of green crops standing out brightly on both banks.

As Mary headed her plane south from Wadi Halfa, she entered the great emptiness of the Nubian Desert. After a short while, her airspeed indicator stopped and her engine started to play up. This was worrying. Mary flew low and then, carefully picking a smooth landing area, put down carefully on the stony, sandy desert ground. While she herself confessed she was no expert, nevertheless she understood enough about her engine to try to sort out the problem. She worked for three hours in the searing desert heat doing numerous checks before her engine roared happily back into life. Very relieved, she then took off for the final hour's flight down to Shereik and Atbara in north Sudan.

The next day, on Sunday 1 April, Mary Bailey continued to follow the Nile 200 miles south and finally, tired, dusty and sandblown from the long flight, she descended and arrived at Khartoum. Her flight down from London had taken twenty-three days. Mary Heath, well refreshed after excellent hospitality and a comfortable bed, was there along with the crowds to cheer the landing and to greet her at the aerodrome. As Mary Bailey rolled to a stop, her thrill of safely arriving must have been somewhat tempered by seeing a glamorous Mary Heath standing in the front of the welcoming group on the runway waving hello. Mary Heath had lost none of her competitiveness and commented sweetly that she was hurt to see Mary Bailey looking so tired and weary, and how gallant it was of her to attempt such a flight when she had never flown out of England before. Mary Bailey, with her aristocratic background, took no notice at all and was the essence of politeness to everyone.

The British community in Khartoum, comprising both RAF personnel and local administrators, loved the two female aviators equally; what a triumph it was for the two women to have flown such distances, one from the north and one from the south. A special celebration dinner was arranged, and Mary Heath rather upstaged Mary Bailey when she arrived in an elegant evening dress. Mary Bailey had brought no special clothes with her; she had kept the weight for the long flight down to the absolute minimum. However, she was not concerned. There were plenty of British fans wanting to talk to both of them and applaud their magnificent flying.

Despite any hidden animosity between the two women, they both enjoyed the comfort and acclaim of the British community in Khartoum, who couldn't do enough for them. Flying so far in an open-cockpit little plane, sometimes for up to eight hours at a stretch; navigating without any communication; crossing dangerous areas where there were few places to touch down; the two Marys were applauded wherever they went in the spreading town.

After four happy days, both women felt they were ready to head off again. There was little talk of who would become the first to fly the route, and really the dangers were too high to risk trying for speed. As it turned out, both women encountered unexpected delays on their onward journeys.

On her way south, Mary Bailey was delayed when, in hot, gusty conditions, she crashed her plane on landing at Tabora in west

Tanzania. The plane turned over and Mary was lucky to escape uninjured. On receiving a telegram about the accident, her husband Abe leapt into action. Through various contacts, a new plane, another Moth, G-EBTG, was finally found and flown out for her. After her enforced and frustrating stay in Tabora, Mary at last set off again on 21 April.

There were still many stops en route, but Mary Bailey finally landed at Cape Town on 30 April to a tumultuous welcome. She had become the first woman to complete the African route and indeed set what is thought to have been a world record at the time; no other woman had flown such a distance.

When Mary Heath headed north out of Khartoum, she followed the same general route Mary Bailey had come out on. Unfortunately, trying to take off from a stopover at Salum, on the Egyptian–Libyan border, she hit some stones and badly damaged the back of her Avian aeroplane. Luckily an Englishman was in the area and he helped to organise local repairs and then called in a team of RAF mechanics for additional help. It all took a few days, though; and then, when she reached Tripoli, Mary went down with a bout of rheumatic fever and had to rest in her hotel, causing further delay.

Nevertheless, once recovered, on she went and made her way back via Paris to land at London Croydon on 17 May, where she was met by a huge crowd and massive celebrations. Although her flight had taken three weeks longer than Mary Bailey's, Mary Heath had become the first woman ever to fly the Cape Town–London route. As she had predicted earlier, this was the most newsworthy of the two flights and made headlines everywhere.

It had been a truly epic flight for both women and helped to put female pilots firmly on the map. This was four years before American Amelia Earhart made her solo transatlantic crossing in 1932.

The story didn't end there though. In Cape Town, after a reunion with her husband and numerous celebratory events and official functions, Mary Bailey took a surprising decision. This quiet, well-brought-up but determined lady decided to fly back to London, and not just fly back, but explore a different route up the west coast of Africa. After leaving Cape Town on Monday 14 May 1928, her adventures went on as she headed up through the Democratic Republic of the Congo, Central African Republic, Chad, Senegal, Morocco and finally over to Spain and home. When the media started to learn about this return trip, interest from the general public grew dramatically. Where was she? Was she safe? Month after month the intrigue and public interest increased.

After eight months of numerous adventures, dramas and also brilliant flying, Mary Bailey arrived back at Stag Lane on Thursday 17 January 1929, having flown some 18,000 miles, and this time she received one of the biggest welcomes ever, outdoing even the welcome that had been given to Mary Heath. The media interest in the later stages of Mary Bailey's flight had been intense, and her safe arrival after such a distance and her reunion with her family was covered by the widest media including across Africa. All Mary Heath could do was look on at the non-stop praise and receptions given to honour Mary's heroic trip, including Mary Bailey's honour of being awarded a DBE in the New Year's Honours list at the end of the month.

Both women continued their interest in aviation after their extraordinary trips. Mary Heath tried for some new records, including a height record in 1929, and a short flight as a second pilot on KLM from Amsterdam to London. But then the company rejected any further requests from Mary to fly with them because she was a woman. Still fired with ambition, Mary Heath tried many other things including flying in America but here, in August 1929, she had a serious accident which pretty well stopped her flying career at the age of 34. Her second marriage to the elderly Sir James Heath had now totally failed and she married again in America, this time to George 'Jack' Williams from St Lucia. They returned to Ireland and became involved in local aviation, including a local airline, but despite all her efforts, her glory days were behind her. She began drinking more and more and in February 1934 was declared unfit to fly by the British Air Ministry. Jack decided to return to the Caribbean, and Mary headed for London where she made several court appearances for drunkenness and even spent two days in Holloway Prison. In May 1939, in shabby clothes, Mary Heath fell down the stairs of a bus and died shortly afterwards. Despite the rather sad ending, she had achieved more than she could ever have dreamed of after her shaky upbringing in Ireland, and her name still lives on in the record books.

Mary Bailey continued to fly and have some exciting adventures before she finally gave up flying after an enforced landing on the edge of the Sahara Desert in 1932. She spent the following years involved with her family and helping her husband Abe, who was becoming unwell. The Second World War was not easy for Mary; Abe died in South Africa in 1940 and Mary's attempt to join the Air Transport Auxiliary as a pilot was squashed because of her age – she had now turned 50. After the war she mainly lived in her sunny house in Cape Town surrounded by friends as well as her flying trophies, and she died in August 1960 just before her 70th birthday.

While the two Marys may not have been the best of friends in life, they will always be paired together in history as the amazing female pilots who flew across Africa.

11

WINIFRED BROWN

1930
RACER AND FIRST WOMAN TO WIN THE FAMOUS KING'S CUP AIR RACE

For anyone who loves statistics, it could be interesting to look at why so many early female pilots were called Winifred.

Winifred Buller was the first when she achieved her pilot's certificate number 848 in May 1912, becoming the third qualified female pilot in Britain. Then there was the big gap of the First World War and also in the early 1920s as society recovered. However, by 1927, things were changing fast. Up until 1926 only nine women had managed to get their flying licence; a year later nine more women qualified all within a few months of each other, and two of them were named Winifred.

Winifred Brown and Winifred Spooner (on whom there is more information in Chapter 16) entered the realms of flying with a new determination. Flight had progressed from simply managing to stay in the air to clever navigation and extraordinary duration. Pilots were travelling further than ever before. Now the two Winifreds were looking for something else. During the previous decade, engines had progressed steadily, and by 1927 both Winifred Brown and Winifred Spooner decided they wanted to push the boundaries in engine performance. They were looking for speed.

Competitions had been established from the very early days of flying and, by the late 1920s, they were in full flight. But with only a handful of women being pilots, female entrants to flying events were rare and in many cases not welcomed. Even by 1930, Winifred Brown was denied accommodation at the Hanworth Aero Club at the start of the prestigious King's Cup Air Race. The organisers had to rethink their views quickly when Winifred actually won this prestigious event!

Winifred Brown wasn't into point-scoring for women, though; she simply loved what she did. She had learned early not to worry too much about the opinions of others. Her mother, while forceful and vocal in many areas, had not been too concerned about her diet, and at the age of 10 Winifred weighed 10 stone. While this resulted in some teasing at her school in Broughton, just north of Manchester, Winifred didn't take offence. She had a cheerful and kind character which won her many friends. She may have inherited this from her father, Sawley Brown. Sawley came from a line of very successful butchers and when Winifred was born, in 1899, he was making a lot of money. He had a gregarious nature and it seems he also had a bit of an eye for other women, even after marriage, which caused a certain amount of family tension as Winifred grew up.

Generally, though, Winifred had a pleasant, worry-free upbringing. She did start to show early individuality when she stole some cigarettes from her father and helped to set up a rebellious Swearers and Smokers club at her school, but she revealed another side of her character when she confessed to her father what she had done.

Winifred became interested in boys from an early age and learned a lot when she volunteered to join the Voluntary Aid Detachment (VADs) during the First World War. She worked as an auxiliary nurse at a local hospital where constant advances from lonely, wounded soldiers helped to turn her from a naïve young girl to a much more mature woman, albeit still with a great sense of fun.

One day, when she was walking down a central Manchester street, she saw an advert that interested her. It was from a coach offering free tennis lessons. Winifred loved the idea of tennis, and then she loved her coach more. It was a short but beneficial affair because, under his tuition, Winifred developed into a useful tennis player and visited various tennis clubs for games. At one point it was suggested Winifred partner Ernest, another young player with promise, in a doubles match. They won and soon Winifred had a new love, and a wealthy one too. Ernest offered to drive Winifred down to tennis matches in Torquay and then Bournemouth in his Rolls-Royce and so the relationship was sealed. Again, it didn't last too long as, soon after, Winifred met another interesting young man eager to make her acquaintance.

Now that she was in her early twenties, Winifred's doting father gave her a car, a green Talbot-Darracq, which offered tremendous freedom. She learned to drive quickly. What a fun time this must have been for Winifred. She had lots of friends through her old circle and now she also had new tennis groups to have parties with. On one momentous day Winifred offered fellow tennis player Ron Adams a lift in her car to a tennis match and another new relationship began.

Perhaps part of Ron's attraction for Winifred was that he had mentioned an interest in flying. Winifred had lots of energy, and the exciting and glamorous world of aviation sounded fascinating. So it was arranged that they would join a friend of Ron's to visit the newly formed Lancashire Aero Club, then based at Woodford Aerodrome just south-east of Manchester. The club had virtually no facilities but it did boast the ownership of a little biplane. As soon as Winifred saw it, she was entranced.

There were no other women in the club, but one of the club members offered to take Winifred up for a flight. G-EBLV was a De Havilland Moth, a two-seater wooden plane with a plywood-covered fuselage and fabric-covered wings. Interestingly it had folding wings, something that had been encouraged by the Air Ministry, which was keen to encourage flying across the country and thought that if planes could be kept in smaller hangars, it might help boost the activity. De Havilland had a tradition of painting the wings and tailplanes of their Moth planes in silver, but they also often painted the fuselage in a specific shade to represent club colours. The London Aero Club had a yellow fuselage, Newcastle red, Midlands green, and the Lancashire Aero Club blue.

Winifred loved the look of the pretty blue and silver Cirrus moth and as they bounced across the ground and rose into the air, something clicked. Perhaps she could also learn to fly. The plane didn't reach vast speeds – its cruising speed hardly went above 80mph – but it was fast enough to whizz around the sky offering an amazing sense of freedom. The pilot let Winifred try the controls and she managed to keep the plane fairly level for a short while.

As Winifred stepped out of the plane, she asked the instructor about learning to fly. Daddy would pay. She was quite correct; her doting father Sawley was excited about his daughter's new interest and happy to get involved. Winifred's stricter mother thought the whole idea was absurd and she was totally against it. Nevertheless, Winifred started having half-hour lessons and steadily learned how to control the little Cirrus Moth. While Winifred didn't show immediate talent, she stuck at it. There was some initial reticence about having a woman join the club, but finally the officials relented and Winifred became a full member.

Now Winifred had two loves in her life: she stayed with Ron Adams but she was also very keen on her flying. The summer and autumn of 1926 was a happy time and by the end of the year she was ready for that momentous occasion, going solo. It went well. After that, Winifred went on with her flying lessons, and by early the following spring she was ready to get her pilot's licence. Winifred passed and was issued with Private Pilot's Licence 1061 in April 1927. Winifred's father was happy to join in the celebrations; it was a great achievement.

Then came an interruption. Winifred had proved to be a good hockey goalkeeper at school; she was happy to admit that it was probably as much due to her size as to her skill. But she was clearly a good defender and after leaving school she had carried on playing hockey for her local and then the county ladies' team. In 1927 she was asked to join the England Ladies' hockey team to go on a tour of Australia. This was a wonderful opportunity for Winifred, now 27 and eager to see more of the world. She was accompanied by her mother and her boyfriend Ron as well. While a mother coming along as chaperone was very acceptable, the team organisers weren't quite so excited about an accompanying boyfriend, but, true to nature, Winifred simply took no notice of the opinion of others and ensured that he was included in the trip.

They booked first class on the P&O steamship RMS *Chitral* and left London in April 1927. Winifred spent the entire summer on her travels, playing hockey right across Australia from Perth to Adelaide and Melbourne, where she managed to borrow a plane and do a flight at Essendon Aerodrome. She hadn't forgotten her skills and evidently gave a good display of controlled flying. Then it was off for more hockey matches in Tasmania and Sydney, finally ending up in Brisbane. There the team separated and Winifred, with her mother and Ron in tow, continued their adventures around the world. They visited New Zealand, Fiji, Hawaii, Vancouver, Niagara Falls and finally travelled back across the North Atlantic to England; in those days this was the most amazing trip for a girl in her twenties.

But this was not as amazing as the surprise that was in store for Winifred when they finally arrived home. Her father had clearly missed his beloved daughter and, as a 'welcome home' present, he offered to buy her an aeroplane of her own. Winifred was incredibly excited by this offer and, as the new year of 1928 approached, she could hardly contain her impatience waiting for the delivery of her new plane. It arrived in February, a brand new Avro 594 Avian III biplane with a Cirrus engine and in a smart red and silver design. Its registration was G-EBVZ.

The Avians, built by local company A.V. Roe and Co., were easy to handle and a very popular aircraft for both training and for general flying. Winifred took to it immediately, getting up in the air and familiarising herself with the controls and feel of the new plane. It was a two-seater, so she could fly with her instructor or she could take her loyal boyfriend Ron up to help her navigate.

In March 1928, just five weeks after she received her new plane, Winifred flew down to Croydon to take part in an aviation display for the visiting King Amanullah of Afghanistan. She was representing the Lancashire Aero Club and, to help her with the navigation, her instructor led the way in another aeroplane.

Back in Manchester, she kept flying, loving it as much as ever. Her mother had come to accept it now, although not with enthusiasm. But then disaster struck.

A flight had been arranged to deliver a can of film to a field near a cinema in Stalybridge, about 8 miles east of Manchester. It was all a publicity stunt for a new film and a large crowd had gathered in the field to watch the arrival. At the last minute, the pilot who had agreed to deliver the film had a problem, and Winifred said she was happy to stand in. With a man from the film company also in the plane, Winifred took off from Woodford Aerodrome and soon spotted the crowds in the designated landing field.

Flying over the ground, Winifred saw that the area was very tight and surrounded by people; but she had been told that landing distances had been assessed before the field had been selected, so no doubt she felt some pressure that she needed to complete the job. She came down carefully and did a gentle touchdown on the grass. However, there was no wind and the plane simply wasn't going to stop in the space available. Conscious of the crowds at the end of the field ahead of her, Winifred powered up quickly to take off again. The crowds thought this was simply part of the stunt and instead of getting out of the way, just stood there watching excitedly as the plane sped towards them. As Winifred lifted off, she just cleared many heads but her undercarriage struck a wall and the plane crashed through, coming to a halt just beyond. Seven children hadn't been able to get out of the way quickly enough and had sustained injuries. One young boy, Jackie Hood, had been killed.

It was a terrible incident and one that must have been truly shocking for a young and still fairly inexperienced pilot. Winifred had knocked herself out, but other than that she sustained few injuries. An inquest was held a month later, and the verdict was death by misadventure.

The plane was soon repaired and, despite even stronger objections from her mother, Winifred got back into her aircraft and continued to fly. It had been a dreadful shock and a steep learning curve for the 28-year-old. The knowledge that she had been responsible for the death of a little boy was something she would have to live with all her life. Just a few weeks later, confidence returned and, taking her flying more seriously, she took part in an air pageant at Blackpool. In one race she came third, which gave her a boost. In August that summer she flew with Ron to Ostend in Belgium. Much of their navigation was done by following railway lines, not unusual in the late 1920s, although she had a few moments of scary uncertainty during the trip when they weren't sure where they were.

Winifred was now taking her flying more seriously, and the overseas trip encouraged her to enrol on a navigation course in Manchester. This was mainly directed at nautical navigation but Winifred learned all she could. Then, developing a small fault in her engine on an easy cross-country flight, she decided to go a step further. She contacted Cirrus saying she wanted to learn more about engines and they agreed she could spend three weeks with them, learning how their engines worked and what needed to be done to maintain them.

Being better at navigation and knowing more about engine performance was a turning point for Winifred and the following year, 1929, was the year her flying career really took off. From spring onwards, Winifred was flying all over the place, attending meetings, air pageants and races. Sometimes with her instructor, sometimes with boyfriend Ron, and sometimes on her own she would take off from Woodford and fly to various venues. In May, she flew up to a Scottish air meet at Gleneagles and in early June she put in a good performance at the Midland Air Pageant at Castle Bromwich. Then, just a few days later, she took off, navigating with Ron's help across the North Sea, to attend the international Light Plane Competition in Rotterdam.

Initially, it had been the fun and partying with other pilots that had attracted Winifred to aviation events; with so few female flyers around she was often surrounded by interesting men and she loved the social aspects and good fellowship of it all. But she also began loving the competitive aspects. After her accident the previous year, now Winifred was showing a more serious side of her nature and was flying with a quiet competence.

The summer of 1929 continued with non-stop flying. In July, Winifred went up to Blackpool to see the planes landing as part of the prestigious King's Cup Air Race. This leading event was first run in 1922 and was part of an overall plan to encourage the development of light aircraft and engine design in Britain. The race was based around a cross-country format and the first route was a race up from Croydon Aerodrome to Glasgow and then, after a short overnight stop, back to Croydon. Since then the race had been run every year. Winifred found the whole event mesmerising; she began to consider the possibility of entering it herself the following year.

Inspired by what she had seen at Blackpool, she continued the summer at a furious pace, attending a myriad of events across the country, including the Manchester intercity air race between Liverpool and Manchester, the Morecombe Air Display in nearby Blackpool and the Newcastle Air Pageant in October. Winifred was clocking up many hours and a great deal of experience. She even came second in one event with an average speed of 78mph, a very good speed for her little plane. While she was well aware that she was not touching the speed of earlier winners of the King's Cup, who achieved averages of well over 100mph, she was gaining experience and confidence all the time and in late autumn she felt she was competent enough to enter the race the following year. After all, a fellow female aviator, Miss Winnie Spooner, had come fifth in the same race that year, and there was no reason that Winifred would disgrace herself.

There was one other factor that strengthened Winifred's decision to enter the race. She had by now become quite famous locally as a female pilot and was very much an integral part of the Lancashire Aero Club where she had started flying. But the club had grown dramatically in the last year or so, and now it was sometimes holding events from which women were banned. This upset Winifred, who thought it unfair. Entering this famous air race would give her more credibility.

With boyfriend Ron and also her father Sawley in full support, during the winter of 1929–30 Winifred made the decision. She would definitely enter the King's Cup Air Race to be held on 5 July that summer.

In the spring of 1930 Winifred continued with her flying and lost a little confidence in a race she entered in April. The event was held by the Hull Aero Club to help celebrate the opening of their new clubhouse. The course to be flown covered a total distance of

30 miles and consisted of four laps around a 7½-mile circuit. Fellow female pilot Winifred Spooner had entered as well, and managed to come second with an average speed of just over 97mph. Poor Winifred Brown was a lot slower and came in at the end of the field. It was a disappointing result. Amy Johnson, another recognised female pilot, also attended the event although she did not take part; she was more intent on answering questions about her planned flight to Australia the following month.

Winifred returned home from Hull depressed, realising that she still had a lot to learn even to catch up with the other female pilots of the day. But her boyfriend, her father and some other friends encouraged her and soon she resumed her happy, optimistic nature. After all, she just loved being in the air. That was really what it was all about; she still enjoyed playing hockey and tennis for the same reason. All in all, Winifred was putting a lot into life and having a great time.

July came quickly and details of the King's Cup Air Race were confirmed. It was to take place on one day only, Saturday 5 July. It started at Hanworth in London, and there were various specified turning points along a course that ran via Hamble on the south coast and Bristol to Manchester and Newcastle before finally heading back via Hull to Hanworth. The route was a total of 745 miles and there were a few stops allocated en route for pilots to fill up with fuel, do various checks and perhaps grab a sandwich.

A record 101 pilots had entered the race. It was a daunting list of the top pilots of the day; many were already famous and most had vast experience. Squadron Leader Augustus Orlebar, who had set the world air-speed record with a flight of 357.7mph in a Supermarine S.6 the previous year, was taking part; so were Geoffrey de Havilland and his son. Many winners from the previous King's Cup races had entered. The planes were handicapped, with the idea of everyone arriving at the finish line at the same time, but it wasn't a precise process and Winifred had serious fears of coming in last.

Winifred was also concerned because her own club, the Lancashire Aero Club, hadn't been particularly supportive of her entering this top event; they thought if she had a poor result it would reflect badly on the club. Winifred had to draw on her natural determination and resilience. She would enter and enjoy the race anyway.

On 4 July 1930, Winifred took off with Ron and made her way down to Hanworth Air Park, an aviation centre in west London. The Hanworth Club had a reputation for running air pageants and garden party fly-ins and was popular with many leading flyers of the day. Unlike many of the pilots, who were all staying at the club and having fun at a special pre-race social event, Winifred had been refused a room. No specific reason was given, but away from all the other entrants, she spent a quiet night at a local pub instead.

The next morning Winifred woke up feeling anxious. Ron was also nervous. He was to accompany Winifred as a passenger and navigator and he knew the race would be enormously challenging. They arrived at Hanworth airfield ready for an early start, took a final weather forecast and again checked their maps. One positive thing for Winifred was that the day had dawned fine and clear. It seemed a good day for flying.

Seeing all the top pilots and powerful planes around, all getting ready for their allocated take-off time, was another nerve-wracking moment for Winifred. But as she finally stepped into her Avro Avian and started up the engine, everything calmed down. It was just another flight. She would do her best.

Carefully calculating winds, and with Ron as a passenger also keeping an eye on navigation, Winifred headed off. She made a good course south to Hamble and turned easily to head directly to Bristol. On landing, she was told she had overtaken a few planes which was quite exciting news and spurred her on for the next sector, up to Liverpool and then on to Barton just west of Manchester. Carefully checking the winds again and her planned course, she flew steadily north to make a good landing at Barton. Here, Winifred's very excited father greeted her with the news that she had crept up to third position in the race.

That was startling news, but Winifred didn't take it too much to heart. She was more than aware that there were some keen competitors all coming up behind her. The positions could change quickly and there were some long legs ahead. As her plane was refuelled and Winifred and Ron checked the maps together, they heard some disappointing news. The weather was closing in and there was thick low cloud over the Pennines, which was cloaking the direct route up to the next stop-off point at Newcastle. This could cause major problems, making navigation very difficult. The pilots would have to alter their planned direct routes substantially to avoid the dangers of flying blind in thick cloud.

Winifred gave her route some thought, and she had a secret weapon. She was now in familiar territory. This was where she had learned to fly, where she had spent many hours in the air. If she could fly east and get across the Pennines through the Woodford Pass, she would once again be in clear air for a direct flight up to Newcastle. It was a risky option. The pass rose to 1,450ft and was known for gusty winds.

Waving goodbye to her father, Winifred clambered back into the plane and off they went again. She made a turn to fly over Woodford, her home airfield, and then headed east. She had made a decision; yes, she was going to try the Woodford Pass.

Charging through the sky, with the wind tearing at her face and clothes, Winifred pushed her plane forward. Heading towards the pass, there were thick grey clouds over the high ground. The pass, however, seemed just below cloud base and appeared clear. Winifred flew on, scanning the way ahead and hoping beyond hope that the clouds hadn't come down to block the route as she surged onwards. As she climbed to clear the highest point in the pass, visibility reduced and the air became wet and misty. She was reaching cloud and the land below her was fast becoming obscured. The ground all around her was hidden in cloud. Her plane was charging through a white, private world. It was touch and go, but she held her course and then, suddenly, they were through. The mist thinned, the air below cleared, she could see the ground. Flying once again became more normal.

It had been a very tense few minutes, but Winifred and Ron could now relax a little. They checked their navigation and then they were off on a steady route up to Cramlington north of Newcastle. Their navigation was spot on and they touched down easily to refuel. It was here that Winifred heard the unexpected news that she was in the lead. She took the information quietly and tried to push any excitement aside. This was the time, more than ever before, that she needed to concentrate on her flying. She was more than aware that they would probably be overtaken in the last push to the finish line. Her main rival, Richard Waghorn, who just a year earlier had won the major seaplane Schneider trophy with speeds of more than 300mph, was just behind. Other planes too were chasing Winifred fast.

As she took off from Cramlington, a plane was taxiing across the runway ahead of her. In normal conditions, Winifred would probably have slowed and gone around again to take off. Not now. She roared off, climbing fast to skim over the plane and head off on her course via Hull back down to Hanworth. Holding the plane steady, she pushed her little engine and rocketed southward. It had been a very long, very tiring day but this was no time to relax her concentration. Keeping tightly on course, Winifred sped on south.

As they eventually approached London and the finishing line, there was a final small drama. As they reached Hanworth, Ron spotted another plane coming up fast behind them. He alerted Winifred, who pushed her shuddering plane forward in a last-minute high-speed dive towards the finishing line. With the engine roaring and her plane rattling around her, Winifred reached a speed of well over 100mph.

They touched down after an exhausting eight hours-plus of flying, relieved to be safely on the ground. Before they could get out of the plane, Winifred saw people rushing towards her. As she looked around, the crowds at the aerodrome were waving at her and seemed to be cheering. Unbelievably, against all odds, an official raced up to the plane to tell Winifred she had won. She was the winner of the prestigious King's Cup Air Race 1930.

Her world quickly became chaotic. As planes landed in a rush around her, Winifred was escorted from the plane and besieged by photographers and people wanting to congratulate her. All the VIPs of the club and aviation in general rushed up to shake her hand. The designer of the Avro Avian and the secretary of the Royal Aero Club wanted to meet her; everyone wanted to say well done to this amazing woman who had just beaten the best flyers of the day to win the country's most prestigious air race.

It was all bemusing for Winifred, who had been cramped up in her pilot's seat all day. Poor Ron, who had assisted Winifred so dutifully throughout the entire flight, became sidelined as the crowds surrounded her. Eventually the couple managed to get together and after a quick celebratory drink at the bar, it was suggested that it might be a good idea if Winifred, with a face smudged with dirt and looking very windblown and battered, freshened herself up for the official presentation. She had her overnight case with her, and she changed quickly into a clean dress and generally smartened herself up. Only now was it beginning to hit home that she had actually come first. News was filtering in of the other entries; some had simply pulled out through engine or other problems; some had got lost; one had run out of petrol within sight of Hanworth. Among the others who had roared in not far behind Winifred, most were totally astounded that they had been beaten by a woman.

The presentation was on the front steps of the grand entrance to the clubhouse, with the crowds spread out on the lawn in front. Sir Philip Sassoon, a well-known politician, social host and aviation enthusiast, was there with many other dignitaries to present the magnificent trophy. Winifred stood to one side as the speeches were made, but they were kept short and then a slightly tentative but beaming Winifred stepped up to say a few words in her soft northern accent.

The presentation over, Winifred could at last relax. From the very early nervous start so many hours ago, it had been one exceptionally long but totally amazing day. Congratulations kept coming in, including a telegram from King George.

Winifred was now offered a room at the clubhouse, but she chose to go back to her hotel. After all, it had been good enough for her before the race. As she woke up the following morning, she realised that overnight she had become a celebrity. When she got back to Manchester, there were numerous official receptions and events to celebrate her win, talks on the radio to give, and even more trips back down to London including a visit to the House of Commons to meet the top politicians of the day. She received a CBE in the following New Year's Honours. Even her mother was pleased.

As the excitement gradually died down, Winifred got back into her old life, continuing to fly as well as keeping up her other sporting activities. She even took up golf. She got a new aeroplane and attended various flying events around the country. However, by the autumn of 1932 her devoted and very proud father explained to his daughter that money was becoming harder to find. Flying was hugely expensive. Winifred took this on board; she was about to turn 33 and she felt she could be ready for a change.

Accompanied by her mother, Winifred and Ron set off for a trip up the Amazon and then she took up sailing, becoming a keen member of the Mersey Yacht Club where she made some close new friends. As her sailing improved, Winifred made several hazardous voyages across the North Sea and on one trip, on a rare occasion when Ron wasn't by her side, Winifred developed a close friendship with a charismatic Norwegian, spending several days with him. Winifred was still living life to the maximum.

In 1940, Winifred's father died and she moved to Beaumaris in east Anglesey, accompanied as always by Ron. Her mother came too. Winifred had not lost her eye for men and this was the home of another very close associate of hers, Dunstan Walker. They had met a few years earlier through the Mersey Yacht Club and enjoyed getting together again in Anglesey.

In spring 1940 Winifred, at the age of 40, found she was pregnant and finally she and Ron Adams were married in a quiet ceremony. The marriage did not last and after so many years together, they split up in 1945. Sailing continued to dominate Winifred's life for many years and she wrote three books about her exploits. As her son, Tony Adams, grew up, he became quite a successful actor, and she moved to London to be near him. Then she moved down to the south coast where she spent her final years supported by the yachting fraternity who knew her for her sailing voyages. Many may not have been aware that this unusual woman was also the first female pilot ever to win the country's most prestigious air race.

12

AMY JOHNSON

1930
THE FIRST WOMAN TO FLY TO AUSTRALIA

By the early 1930s, nearly 150 years after Letitia Sage first took to the air, women were finally being recognised as proper participants in aviation. While there were still very few women involved in all the various forms of flight compared with men, the numbers were increasing fast. There were still boundaries to be pushed, though, and one determined young woman decided to go for the ultimate record: the long-distance flight from England to Australia.

Amy Johnson only obtained her pilot's licence in July 1929, less than a year before she took off for Australia. She had done limited flying and hadn't flown overseas. To attempt a 9,000-mile flight in an open-cockpit biplane across deserts, jungles and ocean was an incredible thing to consider. On her first cross-country flight out of London she got lost; how on earth was she going to find Australia?

Amy wasn't even a natural pilot. After she started flying in September 1928, she didn't go solo until the following June. But underneath her bubbly personality, her attractive looks and friendly girl-next-door character, there was a quiet, steely determination and a fierce doggedness. Amy Johnson wasn't a girl to be beaten.

Her childhood had been happy, wrapped in a loving family in Hull. Her mother had been brought up in an affluent household and ran a charming, efficient home for her family including their first child, Amy, born in 1903, and the three younger girls who came along in the following years. Amy's father was a descendant of a Danish fisherman who swapped the dangers of the sea for a fish import and export business. The company did well and Amy's father continued in the business, leading it to even greater success during Amy's early years.

Like anyone's childhood there were a few knocks – literally, in Amy's case, when a cricket ball hit her in the mouth when she was 14 and broke her front teeth. She was fitted with good replacements but this dented her confidence for many years.

Without her father's financial support, Amy would have found life much more challenging. As it was, her parents could help her to maximise her natural abilities and after school she went to Sheffield University, an unusual step for girls in those days. By this time, at 19, she had already become involved with her first proper boyfriend, Hans Arregger. He was Swiss but involved in business in Hull and played a major part in Amy's younger life; for many years she believed they would eventually marry. Amy's university days helped her develop as an adult and while a lot of her time was spent dancing and socialising, she worked hard enough to achieve a Second Division degree in economics, Latin and French. She also attended shorthand and typing classes and then, at the age of 22, she took a job. This first step was a clear indication that Amy was not a natural conformer. Instead of becoming a traditional secretary or office worker, Amy researched several ideas and finally decided she wanted to become a copywriter, something she felt could suit her abilities and temperament. She was taken on by a local Hull advertising agency but it didn't turn out as Amy had hoped, as she was roped into doing more secretarial work than copywriting.

With her Swiss boyfriend showing a reluctance to seriously plan a future together, Amy started making enquiries about working in London and decided she needed to be there to get a decent job. Her father agreed to tide her over financially, and Amy moved to a small bedsit in London. It wasn't a great time for Amy as she tried to find her feet in the busy capital but finally, through a relation, she got a job at a firm of city solicitors. Here she settled in well and even considered training and taking her law exams. When she joined an old school friend to rent a home, Amy's life took a turn for the better. In early 1928, at the age of 24, with a good, well-paid job and a friend to have fun with, Amy started to enjoy her time in the busy metropolis. She was still pining for her boyfriend and seeing him when, occasionally, he came down to London, but she could sense he was drifting away. Sometimes she played hockey and tennis, she enjoyed dancing and was always ready to consider other ways to entertain herself in the hours away from the office. At the time flying was big news and Amy had been fascinated by the exciting developments that were taking place. On one Saturday, with nothing else to do, she caught a bus to north London and visited Stag Lane Aerodrome to watch planes take off and land. On the grass by the hangars were several club members relaxing in deck chairs as they watched the action, and Amy felt rather out of her depth. The flying was really exciting, though, and after watching for a while, Amy plucked up her courage and approached one of the pilots to ask about lessons. Flying was expensive but Amy thought that if she were careful, perhaps she could just afford it. She signed on as an associate member of the club and put her name down at the bottom of rather a long waiting list to learn to fly.

In the summer of 1928, as Amy turned 25, her long-term boyfriend came down to London to tell Amy he not only had another girlfriend, but that he had actually married her. This hit Amy very hard, and she finally realised that it was over, that it really was time to move on.

Luckily, her name had at last reached the top of the list of people wanting to learn to fly, and a lesson for Amy was arranged for 15 September at Stag Lane Aerodrome. It would be in a Cirrus II Moth. As Amy clambered in for the first lesson, she would have been totally delighted to be trying something so new and so interesting. Her office work had become a little mundane and now there was no man in her life.

From then on, every Saturday and occasionally on Sundays, Amy caught the bus out to Stag Lane for a half-hour flying lesson. She had a variety of instructors; one who was not the most patient left her in tears and, as she headed home on the bus, she wondered if she would ever get the hang of it. But she persevered, saving as much money as she could for the lessons. With her happy enthusiasm, she gradually became accepted at the club and started to socialise with other members in the clubhouse.

Winter weather prevented flying for a few weeks, but as spring arrived, off Amy went again, practising turns and landings. She was just about to be cleared for her first solo when a change of instructors set her back a bit, and it wasn't until 9 June, when she had clocked up nearly sixteen hours' flying time, and nine months after she had started flying, that she finally went solo.

It might have been a slow beginning but Amy just loved it. Gaining confidence in every flight, going up when she could whatever the weather, Amy was gradually becoming an efficient, if not a natural, pilot. Finally, on 9 July 1929, Amy passed her flight test to be issued with her A licence, number 1979.

It was an exciting moment but she was all too aware that she still had a great deal to learn. When she got lost on her first cross-country flight a week later and had to make a forced landing before heading back to the airfield, it confirmed her realistic view of her capabilities. This didn't daunt her but instead fired her up. She started visiting the engineering hangar to learn more about how an engine works and the construction of a plane.

The chief engineer at the hangar, Jack Humphreys, was surprised and impressed by this attractive young girl wanting to learn about engines. He took her under his wing. While she continued to practise her flying, she also began spending more and more time in the hangar learning all she could about engines. Her dreams were materialising; she would become a professional pilot and even perhaps the first professional female aircraft engineer. It was an idea that took over. The dirty overalls and oily face and hands didn't worry her and she started putting more and more time into learning properly about the maintenance of aircraft. The mechanics took to calling her Johnnie, which she loved.

At this time, Amy's younger sister Irene committed suicide. It was totally unexpected and a dreadful shock for the family but it helped to convince Amy's father that helping his eldest daughter do what she really wanted would be a good thing. He agreed to help cover Amy's costs towards becoming a professional pilot. Amy was more than delighted. She was now free to give up her job in the city and simply concentrate on flying. She moved to cheap rooms near the airfield and started working hard on the engineering side as well as continuing to fly whenever she could. She was making new friends and attracting new admirers in the Aero Club. Aviation was quickly taking over her life and Amy was content and also excited. She had become involved in a wonderful new world. By December 1929 she was ready to take her engineering examination. This involved answering technical questions from a panel of five imposing experts, but rather than being intimidated, she had studied so hard she found the test reasonably straightforward. Amy was issued with Ground Engineer's Licence number 1391 on 10 December 1929, becoming the first woman in Britain to achieve the Air Ministry's official engineering licence.

Now Amy Johnson was beginning to stand out: a determined young woman who was steadily creeping up the flying ranks. One day a newspaper reporter happened to be at Stag Lane talking to pilots about aviation when he spotted a woman in oily overalls outside the engineering hangar. He approached Amy, asking what she was doing and what her plans were.

Amy was excited to have an opportunity to talk to the media. From her early days in the advertising agency she knew publicity could help her career. In the interview, she mentioned her desire to become a professional pilot but then decided to add more interest to her comments. She knew the ultimate test for a woman would be a flight to Australia, so she said she was keen to try that too. When the report was published in the *London Evening News*, it created a sensation and was repeated, with photographs of Amy, in newspapers across the country. Her comments had been interpreted into a definite immediate plan – Amy was going to fly to Australia!

Amy quite liked the sudden fame and was proud her parents had seen her picture in the media. However, in her quieter moments, she also had a dreadful feeling. What had she said? She realised she could now become a laughing stock at her precious club if she didn't do the flight.

So the idea of a trip to Australia took a firm hold. The more she considered it, the more reasonable it seemed. After all, it was more than ten years since the route had first been flown by the Smith brothers in a Vickers Vimy. Then, in 1928, just a couple of years before, Bert Hinkler had done the route solo in just over two weeks. Why couldn't a woman also do the route in small steady hops?

Nevertheless, to attempt the long flight to Australia was an extraordinary decision for someone so new to flying and someone who didn't even have her own aeroplane. After seeing the media coverage, however, Amy felt the decision had been made for her. As she was questioned by friends and colleagues about the newspaper articles and about her plans, she confirmed, yes, she was going to attempt the England-to-Australia route. When she started to investigate the flight, she found out quickly that it was vital she left before May to avoid the Far East monsoon period. That meant she had four months to get everything organised. The pressure was on.

Amy filled the first few weeks of 1930 with frenetic activity. Flying practice, of course, and studying further engineering took a great deal of time. Luckily, the head of engineering Jack Humphreys had continued with his great support for this young enthusiast and was happy to coach her personally, which made a huge difference. But now she needed to learn more navigation, plot her route and work out supplies; there were just so many aspects of a long-distance flight. Plus, most important of all, she needed a plane!

Amy didn't waver and didn't stop. Finding the right names and addresses, firing letters off to every possible sponsor, every possible contact, she worked night and day to get things organised. It was incredibly time consuming and exhausting. All the various aspects of planning plus letters, phone calls and making contacts along with normal flying activities: Amy was wearing herself out. Despite warnings from both her father and her friends that she should slow down, on Amy went. Jack became a true champion for Amy and offered even more personal coaching so she was quickly ready to take the next level of engineering certificate. Other pilots and friends helped her with tips and assistance on every aspect. The plane, however, was the burning issue. After numerous disappointments and rejections, at last there was a glimmer of real hope. Her father agreed to put up half the money for an aeroplane. Amy now continued even more vigorously in her desperate attempts to get the rest of the money to buy a plane for the trip, and her drive together with her constant cheerfulness was impressing many people. Even at the highest levels there was talk about this English girl who wanted to fly to Australia. Finally, the Director of Civil Aviation, Sir Sefton Brancker, asked Amy to visit him for a chat. As he learned about what she had already achieved, including the hours she had spent in the engineering hangars, he was impressed by her sheer enthusiasm, as well as her openness about the problems of the flight. Through his intervention, at last a sponsor was found. Lord Wakefield, whose company was involved in the development of the hugely successful Castrol Oil, agreed to cover the other half of the cost of a new aeroplane.

This was finally agreed on 15 April. If Amy had been frantic and working too hard in the first few months of the year, now her life went berserk. She had already done a great deal of work and had decided her departure date should be no later than 5 May in order to get the best weather and miss the monsoons of the Far East. This left just three weeks to get organised.

The plane she quickly agreed to buy was a two-seater wood-and-fabric biplane, a DH.60 Gipsy Moth. It was a good choice. Its owner had already fitted the plane with long-distance tanks for a flight he had made to the tropics. He was also able to give Amy some useful maps. Amy, never having flown overseas before, planned her route with simple common sense rather than experience. Other pilots flying east often made detours to avoid extra challenging terrain and to avoid certain countries where complicated permissions were needed to land. Amy didn't bother with this. Instead, working on a general cruising speed of 80 to 85mph, she simply drew the straightest line possible for the route, checked distances and then worked out the best located aerodromes where she could stop and refuel. After it was sorted, she sent her list of twenty-two stopping points to Shell-Mex to confirm fuel supplies.

Sir Sefton Brancker continued to support Amy in her quest, expediting several flying permits for her; other people involved in aviation helped with advice and information. Chief engineer Jack was helping to supervise the spares she needed to take; a few companies were now coming in to offer various products, realising there could be some benefit from sponsoring this extraordinary trip by a female pilot. Amy tried to interest a couple of London newspapers in an exclusive story, but without success. Nevertheless, it all involved a great deal of contact, meetings, telephone calls and paperwork. Amy only managed to get in a couple of flights on her new plane before her departure date. Everything was being done in a desperate last-minute rush.

When the weekend arrived before the planned departure on Monday 5 May, Amy must have been incredibly tired. She had tried to keep the actual date of her departure secret as already the trip was beginning to get a little out of hand and even calls of encouragement from friends and colleagues were proving a time-consuming distraction. There was just so much still to do.

Her father came down to help with last-minute arrangements and finally all was ready. On the Sunday before departure Amy flew the plane down to Croydon and stayed the night there in a hotel.

Very early on Monday morning everything was inspected. Amy's attention to detail had even included assessing how best to take off with a heavily loaded aircraft. Now, after a final few checks and in front of a small crowd of supporters, she clambered into her cockpit, heavily protected in a fur-collared flying suit, flying helmet and goggles, and waved a cheery goodbye. Her first attempt to take off was aborted. The plane, packed full of gear and equipment and holding a second full tank of fuel, was very heavy indeed. As Amy tried to gain speed down the runway, she realised she wasn't going to make it. She slowed down and turned around for another go. This time, starting right at the back of the runway, she rolled forward down the grass and gained enough speed to gently lift off well before the perimeters of the airfield. Amy was off to Australia.

As Amy slowly gained height, she waved goodbye to England and headed east over the Channel to France. It was going to be one hell of a trip. Amy had no radio, no contact with the ground, no detailed weather reports. There she was in an open-cockpit plane with just a few basic instruments to help her. These included an altimeter for height and an air-speed indicator plus a compass and some maps she had stuffed into the cockpit.

Hour by hour, on she went as the engine buzzed and the propeller whizzed around in front of her. Keeping an eye carefully on her direction and working out landmarks on the ground, it was almost nine hours before Amy spotted Vienna and could touch down, tired but pleased. She had covered the first leg of 775 miles without problems.

The next day Amy took off for an 800-mile flight to Istanbul, but from here on things weren't going to be so easy. When she landed, enthusiastic Turkish helpers tipped her plane on to its nose but luckily without too much damage. The following day, on the 575-mile route to Aleppo, she hit low cloud as she flew through a difficult mountain pass in the Taurus Mountains and was shaken when a wall of rock suddenly appeared out of the cloud in front of her. But with quick reactions she made it through. The following day, on the 460-mile route to Baghdad, she flew into what looked like a thick haze. But then her eyes started smarting, visibility disappeared, the plane dropped violently and then her engine choked and stopped. She had flown into a vicious sandstorm. She made a rough emergency landing on the flat stony desert and rushed around, covering up the engine and air vent to keep the sand out. Then she clambered on to the tail of the plane to keep it down in the grit-filled wind. It was an uncomfortable few hours, but once the storm had gone through, luckily her plane started and off she went again.

On she flew along her route. At some stops, she had to work late into the night to repair engine and structural problems after a bouncy landing, and often she had to battle with paperwork and demands from over-excited officials. Still she headed on. Reaching Karachi, she checked why her engine had been spluttering for the last few hours and found two plugs had been shorting across to each other, creating a very real risk of fire. She fixed them. En route to Allahabad, she couldn't find the airfield and in desperation put down to check her position. She found she was at Jhansi, 200 miles short of her intended stopover. She took off again, but petrol was running short so she put down on a clear parade ground at a military barracks. The landing wasn't easy, with iron telegraph posts and a big sign in her way, and she ended up with a broken wing as well as having to change the oil and spark plugs and find petrol. It was a low moment. But it was all doable and Amy set to work. In the morning, she took off for Allahabad to refuel before she headed off to Kolkata, or Calcutta as it was then. She arrived there, tired and windswept, on 12 May, a week after she left Croydon.

Amy was now beginning to make real news back in Britain. Telegraph contact had been good from most of her stops and, after a week of excellent flying and navigation, now the media was beginning to get interested in the story of the Lone British Girl Flyer.

It had been seven days of hard flying and exhausting navigation but at Kolkata at last Amy could wash and get some sleep. There was an excellent aerodrome that was just being upgraded into a fully fledged airport. Amy's plane was taken away for full servicing by experts and Amy could relax in British company.

If she had known that her flight out so far had been the easy bit, she may have valued her rest more. As it was, after a good sleep and, with some sandwiches, fruit and a flask of tea on board, early the next morning off Amy set again, now turning on a more southerly route for Bangkok.

First, though, she had to cross Burma, now Myanmar, and it was most unfortunate for Amy that this year of all years the monsoon had come in very early indeed. As she flew south, the clouds built up and Amy entered torrential tropical rain. With a range of mountains ahead, she had to climb high into cloud to clear the highest points. The weather was appalling. Amy must have felt very alone, sitting on her seat in the open cockpit as she ploughed steadily on through smothering grey clouds and driving rain. There was no visibility, just the steady hum of the engine to keep her company as she drove her way forward, constantly checking her height and direction. On she went and then finally, hoping that she had gone far enough to clear the high land, she started descending, still wrapped in thick cloud.

At best, she could only have had a rough guess of her position and it would have been easy for her flight to have ended in tragedy here. But as she descended, she suddenly caught site of a gleam below: the Irrawaddy river. She had cleared the mountains. After that, still in torrential rain and hugely challenging conditions, Amy flew really low, following the river to a railway line and then following the railway tracks south. She was still unsure of her exact position but, knowing she must now be near Rangoon, she flew on in an attempt to spot the airfield. But it was getting dark and her petrol was already dangerously low. Amy was also exhausted after flying hour after hour in impossible conditions. In the end, in another desperate moment, she decided she had to land, and spotted what seemed to be a clear piece of grass. As she touched down, she saw the sturdy goal posts and the ditch, but it was too late. The speeding plane came to a sudden halt nose-down in the ditch. Amy had landed 5 miles short of Rangoon. She clambered out, shaky but uninjured, and checked out her precious plane. It had a broken propeller, a ripped tyre, a broken undercarriage strut and a damaged wing. By good fortune she had landed near a technical institute and students and teachers joined local villagers running up to see what had happened. Despite her exhaustion and the language problems, she organised for the plane to be lifted out from the ditch and secured in an area sheltered by trees.

Then she was guided to a bed where she tearfully collapsed into a fretful sleep. It had been one tough day. Waking up to more torrential rain, Amy struggled to the plane and with help from the students, removed the damaged wing and they took it into a workshop at the institute. But the whole situation seemed hopeless. The fabric was ripped, the ribs were shattered, and Amy stood there dripping wet and totally dejected. Was this the end of her dream? What could she do?

Then, suddenly, an Englishman walked in. Introducing himself as a local forestry inspector, he had heard the news that this strange lady had dropped from the sky in a broken plane and thought he could help. He had good contacts and he might be able to get the plane fixed. Amy's relief can be imagined. Suddenly, from being on a tearful point of accepting her trip had ended in failure, she was galvanised into activity and real hope.

With the forestry inspector sorting out broken plane sections and the students in the institute welding broken metal and making new bolts, everything was taken in hand. Amy fixed on her spare propeller and unbelievably, by the following day, and with a great deal of skilled work and somewhat scary improvisation, the plane was just about mended. The plane was then carefully transported to a nearby racecourse so Amy could take off.

After thanking her helpers profusely, and hugely buoyed up, Amy set off again on the next 350-mile leg south-east down to Bangkok. This brought more major problems, as she had to clear high land in the vigorous monsoon, and for some time Amy was flying at well over 8,000ft, charging blind through heavy enveloping cloud. Yet again it was more nerve-wracking flying for Amy as she tried to keep straight and level, and judge when she had cleared the mountains and could start descending. When she did come down, happily she found she was over much lower bush-covered plains, albeit a long way off track.

She adjusted her course as best she could and as she flew on, she suddenly caught sight of some canals. At last, here was a definite identification point. Studying her maps carefully, she worked out her route and finally reached Bangkok safely. Amy was exhausted again. She had been peering ahead for hours, often unable to wear her flying goggles because of the heavy rain. She had been fighting the uncertainty of not knowing exactly where she was, not even knowing if she was safe as she flew blind through the cloud. The trip was beginning to take its toll. Landing, she took a break to have a meal and then worked well into the night with a team of local Air Force mechanics to service and refuel the plane. It wasn't easy, as they didn't have a language in common.

For the next hop south towards Singapore, Amy kept low and within sight of the coast all the way, still flying through torrential downpours. After 450 miles and hours of challenging and exhausting flying, she put down on a stretch of smooth sand on a small airfield. The sand was so soft that her plane almost turned over on landing and she couldn't taxi. With far too many enthusiastic helpers, Amy serviced and refuelled the plane before grabbing some sleep. Early next morning she helped direct a mass of willing hands to move the aircraft on to a nearby hard road. As she hurtled down the road to take off, she only just managed to avoid the crowds which were pushing in from both sides. Once safely in the air, though, Amy had a fairly straightforward flight south following the coast. She arrived at Seletar Aerodrome in Singapore in the late afternoon of Sunday 18 May, thirteen days after she left Croydon. She was given a tremendous welcome, and here at last she could leave her precious plane to expert servicing with British RAF engineers and go off to have a comfortable night's sleep.

Amy could now have taken a day or two for a desperately needed proper rest. She was in good company with everything she and her plane needed, and it shows her steely determination that instead, the following day, off she went again for what she knew would be a challenging flight to Indonesia. Taking off, she headed up again into bad weather which gave her several frightening moments; at one point she said she was hemmed in by blackness. Her navigation – and perhaps her guesswork too – was superb, though, and she managed to find her way across the wide Java Sea to Indonesia. After a stop en route, she flew steadily on to Sourabaya in East Java and received a wonderful welcome from the English and Dutch community based there. Here she had to do some repairs to her engine and then she headed off east for a 925-mile flight to Atamboea Aerodrome on the island of Timor.

It was a very long flight for an aircraft, the longest non-stop sector of the route so far, and when Amy finally reached the island, she couldn't find the airfield anywhere. Petrol was running out and the tropical darkness was descending fast.

It was yet another difficult situation and Amy desperately looked for somewhere she could land. In the growing darkness, she spotted a small grassy clearing and put down. At the same time as her wheels were about to touch down, she spotted the ground was littered with 6ft-high hard anthills. Steering the plane at speed around the obstacles until it slowed and stopped, she landed safely with fast reactions, enormous skill and without real damage.

Her problems weren't over. Now she was in a remote location, alone, uncertain of the exact position, and suddenly large groups of local villagers with red-stained teeth rushed up to the plane. Amy was initially very nervous, not understanding a word of what they were saying, but she quickly realised they were being friendly. With some relief, she accompanied them back to their little village and spent time with them before a Portuguese man appeared, the commandant from the airfield Amy had been looking for. It seems in the darkness she had overflown the airfield and they had, luckily, chased her. Amy got some sleep, fuel from the airfield was organised and then a runway was cleared for the plane.

There was no telephone in this region to report her position and especially in England there was concern about what had happened to Amy. Headlines began appearing about the missing flying girl. The trip was, at last, becoming very big news.

Then, finally, nineteen days after leaving England, with the plane refuelled and a clear runway cut through the thick growth, Amy was ready for the last leg of her trip to Australia. It was 485 miles to Darwin, all across open sea. Amy got into her plane and, with her tanks full of fuel, she lumbered up a frighteningly short runway to just clear the trees at the far end. Off she went again, wind in her face, hands on the control stick, feet on the rudder and constantly checking her direction. After seven hours of steady flying and using smoke from an oil tanker to assess the wind direction, she adjusted her course and then, after untold adventures and incredible skill, determination and perseverance, Amy Johnson finally spotted the long low coast of Australia on the far horizon. As the land became clearer, alone in her cockpit high above the sea, Amy was filled with overwhelming excitement. This was Australia! She touched down at Darwin Airport late afternoon on Saturday 24 May 1930.

Amy, in her wood-and-fabric biplane, had flown for just under three weeks, covered nearly 9,000 miles and become the first woman ever to fly from England to Australia. The welcome was astonishing. It seemed the whole town and more had turned out to welcome this daring Englishwoman. Amy was still only 26; she was attractive with a charming character; her smiles and happiness on safely reaching Australia suppressed her underlying exhaustion and the nation fell in love with her immediately as she gave an impromptu, natural speech. The news was flashed around the world and in Britain people went wild with excitement. Thanks to unemployment and a great deal of poverty, 1930 had been a flat time in Britain. The country was ready for a warm and wonderful celebrity and Amy fitted the bill exactly.

In Australia, Amy instantly became a superstar. Appearances, speeches, official events in her honour, interviews; everywhere she went she was accompanied by numerous officials and huge crowds. Instead of the quiet downtime she so needed to get over her exhausting and at times terrifying flight, she was on the go day and night, being hurried here and there as events were organised across the country. She loved some of it but also at times she was in despair. The demands on her time and energy were non-stop.

After six weeks in Australia, Amy headed back to the UK, first on a P&O passenger ship, the *Naldera*, and then the last section on an Imperial Airways flight. If the Australian celebratory tour was draining, the welcome Amy received when she arrived back in Croydon on Monday 4 August was totally overwhelming. Everyone wanted a piece of this amazing pilot and Amy, on her part, wanted to repay the support she had been given and also earn money from deals, especially from a contract her father had signed on her behalf with the *Daily Mail*. As part of this agreement, a hectic schedule of events around the country had been organised, and a professional promotional agent was employed who totally underestimated the toll and strain involved in a non-stop publicity programme.

Amy and her family were ill-equipped to cope with such stardom, and it is a huge tribute to Amy's strength and resilience that she managed to come through it all, albeit with several near breakdowns on the way. With such public fame and admiration, life could never be the same. On went the circus, with public appearances and flights into events and standing on numerous stages and attending charity dinners until at last, in the autumn, Amy managed to get some time to herself. Finally, by November, things started to die down slightly. Amy got her own flat near Stag Lane and began to recover properly, regaining the joy and optimism of her old self. She wanted to continue with her flying and she started to look at more record attempts. Rather than going solo, for her next trip she decided to join Jack Humphreys, her ever-loyal engineer from Stag Lane, for a long-distance flight to Tokyo. They did a steady hop across Russia and ten days later landed safely in Tokyo. It wasn't reported in any great detail; there was nothing dramatic about the trip and the media had moved on.

Then a special man came into Amy's life. After a very fleeting romance, she married charismatic fellow pilot Jim Mollison. The wedding took place in July 1932 and now there was a celebrity couple for the media to have fun with. Flying continued to dominate both Amy's and Jim's lives. Amy did a long-distance flight to Cape Town in 1932 and early the next year Jim set a record by being the first person to fly solo from England to America. In between flights, the couple enjoyed a vigorous social life. In June 1933, the couple set off for a non-stop flight from England to New York but ran out of fuel and put down on an airfield 50 miles short of the city. Jim was flying, hugely tired, and landed downwind, overshooting the runway and turning the plane on to its back. The couple were okay, although Jim suffered bad cuts and bruises. The following year Amy was named as the youngest president of the Women's Engineering Society, which was one of her most valued achievements; indeed, it was her capability in looking after her engine that had got her to Australia.

They continued trying for various distance flight records but the marriage wasn't going well. They were beginning to lead separate lives and Jim was being recognised publicly for his association with other women. In September 1936 Amy instructed her solicitors to start divorce proceedings.

It was a difficult time for Amy as she tried to reinvent herself, still hopefully in a field of aviation. She moved around a lot, went gliding, sailing and horse riding, and followed up a variety of business propositions. Her money was dwindling, though, and when she managed to get a professional flying job, for the Portsmouth, Southsea and Isle of Wight Aviation Company in 1939, she was greatly relieved and happy. At last, as she turned 36, she was earning money as a professional pilot, the dream she had had from the beginning. Then war was declared. In 1940 Amy joined the Air Transport Auxiliary to help move aeroplanes around the country for the Royal Air Force. On Sunday 5 January 1941, she left Blackpool in an Airspeed Oxford plane, which was to be delivered to RAF Kidlington just outside Oxford. The plane came down in the Thames estuary and Amy Johnson was killed.

There is still ongoing debate about what happened to Amy and why she was so far off course, but the weather was bad with freezing fog and she may just have got lost and then run out of fuel. There are reports of her coming down by parachute into the sea when a rescue was attempted but failed. However, there is still no definite answer and it is an unsatisfactory and sad end for a woman who achieved one of the most extraordinary flights of the era.

13

JOAN MEAKIN AND NAOMI HERON-MAXWELL

JOAN MEAKIN, 1934
THE FIRST WOMAN TO GLIDE ACROSS THE ENGLISH CHANNEL

The 1930s were an astonishing time for aviation; the speed of innovation and development was breathtaking. All forms of flight were moving forward and, as the decade advanced, the world opened up, especially for the wealthy. It became possible to go on a short hop over to Paris, sitting in a comfortable chair and sipping a drink as one looked down on the towns, churches and railway lines not far below; or to dine in comfort on a flying boat before splashing down on remote stretches of water in exotic distant locations. No longer did you have to be an adventurous pilot to fly across the world. In 1935, Imperial Airways and Qantas Empire Airways started their direct passenger route from London to Brisbane – direct in that it went all the way; it still took over twelve days to reach Australia.

Women had already been involved in all the main forms of flight so far, from ballooning and parachuting to airships and powered flight. Now, one of the major forms of flight that was really taking off in the 1930s was gliding. When Dorothy Pilcher tentatively got off the ground in 1897, it was simply an early form of flight rather than gliding as we know it today. It was not until the 1930s, when new designs had introduced better soaring capabilities, that gliding really got going.

Women were enthusiastic supporters – on the ground. Of the 100 gliding certificates issued in Britain in 1930, only three were to women. Canadian-born Joan Bradbrooke was the first when she was issued with licence number 12 in the summer of 1930 and Mary Nichol (gliding certificate number 49) and Katrine Alexander (gliding certificate number 80) both qualified a few weeks later. All three were awarded the basic A licences which involved demonstrating a good flight in a straight line for at least thirty seconds. In the following years, however, more women started to learn to fly gliders, led by the achievements of two groundbreaking women: Joan Meakin, who was the first female glider pilot to fly across the English Channel and introduced looping into Britain; and Naomi Heron-Maxwell, who was the first British woman, and the sixth in the world, to achieve the highest gliding qualification at the time, the coveted Silver C gliding certificate.

In a way, both women followed a similar pattern into gliding, training in Germany and gaining experience through displays with the Alan Cobham Air Circus, but there the similarity ends. Joan's parents had tried to dissuade her from flying; they had already lost a son when he was a cadet with the RAF at Cranwell. But Joan, like her older brother, had been born with an adventurous streak. Once, when she was 5, at the family home in Repton, Derbyshire, she climbed to the very top of a tall copper beech tree and then challenged the grown-ups to get her down. The nurse who looked after her said Joan was always a tomboy, although she had a very sweet disposition.

When the family moved to London, Joan was immediately attracted to the local flying clubs and then the new London Gliding Club. For a time she did her best to follow her mother's wishes and kept away, but it was simply too hard. In 1931, when Joan was 21, she was touring Germany in a little red MG Midget along with an air-minded friend, Ruth Nicholson, and just out of interest they thought they would call in to a gliding event at Wasserkuppe.

In the 1920s and '30s Wasserkuppe, 80 miles north-east of Frankfurt, was a leading centre for aviation. Famous names such as Willy Messerschmitt and Hanna Reitsch spent time there. When Joan arrived, she was taken aback by what she saw: the new style of gliders, the capabilities of the pilots and the amazing flights that were being achieved. They also offered training courses. Joan and her friend carefully counted their money and then signed on. They stayed for two weeks and in that time Joan showed herself to be a quick learner. At the end of the course she demonstrated good control and a successful long flight.

After that, there was little stopping Joan. Back in England, she flew Fred Slingsby's innovative new glider, the British Falcon, and then, in autumn 1933, she travelled back to Germany to attend Wolf Hirth's acclaimed gliding course in Hornberg. Wolf Hirth was recognised as not only being a top glider pilot but also a bit of a character. After he lost a leg in a motorbike accident, he had his fibula from the amputated leg made into a cigarette holder. Along with excellent instruction, Wolf had added his own unique requirement: he made his students perform several loops in the air before completing their training. Joan was learning on a Grunau Baby sailplane, with a thick aerofoil that gave good lift at slow speeds and a gentle stall. After catching thermals and practising soaring, she completed the course quickly and it was time for her to do the final loops. She just loved doing loops from the first, slowing gaining speed and then pulling back on the controls and lifting the front of the glider right up and over the top. To pass the course, Joan successfully achieved three excellent loops.

By now her parents were beginning to become concerned, but back in England Joan carefully explained the details, assuring them gliding was so much safer than powered flight. Her enthusiasm and excitement shone through, and her parents finally accepted that they weren't going to dissuade Joan from her love of flying. Early in 1934 her stepfather kindly offered to buy her a glider of her own. Joan, of course, was delighted, and settled on one of the newest designs of glider available at the time, a German-made Rhonbussard. These aircraft offered good performance at a reasonable cost.

But first she had to pick up her glider from Darmstadt in Germany, and once more Joan's stepfather made a contribution to her career: he suggested she should fly it back across the Channel. It would be an interesting challenge, plus it would save the expense of packing up the plane to transport it by road or rail. While Joan was by now a very capable pilot, with the equipment of the time there was no way she could soar over to England unless she were under tow. No one would manage to do an unaided soaring flight across the Channel until five years later, when Geoffrey Stephenson flew across to France in April 1939, and it would be another eighteen years before exceptional glider pilot Anne Burns finally achieved a free glider flight over the Channel in 1957. So a plan was devised that Joan would collect and fly her plane back with the assistance of a powered aircraft.

Two experienced German pilots, Roeder and Maier, agreed to do the tow in a German Klemm monoplane. After Joan had excitedly tested her new glider, she was ready to leave. She got into the cockpit and signalled she was ready. The plane in front of her started up and then roared off. With a bit of a jerk, Joan was pulled up into the air behind it.

Heading north, soon they hit some bumpy weather as the two planes cleared the Taunus mountain range, but Joan controlled her glider well as she lifted and sank at the end of the long tow rope, and they made Cologne after one and a half hours of steady flying. Then they headed off again for another hour-and-a-half flight to Ostend, where they landed for a break and took time to make sure everything was ready for the Channel crossing.

When they left Ostend, they headed down a course along the coast south to Calais before turning to cross the Channel. They were flying at around 4,000ft and Joan was being very careful to keep her glider under control. Flying a soaring craft behind a powered aircraft and keeping a steady level course is no straightforward matter, but Joan was concentrating hard. The weather became hazy but then, with some relief mixed with elation, Joan spotted the English coast near Dover and soon she could make out the harbour.

Crossing the coast, the planes turned westerly and flew to Lympne in Kent and then the tow line was released. Joan was now back in familiar territory, gliding alone in reasonable weather. She made three beautiful loops, circled the aerodrome and then made a perfect, gentle landing, becoming the first woman ever to have glided across the Channel. Probably no one at the airfield who had rushed over to watch her land had ever seen a glider loop; to see a woman do three consecutive loops after a cross-Channel flight was hugely exciting.

Just two months later, Joan was ready to make more records in her beautiful new glider. On a warm day in June 1934, after a tow to 4,500ft above Bristol Airport, she successfully made an astounding eighteen loops, three more than achieved by the previous women's record holder, the famous German aviator Hanna Reitsch.

After that Joan became a well-known professional glider, working for a while with Alan Cobham's Flying Circus and becoming recognised for her aerobatics as well as a leading competitive pilot. She married a fellow aviation enthusiast, Ronald Price, and continued with her interest in gliding until well after the war, before eventually retiring to the Isle of Wight.

NAOMI HERON-MAXWELL, 1936
A FREEFALLING PARACHUTIST AND FIRST BRITISH WOMAN TO ACHIEVE THE ULTIMATE SILVER C GLIDING CERTIFICATE

While Joan was gliding across the Channel, a friend of hers and another determined young woman, Naomi Heron-Maxwell, was building up her experience to become the first British woman to qualify for the top Silver C certificate in gliding. It was some build-up. Naomi's life was extraordinary from the start. She was born in 1913, the daughter of Sir Ivor Walter Heron-Maxwell of Springkell, 8th Baronet. Springkell was the family's traditional Scottish home, but it had been sold long before, and the Heron-Maxwells had based themselves in southern England. Naomi's father was a military man, distinguishing himself in the First World War. Naomi was the second of his four children and the family spent a short spell in Russia when she was very young; then it was back to

England for a good education. With adequate family finances, Naomi was also introduced to outdoor activities such as skiing and riding, which she loved. In early 1928, when Naomi was 14, her father died unexpectedly. It was a dreadful shock which also dramatically reduced the family's income. They continued to live comfortably but money was now tighter; when Naomi was 19 on a trip to Malta with her mother, they travelled on the boat second class.

Dreaming of a fun-filled life ahead, Naomi needed a job, and initially she settled for secretarial work, a common occupation at the time. But her restless nature wasn't satisfied, and by 1934 she decided she needed more action in her life. Along with riding a motorbike, Naomi had been excited by all the recent aviation news and thought it would be wonderful to learn to fly. It says a lot that her mother, who had already lost her husband, didn't try to dissuade Naomi from what, in those days, was still a very risky activity. Instead, her mother, who hated idleness, simply said she thought Naomi could have thought of something more intelligent to do.

A few months before her 21st birthday, in spring 1934, Naomi booked lessons at the Abridge Flying Club just east of Loughton in Essex. The club had only opened the previous year and was offering lessons in a Gipsy Moth. Initially, things didn't go quite as planned. On her second flight, on landing, Naomi turned the plane over, causing considerable damage to the aircraft but luckily not to herself. If anything, she became more determined and she devoted herself to improving her skills. She learned about the plane's engine as well and then, through friends and contacts, she met John Tranum. She couldn't have found a better person to excite her about aviation in general and a new activity – parachuting. John had been brought up in Denmark but had spent a lot of time in America and had become one of the leading parachutists of the era. He was very knowledgeable about all the latest developments in parachuting, including delayed drops and ripcord openings.

Throughout the 1920s, opening a parachute manually by pulling on a large ripcord handle on the harness had gradually taken over from the static line system. An increasing number of intrepid showmen were falling off aeroplanes and counting to three or even more before pulling the large ring ripcord. There was, however, still a great deal of scepticism about delayed drops and there were some who continued to believe there was a risk that the jumper would become unconscious because of the speed of falling through the air. Some traditional parachuting displays from balloons were taking place throughout the 1920s, but there were very few women involved. Really only June Williams, a young woman working as a typist in London, was getting to grips with jumping from an aeroplane with a parachute using a ripcord, and she mainly did what was termed as a 'pull off'. Here, the parachute would be packed into a bag worn by the parachutist and, when the time was right, they would clamber out on to the wing of plane, pull the rip cord while still holding on, and then the opening parachute would drag them off the wing.

By 1932, an adventurous German woman, Lola Schroter, was demonstrating clearly that falling below the plane before pulling the ripcord could work really well, and she had been breaking height records over Germany. John Tranum liked this system, and when he spoke to Naomi about all the potential, Naomi thought it sounded interesting. In early summer 1934 she agreed to do a jump. The plan was to clamber out of the plane and jump off, keeping one hand tightly holding the large ring ripcord handle situated on the front of her harness. Then she was to count to three before pulling it firmly. Thanks to the few fixed-wing flights she had done, she had some idea of what it was like being up in the air, but even so this was a lot to ask of a 20-year-old. When all was set and Naomi climbed out on to the wing, she was totally petrified and hung on. But there was no way she could fight the slipstream and climb back into the plane, so after a couple of seconds, she firmly gripped the ripcord handle and fell backwards off the wing. She gave the ripcord a strong jerk and the parachute opened perfectly.

After that there was no stopping Naomi; she loved it. It was cheaper than flying and also, to her delight, she found she might be able to actually earn money as a display parachutist. That would be better than working as a secretary. That summer Naomi managed to do a few displays, earning enough money to keep her flying going. Towards the end of a busy summer, in early September, things took a big turn upwards. Naomi passed her final flight tests and became a qualified pilot with aviation certificate number 12,254, and she was also suddenly given an opportunity to speak on the radio. This was just before doing a parachute show in Lympne in Kent and she spoke about aviation with clear enthusiasm.

It was a fortunate opportunity for Naomi: for Sir Alan Cobham heard the broadcast and quickly recognised this articulate and well-spoken woman could add value to his aerial circus show, which was giving displays across the country. He arranged a meeting with Naomi and the deal was done. Naomi was to join his show for 1935 at £7 a week plus an extra £2 for every jump she did.

Naomi was excited; her life was beginning to take shape. Confident of a financially secure summer ahead, she took off to the Alps for a few weeks of skiing and socialising. But then a letter changed her plans. The publicity manager who worked for Alan Cobham had written to suggest that while Naomi was in Germany, she should take a course in gliding. Germany was still recognised as the leading centre for gliding at the time. The idea was that when she wasn't jumping, Naomi would be able to help the show's glider pilot, Joan Meakin, who was also booked for the summer. Naomi agreed to this and contacted a well-known gliding school, only to be told that Hitler had forbidden women to glide to free up more spaces for men. Luckily, however, during her enquiries Naomi met another gliding instructor who agreed to take her on. At the end of February she travelled to a gliding school in Hesselberg in central southern Germany to join twenty men on a course. They loved having a woman in their group and Naomi found she had a huge group of supporters and soon admirers too. Every day they all set off from their accommodation to march up a steep hill to the high glider base. With wind and snow a regular feature, Naomi didn't get a lot of gliding done but on 7 March she had one flight where she managed to stay in the air for twenty-nine seconds, which really delighted her. She was finding she loved being in the air and controlling her movements without the need of an engine. Having such an attentive crowd of fellow students around her must have helped her enthusiasm as well.

Back in Britain for the start of the air show season, Naomi found being part of a professional touring company was more hard work than excitement. There was a great deal to learn. In April it was arranged for Naomi to do her first jump and soon it was clear to Ivor Price, another professional parachutist employed by Alan Cobham and the brother of Joan's husband Ronald, that Naomi needed some help. Instead of jumping off the wing in a haphazard fashion, Ivor took her in hand and explained the system of doing a pull-off, pulling the ripcord while still holding on to the wing. Naomi wasn't over keen on the pull-off system, saying that the jerk left her shoulders in a mass of bruises, but that was what was wanted. Then the couple planned some double jumps, when two parachutists leave the same plane but from opposite wings. The crowds loved this.

April and May 1935 were busy for Naomi as she jumped regularly with the show. She was slowly becoming quite experienced and also learning to cope with the usual hazards of parachuting at that time, such as an unfortunate landing in a pond. The show, involving pleasure and aerobatic flights, gliding and parachuting, was booked for almost non-stop events all around Britain. Then, on 30 May, Naomi went up for a double jump with Ivor Price. They both left the plane at the same time and for Naomi, everything went smoothly. Ivor's parachute, however, streamed in the air and would not open. He crashed into the ground and died.

The death was a dreadful shock, but the show must go on – after all, flying was a risky business – and so Naomi agreed to continue jumping. A replacement male jumper was brought in and off they went again. Only two weeks later, though, Naomi herself had a fright. Naomi was jumping a Russell Lobe design of parachute which she didn't like, as it opened without a pilot chute to drag it out and, on opening, Naomi had experienced lines being caught over the top of the canopy. On this particular jump, 15 June, she was trying jumping with a second, back-up reserve parachute on her front, a new GQ model which she liked, but it altered the positioning of her main harness. Also, with her new partner, she found she was in a different position on the plane and needed two hands to hang on to the strut on the wing. So she reverted to a freefall jump, dropping off the wing first and then pulling the ripcord. She had done this successfully before – however, on this jump, wearing the new equipment, it took her a while to find the ripcord and pull it, and in that time she had lost a lot of height before her parachute opened. Alan Cobham didn't want any more accidents. Naomi was asked to take a short holiday while everything was checked.

Naomi decided to use the time to travel back to Germany and meet up with her old gliding friends. This was in June 1935 and Naomi was becoming increasingly aware a new Germany was taking shape. She attended a rally and listened to a two-hour speech by Hermann Göring. She described him as a fat little man with a chubby childish face.

The gliding school was now fully booked, and to begin with the only gliding Naomi managed to do was helping to deliver training gliders back to their base at the bottom of the hill at the end of the day. But lying around watching gliding, together with sunbathing and swimming, wasn't a bad way to spend a holiday. Naomi was learning a great deal just listening and talking and watching. Occasionally she managed to get in the air and, early in July, she finally managed to soar as she had dreamed, staying in the air for thirty-eight minutes. It was a wonderful moment and encouraged Naomi to think about getting that coveted Silver C licence.

Britain's Royal Aero Club had started issuing certificates for gliding in 1930, with the first A certificate being awarded in March of that year. This was simply for a straight-line flight of at least thirty seconds' duration. The B certificate involved two flights of at least forty-five seconds plus another flight to demonstrate turns in both directions. The C certificate required a flight of at least five minutes. By 1935 a handful of women in Britain had already achieved all this. What Naomi was going for was the Silver C. This was a dramatic step upwards from the ordinary C certificate and involved an altitude gain of 3,000ft, soaring for a minimum of five hours and flying cross-country for over 30 miles. At the time Silver C was the highest official qualification possible.

As Naomi slowly improved her flying, things came to a sudden halt. First the school received an official letter asking details about the female flyer and also stipulating that she must not be allowed to do any more gliding unless permission was given. Then, Naomi got a letter from the Cobham Air Circus asking her to be back with the show in two days' time.

It was time to head back to work. On her return, Naomi found some changes had been made. Joan Meakin, the glider pilot giving displays, had become a good friend but now she had been opted out into a separate half of the show giving different displays around the country. Naomi missed her friend and was beginning to wonder if she hadn't also lost her zest for thrills. On one jump she had a line over the parachute, turning the canopy into two bulbous halves. This still gave her a safe descent rate, but she didn't know this until she hit the ground and found, to her surprise, that she was okay. Then came a fateful day at the end of July. The show had moved to a field near Hunstanton, and Naomi was packing her parachute when she heard a bang. Eric Collins, the glider pilot in the show, had crashed. Naomi rushed over to see what had happened and saw Eric lying there, dead. Naomi became hysterical. It was a dreadful moment.

Again, the show had to go on. The 1930s was a time of great advancement in aviation, but also a time of many accidents. Naomi went on with her jumps. Then, towards the end of August 1935, she sprained her ankle badly on a landing and while she recuperated, a man called Frederick Marsland joined the tour. He used a parachute Naomi had previously complained about, and when he opened it, several lines were across the top of the canopy, preventing it from fully opening. Marsland crashed down, incurring terrible injuries, and died a week later.

Just a few days afterwards, a passenger flight with two ladies on board had a mid-air collision. Naomi decided she had done enough with aviation for the season and went home to her mother's comfortable London house. A lot had happened in a year. Naomi was still only 22, but had completed over 100 jumps in a short time and had quite a few dramatic incidents. She also had a serious boyfriend and they had become very close. Now he asked Naomi never to jump again and she took his wishes seriously. Two weeks later he was driving to a friend's wedding and crashed. He was rushed to hospital and died with Naomi holding his hand.

What a year. She had been proud to be part of the Air Circus and its aim of bringing aviation to the masses, but the deaths and drama were offsetting the adventure and fun. It was nice to be home, back in her normal circle of friends and social events.

In December, after an afternoon's shopping, Naomi returned to find her glider pilot friend Joan Meakin – now Joan Price – on her doorstep. They had much to talk about and it was good to catch up. Naomi learned that Sir Alan Cobham had had enough and was giving up running an air circus. A new air show was to be formed the following year, but without any parachuting. Naomi had been vaguely thinking what she was going to do next; going back to secretarial work really had little appeal. Perhaps she could join the show helping out in some way and backing up the gliding when Joan needed time off.

Naomi's mother thought a change of scenery would help Naomi after a difficult year and had managed to arrange a ski trip to Davos. She would be acting as a chaperone for two girls with all expenses paid. Going with them for two weeks on the snow suited Naomi perfectly and, as she challenged herself on all the long runs and made new friends, the bad memories of the summer gradually receded. After the holiday, Naomi decided not to accompany her mother back to the UK but return via her old friends in Hesselberg. One of her friends there, Charly, had seriously fallen for Naomi, and he met her at the station and they travelled up to Hesselberg together. But the gliding school had now been taken over by the military and there was no opportunity for Naomi to do any more flying there. It was suggested she write to a couple of other schools and Naomi did this while spending time with Charly. He introduced Naomi to his mother and asked her to marry him. This was difficult for Naomi. She was very fond of him, but it was only six months since the earlier love of her life had died. Also, it would mean giving up everything she had in England and settling down in Germany.

She felt this wasn't what she wanted to do and returned to England. Gliding had taken its hold, though, and Naomi immediately contacted Fred Slingsby, an experienced glider pilot who was beginning to make gliders of his own. She went up for a flight with Fred, soaring for half an hour in a Falcon III two-seater, and found the controls quite heavy compared with the German gliders she had flown. While contemplating trying to join an air circus as a glider pilot, Naomi received a letter from a gliding school near Darmstadt, giving her permission to fly in Germany.

Naomi left immediately. She took a train to Darmstadt and a taxi to Griesheim, and booked herself into a room over a small shop. Then she went up to the flight area eager to meet everyone and get going – only to find the place deserted! Luckily, back in the town she finally found someone to talk to, linked up with some others, and things were soon sorted. Students were being combined from a couple of other schools and training would start soon.

After four or five days, suddenly it was all action and Naomi found herself again surrounded by men. There were two instructors, and one organised a special course for Naomi. She started off with a winch launching in a Falcon glider. She handled it well, had a short flight and then turned and made a good landing. The next day, after a similar launch, she lost speed on a turn and landed the glider tail first, causing some damage. She was cross with herself; it wasn't a great start, but Naomi consoled herself with the thought that the Falcon wasn't the easiest to fly. Ideally she wanted to get into a glider with more sensitive controls.

When she wasn't flying, Naomi was busy pushing machines around the high airfield, often in a steady wind. Eating in the canteen with the other students, it was a full-on and intensive course, but Naomi managed it all well. By now, chatting away in German was easy for her, and she enjoyed mixing with the other students as well as all the new challenges of gliding. There were a couple of no-flying days due to the weather and then flying recommenced.

At the beginning of May 1936, there was a big breakthrough for Naomi; she would be allowed to be towed up in an aeroplane instead of launching from a winch. On her first flight being aero-towed, Naomi became very concerned as she wasn't sure when to drop the cable and found she could hardly see the plane that was towing her, let alone the expected signal about when to release. In the end, she simply released the cable anyway and turned and came in for a smooth landing. The second time she felt much easier about it and it all went very well. She had two more aero-towed flights on the Saturday and two more on the Sunday. With non-stop instruction and consistent flying, Naomi was building up her experience and her skills.

At last she was considered good enough to move on to the Buzzard glider, a more responsive plane with lighter controls. Immediately Naomi found flying dramatically easier; the very first time she flew it she stayed in the air for over half an hour. Now at last she thought her aim to gain that coveted Silver C certificate might be within reach. She needed to do a duration flight, an altitude gain of 3,000ft and a long flight of over 30 miles. The long-distance flight was considered the most difficult to achieve.

Naomi had some luck. It was her fifth flight in the Buzzard glider and she was going for her height requirement. She steered towards a large lumpy cloud and started circling, hoping to get lift. Steadily she rose and she was pleased she might achieve the required height gain. Then, suddenly, she was engulfed in thick grey cloud. Naomi hadn't realised it was a thunderstorm above her with rapidly rising air currents, and she found that her little glider was unexpectedly and vigorously being lifted at a rate of 4m per second. While she was now easily obtaining the required altitude gain for her Silver C, Naomi found she was losing control. Her little glider was being tossed about all over the place and the stress on the aircraft frame was immense. She made a quick decision and put the plane into a really steep descent, desperate to exit the turbulent action of the air currents. After what seemed an age, the earth began to reappear through the cloud. A big relief, and as she managed to pull the plane back into a level flight, she looked around for the airfield below.

With horror, she realised that she recognised nothing at all; she had no idea where she was. The storm was still brewing behind her and the wind was picking up. Naomi flew along at high speed, keeping low to avoid the clouds, and finally she made it into calmer weather. But she was now heading for hills and woods. She needed to land. Looking for somewhere flat and open, she flew on for a while until she saw a suitable piece of ground. Avoiding high tension wires, Naomi landed in a field of corn and breathed a huge sigh of relief. That had been a very scary flight indeed.

Naomi was quickly surrounded by crowds who told her where she was and helped to guard her plane while she went to the nearest phone box to call the airfield. They sent a trailer out and Naomi was really worried she would face a row as she had gone off cross-country without papers and without permission. However, she learned that the thunderstorm had made it impossible to land at the aerodrome after she had left, and instead of having to explain her actions, she found she was being congratulated by everyone on her long-distance flight. She had achieved 34 miles, just enough as a qualification for her Silver C. She had also achieved the required altitude gain.

It was an amazing piece of good luck for Naomi and she found the other students at the airfield were keen to hear all about her experience. Now, all she had to do for her certificate was the five-hour duration flight. Here, Naomi proved her capabilities as a pilot, because after being towed up to 3,000ft and releasing, she found no up-currents anywhere. She managed to get into a few thermals but never achieved more than a very gentle climb, although this was enough to keep her up. She had to achieve five hours of flight, so round and round she went, leisurely circling above the airfield. The most difficult part of the flight for Naomi was the tedium. Hour after hour she sat there, controlling her little glider but getting cold and getting bored. She had had nothing to eat since breakfast and now it was late afternoon, plus she had cramp in her foot. But every minute she was up, she knew she was nearer to the Silver C. On she flew, and finally she reached the five-hour mark. In case there was any question over ratification, she stayed up just a little longer.

Then she came down to make a smooth landing and to become the first British woman to achieve the Silver C award. She was also the sixth woman worldwide and only the 208th in the world to have achieved this. She had made some close friends among her fellow trainee pilots and it was definitely a time to celebrate. In two short years, Naomi had become one of the first women to jump using a ripcord, a qualified pilot and now a qualified glider pilot at the highest level. She still hadn't turned 23.

During the rest of the 1930s, Naomi continued with her gliding, improving her skills and, along with Joan Meakin, attending the first international or world gliding championships in Wasserkuppe in July 1937. They enjoyed the event, but were beaten by the more experienced European pilots, including the famous Hanna Reitsch, who set a new long-distance record for women with a 220-mile flight. In March 1938 Naomi married fellow pilot Cecil Allen, who sadly died less than a year later after problems connected with a duodenal ulcer. Joining the ATA in the 1940s, Naomi lifted her flying skills to become a useful air ferry pilot.

After the war and dissatisfied with life and the weather in Britain, Naomi moved to California, where she married a businessman involved in real estate. At the age of 45, she suddenly found herself pregnant and was delighted to become an American mom. She lived in southern California for the rest of her life, swimming, playing tennis and also chatting about flying when she could, especially about the heady days when she managed to be the first British woman to gain that precious Silver C gliding award.

14

VERONICA VOLKERSZ AND DIANA BARNATO

VERONICA VOLKERSZ, 1944
THE FIRST BRITISH WOMAN TO FLY A JET

By the late 1930s, all the key breakthrough firsts for women in aviation had been achieved; but more opportunities were opening up, especially with the new types of aircraft that were arriving on the scene. But it was the advent of the Second World War that offered an opportunity for the next really big steps for British women in aviation.

These opportunities might not have arisen if it had not been for the groundbreaking efforts of Pauline Gower (on whom there is more information in Chapter 16). She had been one of the outstanding female pilots in the 1930s and, when war was declared in 1939, she felt there was a role for women. The RAF was very resistant to female pilots, so Pauline turned her attention to trying to get them accepted in the newly formed Air Transport Auxiliary. This was a civilian organisation set up to help move aircraft around Britain, an essential requirement during the war years when planes from factories and maintenance areas needed to be moved to frontline airfields across the country.

Despite the demands of war and the need for more pilots, there was some surprisingly strong opposition to women becoming involved in flying roles. As one journalist commented at the time: 'Women anxious to serve their country should take on work more befitting their sex instead of encroaching on a man's occupation.' But times were changing, and despite the appalling concept that the dusting and ironing might not be completed properly, Pauline was given authority to set up a women's section and appoint eight female pilots to the Air Transport Auxiliary.

They would only be allowed to fly a limited number of appropriate light aircraft; they would need to be based away from the men and they would need to be trained separately. Of course! But it didn't take long before the necessity of war took over and more women were allowed to join. As the situation became more desperate and the numbers of pilots became critical, women were also authorised to fly a wider variety of aircraft, including Hurricanes, Spitfires and Wellingtons. Pre-war pilot Lettice Curtis was the first to fly solo in a four-engined aircraft, a Halifax, and – as a small example of what the women of ATA were accomplishing – by 1942 she had flown over ninety different types of aircraft.

By 1944 there were 166 women pilots of many nationalities in the ATA, or the Anything to Anywhere as they sometimes called it. They were gradually becoming famous for their success in quickly adapting to new aircraft and flying through all conditions without radios to get the job done. The extraordinary exploits and achievements of the women pilots in the ATA confirmed without doubt that women had a rightful place in the air.

As the war years drew to a close, the aviation world became absorbed by the concept of speed. Britain's first jet plane, the Gloster Meteor, came just a little late to play a major role in the war years, but of course the interest was huge as pilots and the general public got to grips with an entirely new form of flight.

Just two weeks after the Japanese surrender and the final end of the war, 28-year-old Veronica Volkersz became the first woman in Britain to fly one of these powerful new jet planes. It was the most unlikely event for this extremely well-brought-up British girl, a debutante who had been presented at Buckingham Palace in 1934 and selected as Queen of Beauty at a major Plantagenet pageant, and who had listed gardening and painting, especially in watercolours, as her main interests. But perhaps this was more how the media of the time thought she ought to be; for underneath her innocent pretty persona was a streak of strong adventure. As she reached her twenties, she was well aware of the growing conflict in Europe and started flying with the Civil Air Guard. This organisation had been set up by the UK government in July 1938 to encourage and offer financial support for pilot training in preparation for the possibility of war. Veronica started her training at Marshall's airfield near her home in Cambridge, initially on Gipsy Moths. She was not alone; in 1939 there were over 2,400 Civil Air Guard pilots, of whom ninety-three were women.

After a short spell driving ambulances for the London Ambulance Service, Veronica applied and was accepted to join the ATA in 1941. Like all the ATA pilots, she flew a wide range of powerful aircraft and was soon a very accomplished pilot. In August 1945 Veronica happened to be posted to an ATA ferry pool which was the first to deliver jets. This all looked new and exciting and Veronica asked the flight captain if she could ferry one of the new Gloster Meteors. Veronica was in the right place at the right time and, on 15 September 1945, she was handed a chit to deliver Meteor III EE386 from RAF Moreton Vallence Aerodrome in Gloucestershire to a squadron at RAF Molesworth, north-east of Northampton.

She had no special training other than the usual little book of *Ferry Pilots' Notes*, but one of the pilots at the airfield showed her around the plane and the cockpit. Veronica noted that really it was fairly conventional in design and the controls seemed much the same as those of other aircraft, although she was very aware that there were no propellers! There was still a bit to learn, though. Britain's first jet plane was fast, with a maximum speed of over 400mph; the fuel gauges could go from full to empty in thirty-five minutes; the plane could drop like a brick when the power was reduced on landing.

Nevertheless, with no further training, on 15 September 1945 Veronica stepped into the Meteor. The cockpit felt reasonably familiar and she was not unduly concerned. As an ATA ferry pilot, Veronica was used to jumping into a huge range of different aircraft with different cockpits and in many ways this was just another aircraft. That was, until she started up the powerful turbo-jet engines. It was definitely noisy, but the breathtaking difference was on take-off. As Veronica released the brakes, the plane hurtled forward with enormous speed and power. She was off the ground in no time. After that, however, the flight was fairly straightforward – and short. It was only 90 miles from Morton Vallence to Molesworth, and Veronica found the actual flight and even the landing straightforward. Veronica had become the first British woman to fly a jet, but there was no big acclaim. The ATA girls were just continuing to do the remarkable job of flying different aircraft when required. The ATA was disbanded at the end of 1945, but many of the women wanted to keep flying.

While flying a jet was a big step forward, after the war ended the main talk among the pilots of the day was the potential of supersonic flight: going faster than the speed of sound. American pilot Chuck Yeager was the first officially recorded pilot to fly through the sound barrier in 1947; the following year it was reported that British pilot John Derry had also managed to go supersonic.

No longer were women going to be sidelined, and several female pilots were now looking at whether they too could attempt the holy grail of the sound barrier. It wasn't going to be easy; they had to get access to the right plane. There were three Jackies who firmly set their sights on becoming the fastest woman in the world: an American, a Frenchwoman and an Englishwoman. American Jacqueline Cochran finally achieved supersonic speed in May 1953 in an F-86 Sabrejet. Just three months later French pilot Jacqueline Auriol also made it in a Dassault Mystere-II. Before their successful flights, Jackie Moggridge, a hugely experienced pilot who had joined the ATA at the age of just 19, had been determined to get the record for Britain and did everything she could to get access to an appropriate plane. Despite letters to Winston Churchill and even to the Duke of Edinburgh, it was not to be and Jackie never managed to obtain permission to make a supersonic flight.

DIANA BARNATO, 1965
THE FIRST BRITISH WOMAN TO FLY THROUGH THE SOUND BARRIER

When, a decade later, Diana Barnato Walker finally achieved the record of being the first British woman to go faster than the speed of sound, it was a fitting conclusion to a remarkable story. Her grandfather, Barnet Isaacs, was a colourful character from the poorer areas of the east end of London who sold apples from a barrow. This offered limited profit and so Barnet started juggling to make more money. Then he decided he wanted to be an actor so, along with his brother, he arranged to take part in a show at the local music hall. He chose a serious segment from Shakespeare's *Othello*. As it turns out, the brothers were good, but not in the way they wanted. The audience thought it a comedy act and laughed themselves silly watching these two youngsters trying to be serious actors. When they were reluctant to come out on the stage for the final curtain call with the rest of the cast, the audience started shouting 'Barnet too'. The name stuck and Barnet and his brother became known as the Barnetoo brothers. They liked the name and adopted it; otherwise Diana Barnato would have been born as Diana Isaacs.

When the brothers heard of diamonds being found in the Kimberley in South Africa, they were off. There had to be a better way to earn money, and indeed there was. After a few years Diana's grandfather Barnet had traded his way up and finally, after a deal involving the De Beers mining and Cecil Rhodes, walked off with a cheque for £8 million.

Barnet passed on some of his colourful character as well as much of his fortune to his son, Diana's father Woolf Barnato. Woolf married a charming American lady from New York and in 1918 Diana was born into a luxurious home in central London. Soon after, Woolf became acclaimed as a top racing driver with an outstanding achievement of three consecutive wins in the twenty-four-hour Le Mans race. He wasn't quite as good at marriage, and Diana's parents divorced when she was 4. Diana took it all in her stride. She was naturally a happy, self-contained person and it helped a lot that money was not a problem in the family. With both parents finding new partners, Diana was brought up with nannies and animals in cheery, loving home surroundings, mainly living with her mother but with regular visits to her father's exciting property in Surrey where she could ride her beloved horses and was allowed to attend formal dinner parties from a young age.

Riding, skiing, going on exotic holidays and finally putting on a beautiful white dress to be presented at court in 1936, Diana was following the route of other wealthy young Englishwomen. Pretty and with an interesting character, she never lacked admirers. Sitting in a charming frock sipping a cocktail while chatting and laughing with friends was a perfect way to spend an evening. However, while Diana enjoyed all the dances, parties and social events, the customs of the day also meant that she had to be carefully chaperoned. As she turned 20, she thought flying could help to give her more freedom. She had already visited Brooklands to see her father and his friends racing around the highly cambered track, so the Brooklands Flying Club was the obvious place to go. They were offering flying lessons for £3 an hour and Diana signed on. With the confidence of youth and money, plus clear natural ability, Diana quickly mastered the Tiger Moth and went solo after just six hours' instruction.

Diana's parents weren't overly keen on their daughter flying, and instead of giving her more money for aviation, her father bought her a silver-grey 4.5-litre Bentley for her 21st birthday in January 1939. That gave Diana the potential for lots more fun. When war was declared, in September 1939, the first few months hardly affected her. She volunteered to be a Red Cross nurse but wasn't needed immediately and, in January 1940, decided to drive across France with a friend for a skiing holiday. The situation in Europe wasn't as carefree as perhaps Diana had assumed, and when they returned to Britain she joined the VADs, first working as a nurse and then, thanks to her experience, driving an ambulance.

When Diana heard about the Air Transport Auxiliary, she liked the sound of it. It might be more fun than driving ambulances. But she only had ten hours' flying; she was not exactly an experienced pilot! Thanks to her wide social contacts, though, Diana had a couple of male admirers who knew some key people and, with a few chats in the right places, she was offered a flight test for the ATA in March 1941.

Underneath Diana's reputation as a bit of a party girl, there was a quiet determination, and before her test she worked really hard to revise everything she had learned during her pilot training. Her check flight was in a Tiger Moth based at White Waltham airfield just south-west of Maidenhead. With the examiner on board, Diana did a very careful half-hour flight before making an excellent landing back at the airfield. With the test over and Diana feeling a little bit confident that she could plan a future in the ATA, she celebrated by going riding. It was an unfortunate decision and, the day after the test, she had a problem jumping a fence and crashed to the ground. With a broken jaw and other injuries, Diana was still receiving treatment in hospital when she received a letter saying she had been accepted into the ATA. It was not an auspicious beginning and it was six months before she could start her ATA training. In that short time a boyfriend had been shot down and killed, and another close friend lost both his legs when his ship was torpedoed. Suddenly the war was beginning to hit home.

Diana was ready for the new challenge and, as a member of the ATA, she carefully built up her hours, becoming a responsible and careful pilot. The role of ferry pilot suited her and, like the other exceptional pilots in the organisation, she had some extraordinary and sometimes terrifying experiences. But she flew on, delivering aircraft wherever they were needed in all but the very worst conditions.

Diana hadn't totally lost the carefree spirit of her upbringing and, after she was posted to Hamble near Southampton, she gained a bit of a reputation for still being a party girl. She would occasionally make a detour with the plane she was delivering to have lunch with a friend; on other days she would catch a train to London for an evening party, getting the early train back at the crack of dawn to start another day's flying. It wasn't all lighthearted fun, however: there were many moments of real tragedy when fellow pilots were killed. Sixteen female pilots in the ATA died during the war. Worse still, Diana became engaged to a Spitfire pilot who crashed in Essex; and then, in May 1944, she married another handsome war hero who died in an aircraft crash just eighteen months later. Diana, despite her positive outlook on life, was having a very tough war.

When the ATA disbanded, Diana had delivered 260 Spitfires and had also flown a huge range of aircraft from Typhoons, Mustangs and Hurricanes to Beaufighters, Mosquitoes, Wellingtons and Lockheed Hudsons. She would have loved to have tried for the women's air-speed record but, like Jackie Moggridge, she could never obtain the necessary permissions or aircraft.

Then, by the late 1940s, all the activity, the excitement and the heartbreak were over. Diana pondered what to do with her life and, realising her only skill was as a pilot, decided to continue to fly. She thought that being able to fly passengers could open up a new future, and so she enquired about taking her commercial or B licence as it was then called. Another handsome war hero whom she had known on and off for many years had also made the same decision and they decided to do the commercial pilot's course together. Whitney Straight was very much in the same mould as Diana's father: adventurous, charismatic and for a while dedicated to racing cars. Flying, however, was his key interest and, as a member of the RAF in the war, he was fearless and determined, surviving many dramatic events. When Diana and Whitney decided to study together for their commercial licences, Whitney was already married with two daughters. However, spending a lot of time working on their flying theory together in Diana's London house, they established a lasting friendship – and more – and Diana gave birth to their son, Barney, in 1947.

The studying was a success, for they both passed their commercial exams and soon afterwards Diana was approached by an old flying colleague. Would she help out with the Women's Junior Air Corps? The Ministry of Education had helped to set up this organisation to make girls into good citizens as well as introduce them to aviation. Diana thought it sounded excellent. It only involved weekend work, when she would be required to take the young girl members up in the air for a very short time just to experience flight.

Looking after Barney and enjoying an active social life in the week and then flying girls at the weekends soon became a steady and enjoyable routine for Diana. After the hectic drama and sadness of the war years, a social life of parties and hunting interspersed with a really useful job of introducing excited teenage girls to flight, worked very well for Diana. As she brought up her young son, the years went by happily. Despite her wartime experiences, she was not averse to romance and, in 1954, she was cited in a divorce case. But she made no permanent new attachments and then, in 1963, a couple of events occurred to add unexpected excitement to her life.

In May, when Diana was 45, she was awarded the Jean Lennox Bird Trophy for her work with the Women's Junior Air Corps. It was presented to her by Lord Brabazon of Tara who was the first pilot to achieve the Aero Club's aviation certificate in 1910. Three months later Diana achieved something that top British female pilots had been looking at for more than a decade: she went supersonic.

It all started when, flying for the Women's Junior Air Corps, Diana spent a weekend at RAF Middleton St George, just outside Darlington in north-east England. After a hectic day flying the young girls in difficult foggy conditions, Diana relaxed in the bar at the RAF officers' mess. Also based at the airfield were several RAF pilots on a conversion course to the English Electric Lightning jet, and of course they all got talking. The discussion inevitably veered towards women flying supersonic and Diana having a flight. A wing commander at the airfield seemed very supportive. The idea took hold with Diana. She had already flown so many aircraft, and an opportunity to add one more to the list and to fly this fabulous Lightning, to fly faster than she had ever done before, was hugely exciting. But a group of enthusiastic senior RAF officers at an airfield was one thing; Diana knew she would also need official permission first. Luckily she already knew the then Minister of Defence, the Right Hon. Hugh Fraser; she had met him on several social occasions and she managed to arrange an official meeting.

Making sure she looked her best, in her smart Women's Junior Air Corps uniform with her long flowing hair tightly rolled up off the collar, Diana presented herself at the Ministry of Defence. She had planned her request carefully, and had tried to clarify some ideas about why she should be given permission to fly the aircraft. However, much as she tried, she couldn't really come up with any really strong rationale. She did, however, manage to come up with twelve weak reasons why she should fly the aircraft, and she carefully wrote them down on a tiny card to take with her to the meeting in case she needed a prompt. When Diana was shown into the smart ministerial office, with its deep green carpet and leather chairs, and with the minister sitting behind a huge desk in front of a dramatic view of the Thames, she found it all rather intimidating. She saluted and, standing to attention, she managed to get through her twelve reasons. As she said after, all her reasons were pretty weak, and she finished up lamely, simply telling the minister: 'I really do want to fly the Lightning!'

The Right Hon. Hugh Fraser listened carefully, and quickly realised there could be an additional benefit for the RAF that Diana hadn't included in her twelve reasons. Publicity! Nearly 185 years after Britain's first woman had got off the ground, women in aviation could still be big news. Hugh Fraser knew the country was hoping to sell the Lightning overseas, and he thought that showing a woman could fly one would emphasise how easy it was to control and this would add to the aircraft's commercial value.

Permission! Diana walked away from the meeting hugely excited but also slightly daunted. Now it was all about detail and, unlike all the planes in the ATA, stepping into a Lightning wasn't simply a question of checking the *Ferry Pilots' Notes*. It had been easy to be enthusiastic about flying this rocket of a plane in an RAF bar; the reality was very sobering indeed. Diana, however, was by now totally determined and committed. She had experienced some real flying dramas during the war years, including being shot at by a German Messerschmitt 110 and another time when she landed a plane on fire; surely she could handle this.

First, arrangements were made for Diana to visit RAF Upwood, south-east of Peterborough, for a medical check. This included an altitude test in a small pressure chamber. Diana was accompanied by a doctor and an RAF officer while she experienced simulated different levels of altitude. She was fitted with a pressure helmet and various pieces of equipment and taught what they were all for and how to use them.

The next step was to go up to Middleton St George to do some hours on the Lightning simulator. The whole experience was very new for Diana and a million miles away from the flying she had been enjoying both in the war and also with the Women's Junior Air Corps girls. The Lightning was a unique design with highly swept-back wings and, fitted with powerful Rolls-Royce Avon engines, it offered exceptional power and rate of climb. Pilots had already compared it to sitting on two rockets. The plane could climb at 20,000ft a minute and reach a ceiling of 60,000ft.

As Diana got used to the simulator, things didn't go as well as she hoped. She was by now 45 and several times she felt weak and ill, suffering from the power and height as she practised handling the fast and lively plane. Here Diana showed enormous determination; she battled through her health issues and continued spending many hours on the Lightning simulator until it was felt she was finally ready for a real flight.

The RAF's idea of using Diana to help publicise the aircraft had not gone away. Their publicity machine had done its bit and there was huge media anticipation about Diana's first proper flight in the Lightning, or an attempt to break the Women's Speed Record, as the RAF also called it.

When the day finally arrived, on 26 August 1963, the weather was perfect, with a clear blue sky, a few dotted white clouds and the wind straight down the main runway. Diana was to fly a two-seater version of the Lightning XM996 and a check pilot, Squadron Leader Ken Goodwin, was to accompany her in the plane. Diana, though, would be in control.

First, Diana had to negotiate her way through the cameramen and reporters and quite a bit of time was taken up as the press men demanded pictures of her waving from the steps up to the plane, of her standing in front of the plane and numerous other poses. Diana did it all with good grace but her thoughts were all on the coming flight. She had managed on the simulator; really this shouldn't be that different!

Finally she climbed up to the plane and clambered into the high cockpit. There wasn't a lot of room. Diana carefully strapped herself in and checked her helmet. Ken Goodwin followed her in. There were a myriad of switches and instruments to check, and then, finally, everything was ready. The time had come.

Starting the engine was like lighting a firework and, after final checks, suddenly they were off, thundering down the runway and up. The feeling of sheer power was breathtaking. Diana followed her instructions exactly with ninety seconds in reheat to increase thrust and turning on to an easterly course to fly over the sea rather than land. Now it was time to climb and suddenly Diana found herself tearing up almost vertically into the sky. Looking at the vertical climb indicator, she saw it was virtually off the clock. Diana had been concentrating hard on keeping an accurate course but after only a very short while her check pilot Ken drew her attention to the altimeter. They were reaching 42,000ft. This was too high. Diana was only wearing a pressure helmet, not a pressure suit needed for that level of flight. She hadn't been cleared to go up so high!

There wasn't time to look around; there wasn't time to think about anything. This was one incredibly powerful, incredibly fast, very responsive plane. Diana concentrated fully on the controls and the instruments. Lighting the afterburners again, Diana started a shallow descent, building up speed. At 30,000ft, Diana started her run, tearing through the sky as the roaring plane hurtled them forwards. Firmly strapped in and keeping control, Diana saw the instruments starting to shake; then they started waving all over the place. Still she held tightly to her speed as they flashed onwards across the empty sky. Then, suddenly, everything became calm and quiet. Instantly, the instruments came back to normal and Diana was enveloped in a calm and tangible silence. Far below were the tops of broken clouds. They were flying smoothly and, to Diana at the controls, quietly through a clear blue sky. They had reached 1,262mph, or Mach 1.65. They had made it through the sound barrier!

There wasn't any time to enjoy the moment. Diana's check pilot Ken pointed out that if they didn't alter course, they would soon be in Norway. It was time to go back. Turning gently, going back to subsonic speed and slowly descending, Diana brought the Lightning steadily back to the English coast and Middleton St George. Slowing down, she made a careful landing, released the drogue chute and brought the plane to a stop.

She had done it! But suddenly, as the powerful plane stopped, Diana felt really sick and faint. She released her helmet quickly and opened the hood to get some fresh air. This wasn't the triumphant landing she had hoped for. Deep breaths. Calm down. As she slowly taxied towards the waiting crowds, she felt slightly better and managed to handle the congratulations and numerous media photographs. Diana had become the fastest women in the world and the first British woman to break the sound barrier.

There were celebrations and acclaim, of course. Her speed was verified and it became official that Diana had flown faster than any woman in the world. But Diana was not feeling right. After she got home, it didn't take long to realise that the feeling of sickness Diana had experienced immediately after the flight wasn't due to the speed, her nerves, or even relief. After some checks, it was confirmed that Diana had cancer.

She was in hospital for many weeks but, after three operations, she managed to make a good recovery. Eventually Diana was well enough to start flying again and also continue her help with various aviation organisations, especially with the ATA Association and the Girls' Venture Corps, a new name for the original Women's Junior Air Corps. Settling at her property in Surrey, Diana loved her garden as well as her farming activities which included hands-on help with her sheep. Riding also remained a big interest and Diana became Master of the Old Surrey and Burstow Foxhounds for thirteen seasons.

Diana Barnato Walker died, aged 90, in 2008. Since 1963, men may have landed on the moon and people are now regularly flying around in space; but none of the progress can take away the fact that for a while Diana was the fastest woman in the world and the first British woman to fly faster than the speed of sound.

15

HELEN SHARMAN

1991
THE FIRST BRITISH WOMAN TO GO INTO SPACE

When Letitia Sage finally got off the ground in 1785, little could she have imagined the events that would be taking place 200 years later.

New technology, new materials, totally new concepts; as the second half of the twentieth century advanced, the world of aviation had progressed into a very different world. New fabulous aircraft were being launched that would change flying forever. Increasingly, women were playing key roles in all aspects of the aviation industry, from engineering and design to flying, and no longer was their involvement causing raised eyebrows.

At the same time, two new areas of aviation were beginning to make dramatic progress. One was the development of air sports, featuring a myriad of fun and exciting ways to fly through the air, and the other was an attempt to venture into space. Both made major advances throughout the second half of the twentieth century and both eventually gave women fantastic opportunities to explore the air in exciting new ways.

It wasn't plain sailing for British women, though, either in air sports or getting into space. Parachuting was one of the activities that, after the war, was developing fast into an air sport. As the 1950s arrived, freefall was becoming commonplace and competitions were being organised for landing near a target and also for manoeuvres in the air before the parachute was opened. The first World Parachuting Championships took place in what was then Yugoslavia, in 1951, and Britain sent a team of two men. There were no female British jumpers to choose from. In the 1964 British national championships, there were only three female competitors and their equipment was all ex-military, heavy, cumbersome and difficult to operate. For the handful of women who were would-be parachutists in the 1950s and '60s, just walking to the plane in all the kit was a major challenge!

It was not easy for women to participate in the other new aviation activities, either. By 1960, an American had invented a propane burner as an easy way to create hot air which set the scene for the sport of hot-air ballooning to take off, but this took a while to get going. By 1966 there were only a handful of modern hot-air balloons flying in the world and opportunities for women to fly them were minuscule.

Hang gliding as we know it today was a latecomer in air sports and really started when a NASA engineer and others created a new type of flexible wing called the Rogallo wing in the late 1940s. The concept progressed only slowly and it wasn't until 1963, when an Australian built a new easy-to-control glider, that modern hang gliding really started. By the early 1970s, hang gliding was attracting a lot of interest in Britain but initially this was mainly among men. Women were far fewer in numbers, and at the inaugural British Hang Gliding Championships in 1975, out of over 200 registered hang-glider pilots, there were only a couple of serious female entrants.

However, by the time the 1980s arrived, there had been a dramatic change. New materials and new ideas had evolved quickly. Women were now joining hang gliding, microlight flying, parachuting and ballooning in good numbers. Another new idea, paragliding, which involved soaring under a frameless soft wing, was beginning to attract women as well as men. While gliding and parachuting had been holding world championships for many years, now the additional new air sports were also starting to hold international competitions. British women were now really showing their abilities, achieving podium places and various world records in all the air sports.

It took a little longer for a British woman to participate in space flight. When Yuri Gagarin first zoomed off into space to orbit the earth in April 1961, and then when Neil Armstrong and his team landed on the moon in July 1969, space exploration became the big new interest among aviation-minded people. However, one had been a Russian operation and the other American; what hope would there be for a British woman dreaming of the stars to venture up into space?

When Helen Sharman was born in May 1963, the idea of space travel was remote. Her dad was a college lecturer and her mum had been working as a nurse. Living in a pleasant semi-detached house in Sheffield, life for young Helen was a typical happy childhood of the 1960s. Local school, riding a bike, playing a recorder, learning to swim, messing about with friends and with her younger sister, Helen grew up steadily without drama. She was bright, though, and at her local Jordanthorpe Comprehensive School, she elected to include chemistry and physics in her subjects at A-level, the only girl to choose these courses. But she didn't see herself as different in any way. She was happy to work hard – hard enough to be accepted into Sheffield University to do a chemistry degree. She liked the subject, but more than anything Helen just loved learning and experimenting in new areas.

As she completed her degree, she had no real idea what she wanted to do. A degree in chemistry was not the most usual qualification for women, and Helen was quickly offered a range of opportunities. For a scientist, Helen made her decision on rather an unscientific basis! She decided to take the job that was based in London because, although the salary was not the highest, it would give her a chance to experience the fun of living in the capital.

A month after she turned 21, Helen left the university with a 2:1 degree and headed down to London. The job she had chosen was with the giant industrial group General Electric Company and she stayed with them for three years. Her work involved a range of duties including research on materials used in cathode ray tubes.

Helen found it all interesting but, after a short time there, she was keen for an additional challenge. GEC were happy to support her, and Helen enrolled at Birkbeck College in London to do a PhD. It would involve her in a day release from her job and a lot of extra work as she investigated the luminescence of rare-earth ions in crystals and glasses. Helen was happy to take it on, though. With an interesting job and now with new things to learn and new research challenges, her life was going well.

Helen was steadily establishing herself as a very capable scientist. In 1987, she left GEC to join Mars Confectionery in Slough while also continuing with her extra research at Birkbeck University. Her work in product development at Mars was very different indeed from looking at cathode ray tubes but just as interesting for Helen, and it provided another exciting new challenge. As she said at the time, it was no good understanding the chemistry of emulsifiers in your ice cream if the toffee falls off the ice cream before it has had a chance to harden. As she turned 26, she had found a nice boyfriend, she was content in her studio flat in Surbiton, south London, and her life had a regular pattern of driving to Mars and then either home or on to Birkbeck college to do more research for her PhD.

Everything changed on one pleasant evening at the end of June 1989. With the light summer evenings of England, there was a lot of traffic about. Driving home from her work in Slough to her flat, Helen was caught in a traffic jam on the A308 Staines bypass. She fiddled with her car radio to find some music, and as she turned the radio through the channels, an advertisement caught her attention: *Astronaut wanted. No experience necessary.*

The advert had been designed carefully to be brief but to attract attention. Short and to the point, it simply stated that a position was being offered and there were a few basic requirements: applicants must be under the age of 40 and have an ability to learn a foreign language, a high standard of fitness and have had a formal scientific, engineering or medical training. At the end of the advertisement, there was a telephone number for anyone to contact if they might be interested.

Helen jotted the number down on the back of an old petrol receipt and then, as the traffic began to move again, she drove home to get on with her life. When the weekend came, Helen decided there was no harm in finding out more about that extraordinary advert, and she gave the number a call. She got through easily and the voice at the other end wanted to know a few personal details about age, address and the degree she held, whether she spoke any languages and whether her job involved a hands-on approach or just paperwork.

Helen's questions to the woman at the end of the phone didn't result in a lot of information back; it was some space project between Great Britain and Russia. But to try to find an astronaut through a radio advert? It all seemed totally unlikely, but it was intriguing. Helen, however, wasn't the only one a little puzzled but also interested. Unknown to her at the time, over 13,000 calls were received in response to the advert and from the basic answers given, 5,500 people were selected to receive official application forms.

Helen was one of them. Early the following week an official application form dropped through her postbox and then things started to become a bit clearer. The project was for the UK Soviet Juno mission, a commercial enterprise to be funded by British companies. They would pay Glavkosmos, the Soviet Space Administration, to take a British astronaut up to Mir, the Russian space station. Mir had been launched five years earlier in February 1986, and the plan was for someone to travel the 250 miles up to Mir and spend a few days with the team as it orbited the planet at an astonishing 17,800mph.

It was an extraordinary idea. When Helen picked up and looked at the application form, while it appeared interesting, it was incredibly long and detailed. It would all take up too much time to fill in properly. Helen popped it into her briefcase and forgot about it as she carried on with her normal activities. Occasionally, she thought she ought to really get the form out and perhaps fill it in, but the days and then the weeks went by as more immediate jobs came up that needed to be taken care of. This was nearly the end of the story of Britain's first woman in space. Helen's job at Mars, and her research work, were far more interesting than form filling.

It was almost by chance that, in the middle of an experiment at Mars, Helen pulled out some papers from her briefcase and the form also fell out. She noted the closing date was in a couple of days, and decided to fill it in. She never thought for one moment that she would actually become an astronaut, but it wouldn't do any harm to complete the form. It was just an interesting challenge and she loved challenges. It took her three hours but then she posted it off and forgot all about it.

Again, Helen must have given some good answers, because from the 5,500 application forms sent out, only 150 names were selected for the next stage. When Helen received a call to attend a medical for the Juno Space Mission, and she told her colleagues she needed a day off, they all laughed. Helen laughed too. It was ridiculous, of course. No one, least of all Helen, was taking it very seriously.

After her first medical, Helen's ideas began to change. It was, of course, incredible to think that a normal British citizen could actually be sent up into space, but that seemed to be the case. The more Helen thought about it, however, the more extraordinary it sounded. Astronauts work with highly technical equipment; they are incredibly knowledgeable; how could a normal person just hop up to a space station? It did seem, though, with this project, one lucky person might, just might, have the chance to go into space.

Suddenly, from going along with the selection process in a fairly casual way, Helen began to think about it properly. To be selected and train as an astronaut would be the most amazing and interesting challenge. Over the next three months there were more interviews, psychological tests, presentations and even more medicals. It was intrusive, time consuming and very wearing, but Helen kept going, fitting it all in with her busy work. Gradually, step by step and test by test, applicants were being dropped, but Helen was still there. By mid autumn Helen found she was down to the last thirty-two. Now her colleagues began to take it seriously. What was this clever young scientist up to?

There was a final round of medicals and tests, and this time Helen was determined to do her very best. The more she thought about going into space, looking down on the earth, experiencing being so far away from the planet she called home, the more she found the whole thing fascinating. Always at the back of Helen's mind, though, was the belief that really it was all a bit of a dream. Going up into space, indeed!

Because the mission was a commercial venture, publicity was key to help repay the investors, and the media was being rolled in to lift public awareness of what was going on. Suddenly, Helen found she would get a call from a reporter at work, or an email requesting information or an interview. It wasn't long before a journalist came up with the great heading 'The Girl from Mars' and this fun title created more interest. This was all a bit too intrusive and Helen was unprepared for the incredible public and media interest in the project. It also disturbed her work. Was it all worth it? Thank goodness Helen's employers were being very supportive.

After four months of checking and testing and meetings and presentations, the last four names in the selection process were about to be announced. These four would then have to go to Moscow for two weeks of further checks before the final two potential astronauts would be named.

After so much time and effort, Helen was a little nervous; by now she desperately wanted to be selected. But other applicants had more appropriate qualifications; they seemed more suitable; they were men! Would her name be on the list? Going to work in the morning as normal, she was in for a surprise. She hadn't heard anything herself but suddenly TV crews descended on Mars causing disruption in the chocolate lab. It seems she had indeed made the last four; she had been selected. She received the official news at a London PR company that evening. Together with three men, she would need to leave for Moscow shortly for some further medical and psychological checks and testing. After that, two of them would be selected for the final training. From the final two, one would go into space and one would be the back-up.

The whole thing was extraordinary and now it was hectic too, arranging more time off from work and getting ready for a trip to Russia. Helen spoke no Russian – what would it be like? When, in early November 1989, Helen finally stepped on to the Aeroflot plane at Heathrow Airport, she quickly fell asleep. The adventure, which had started so lamely in a traffic jam near Slough just five months before, was about to begin in earnest.

The two weeks in Moscow were a bit of a let-down. After such a build-up, the four found themselves housed in a hospital, albeit with reasonable facilities, but with no contact to the outside world. There was an oxygen supply by Helen's bed which was a tad unsettling, and even worse, in the mornings Helen wasn't allowed up until her blood pressure, pulse and temperature had been taken. The food was very different too; breakfast was corn and dumplings with cheese and bread; there was more starch for lunch. This was nothing like the careful diet Helen normally followed. The four became bored and frustrated, waiting around in their hospital rooms with nothing to do but watch incomprehensible Russian TV. Going into space seemed a very distant dream.

Gradually the four were called out for medical tests and then psychological tests and slowly things started to happen. On one exciting day, the group was told of a planned trip to Star City. This was a small purpose-built military town about an hour out of Moscow and was the official base for cosmonaut training. A visit here was at last getting near to the real business of space travel.

When they arrived, Helen and her three companions were given a great welcome and generally treated as VIPs. They had to succumb to yet another range of medical tests including sitting in a spinning chair for balance checks, but then they were given a slap-up lunch with cognac and champagne plus a trip around the city, which included seeing a mock-up of the Mir Space Station. Suddenly, to envisage what it might be like to actually travel up to this station and to orbit the planet gave them all a terrific boost. Only one of them would finally be selected; another would undergo full training in Russia as a back-up and the other two would remain in the UK as further back-up. The stakes were very high indeed and the four of them went back to their hospital rooms in a determined mood and a much happier frame of mind. All they were going through was more than worth it.

Once the Russian checks were finished, they returned to London, arriving on Friday 24 November 1989. The decision on the final two names to undergo full astronaut training was made quickly in Moscow. Because of the commercial aspect, in Britain a big television programme to cover the announcement had been planned, with Helen and her three colleagues in attendance. The programme, after a summary of the lives of the applicants, would flash over to Moscow for the final announcement. It was an exciting build-up but not the easiest way for the final four applicants to learn who had been selected. When the cameras switched to Moscow, the four applicants together with thousands of viewers across the country all learned that the final two selected to complete their training in Moscow would be Tim Mace – and Helen.

If Helen's life had been busy before, now it was chaotic. Depending on which way the announcement had gone, she could have been stepping back into her life, living in her little Surbiton flat and continuing her work as a research scientist at Mars. Instead, just five months after she had listened to the advert, she had under a week to sort her life out before returning to Moscow for eighteen months of training before the planned space flight in May 1991. Seeing her family, sorting out her work and flat and saying goodbye to her boyfriend took all her time; trying to deal with the non-stop media requests was almost too much.

Finally, the following Thursday, 30 November, Helen stepped into the plane and headed back to Russia. An intense few months lay ahead, all in the hope that she rather than Tim would be chosen for the final mission.

Helen and Tim were given flats to themselves in Star City, each with a living room, two bedrooms, a kitchen and bathroom: luxurious by many Soviet standards. There was a colour TV, albeit only showing various shades of green, and Helen could cook her own meals although there was also a canteen available in the complex. The training commenced immediately. Helen's first Russian language lesson was hugely challenging, but it was a necessity as many of the future technical lessons would be in Russian, and the early weeks were spent on picking up the language as fast as possible. The British pair were also soon involved in all the other areas they needed to cover before they could venture into space, and the list was extensive: technical and scientific theory of space, orbital dynamics, propulsion, materials and structures, fuel systems in the rockets, life-support systems, robotic systems. A huge range of complex class lessons were offset by sport and physical training and Helen was impressed by the superb facilities at Star City. Together with Tim, she went swimming, running, cross-country skiing and also did work in the well-equipped gym. The training was relentless; there was just so much to learn and so many aspects to cover.

Along with theory, Helen and Tim had to experience weightlessness, do two parachute jumps, and even a practice landing in a remote area of ocean. Day after day and month after month Helen and Tim studied and trained. Inevitably they became close friends, but Helen also found the Russians she met were generous and hospitable. As 1990 sped by, her Russian improved and Helen began to make her own friends. In her little spare time, she would visit the exhibitions, museums and concert halls in Moscow. It wasn't easy getting back to Star City from the capital, and her trainers discouraged her from using the railway.

By August 1990, Helen had had enough. There was a massive amount to learn and it was very hard work indeed. While it was all incredibly interesting, it was also a very enclosed, very organised environment and Helen felt she needed more freedom in her time off. She was told about a shop in Moscow which would import Ford motor cars from Finland, and so she phoned Helsinki and ordered a basic Ford Escort. It was quickly put on a train to Moscow and Helen was delighted by how easy it had all been. That was until she found the car would be impounded until it could be issued with number plates. It took a month to sort it out, but then Helen's life improved a lot as she could visit friends and attend events in Moscow and then simply drive herself home.

While Helen's life was dominated with lessons and training and new experiences, she was able to get back to the west six times during her eighteen months in Star City to see family and friends, including a long weekend in Paris and Christmas 1990 in America. Her family and a couple of friends also made the journey out to Star City, so Helen was by no means cut off from the world. But the training went on relentlessly. At one point this was not helped by rumours that funding for the British flight had failed and for a while they lived in fear that they would be called back to London.

After a year of extensive training, Helen and Tim entered a new phase of their preparation – crew training. Along with a myriad of facts and technical information, this included a lot of time in simulators, going through procedures time and time again until they became automatic. The idea of venturing into space was becoming very real indeed. However, while they had both been treated as equals so far, despite all the incredible hard work they had both put in, they were increasingly becoming aware that only one of them would be finally selected for the mission.

In February 1991, the pair were called back to England. In separate rooms in a London hotel, they were quietly told that Helen had been selected for the space mission and Tim would be the back-up. Suddenly for Helen, all the training, the anguish, the hours of exhausting hard work and concentration, and the physical challenges she had put up with, were worthwhile. All being well, she was going to go up and stay on a space station! It was a wonderful moment for Helen and it took a while for it to sink in that she had actually made it. But she was also immediately concerned for Tim. After being through so much, how would he take the fact that in all probability, he would never get off the ground? Tim, in fact, was hugely supportive, congratulating Helen and giving her every encouragement. The following morning they had to go down and meet the media. After numerous media interviews, Helen hired a car and whizzed up to see her family in Sheffield. Helen was going to be an astronaut. It was still unbelievable really. Then it was back to Russia to complete the training before the planned launch in May.

The plan was for Helen to travel up to Mir in the Soviet Soyuz TM-12 space capsule. This would be launched from the Baikonur cosmodrome in Kazakhstan, at that time part of the Soviet Republic. Travelling with her would be cosmonauts Anatoly Artebartski, the flight commander, and Sergei Krikalyev, the flight engineer.

Now, there was a new vigour and a new intensity of purpose as Helen and Tim went through further training. By the end of April 1991 they were declared ready, and to celebrate they were given an official tour of the Kremlin.

After so long, it was time to say goodbye to Star City. Helen and Tim were transferred to the science city of Leninsk, around 650 miles south-east of Moscow and deep in the desert steppes of Kazakhstan. Here, the final instructions, the final practices, the final checks all continued. There was no sightseeing. The pair were now in full quarantine, to ensure they didn't pick up any germs or sickness this close to the launch.

In early May, two weeks before launch, Helen and Tim were transferred to the actual launch site at the nearby Baikonur cosmodrome. On arrival, they were met with typical efficient but unhurried Russian activity. Scientists, technicians, trainers, medical staff, general workers and of course reporters – the place was swarming with people all intent on specific tasks. The preparations went on. A few days before launch date the Soyuz capsule was erected on its launch pad and then, on 18 May 1991, less than two years since Helen had heard the advertisement on the radio, the day arrived. It was time to put on the space suit and fly off into space.

Helen's family had flown in to see the launch but getting near anyone was impossible. Everyone was wearing masks; there could be no final risk of Helen catching an infection; she had already had an alcoholic rubdown to get rid of any germs or bacteria. Now, in the cosmonauts' basic buildings near to the launch area, Helen changed into fresh underclothes and was fitted with an electrocardiograph chest belt to wear throughout the launch. Then she put on her training suit and finally her carefully measured spacesuit. This comprised a rubbery internal layer, airtight and wired for strength, covered by another tough outer layer. It wasn't an easy garment to move around in. Checks, including pressurising up the spacesuit to ensure it was airtight, were continuous.

While Tim, after all his training, now took a back seat in the proceedings, Helen got together with Anatoly and Sergei, the two other cosmonauts who would be travelling up to the space station with her. There was a final press conference, and then it was on to the bus to be transported over to the launch pad. As Helen boarded, her mother appeared by the door. It was lovely to be able to give her mum a quick hug, but then Helen was in the bus and off they set, leaving the crowded busy scene behind. As they approached the launch area, Helen had her first proper look at the Soyuz capsule that was to be her home for a couple of days before they docked with the Mir space station. Standing tall with a white tip, its supporting gantries had now been released. White condensation was pouring off the capsule's surface.

Clambering out of the bus, the three stepped into a small cage and then were steadily lifted high up to stop at a small platform by the entry hatch. Moving in the suits and a large helmet was tricky. Inside the capsule there was little spare space. Slowly and carefully the three managed to clamber down into their specially moulded well-fitting seats. Eventually, when they were settled, the hatch was closed. It was time to go.

Nothing was going to be quick. Each of the astronauts had a long list of checks they had to perform and every so often Helen felt a shudder in her seat as something was detached from the connections on the outside of the rocket leading to the capsule. With all the checks completed, there was still another twenty-five minutes before the rocket would actually be launched. Would the team like to listen to some music while they waited? Light Russian pop music began playing over their speakers as the final preparations were made. Then it was five minutes before take-off time and the team resealed their helmets.

A rumbling deep below was the first indication that the rocket engines had been ignited. The roaring accelerated and the capsule began to vibrate. As she sat cocooned in her specially fitted space seat, slowly Helen began to feel the increased pressure of acceleration. They were on their way. Under three minutes into the flight, a fairing that protected the craft from the earth's atmosphere was jettisoned. Suddenly Helen could look out through a little window.

In such a short time, they had climbed to an incredible height. Helen could see the curvature of the earth, the brilliant blue of the Pacific Ocean, and upwards, the blackness of space. Chunks of ice were falling off the fuel tanks, and now, as the capsule turned, so did the view. There was a sudden bang as the second stage separated and the third stage fired. Strong acceleration pushed them down in their seats. G forces rose and at last Helen had a real feeling of speed. After just under nine minutes of flight, the third stage cut out and was jettisoned. The crew were now feeling weightless.

The next two and a half hours were taken up with a long list of checks as Soyuz orbited the earth. Then the team could relax a little. It would be two days before they would reach and start docking with the space station Mir. In the meantime, they could get out of their space suits so that things were more comfortable in their living quarters in the capsule. It was a very small space but feeling weightless meant they could make use of all the room.

Helen had experienced weightlessness in training, but only for very short periods. Now she could experiment properly, learning how to turn and move across the capsule in control. It felt good, but there were some strange things to cope with. Everything had to be secured so it didn't float away. Food was in tins or in tubes; fruit juice was in tubes; drinking water was from a pressurized tank with individual mouth pieces – although the team had a bit of fun releasing a few large droplets of water to float around the cabin and be caught in the mouth. Now out of their space suits, the team could use the toilet on board. The little pull-out receptacle had a gentle suction, so as long as you held yourself on in the right position, nothing would unexpectedly float off into the cabin. There wasn't a lot of privacy on board, though.

Helen's training had been so thorough that nothing came as a surprise, yet it was all slightly different as this time it was real. The sense of time changed as, at the height they were now orbiting, darkness lasted for just forty minutes and occurred sixteen times a day. Their clocks had been set to Moscow time and they acted accordingly. That evening the team were tired; it had been one long day. Sleeping bags were tethered and Helen fell asleep at once.

The following day the results of feeling weightless were beginning to have an effect. Without gravity, bodily fluids tend to move towards the upper chest and head, and Helen's face became puffy. Her eyes felt as if they were bulging as well. Special elastic straps had been issued as part of their normal clothing for the trip, but they didn't totally stop the problem and it was some days before Helen's body settled down and she felt comfortable again.

There were continuous tasks to do, including regular contact with mission control, and also specific technical tasks, from checking oxygen levels to orbital adjustments for the capsule. A second night on the capsule, and then it was time to get ready to dock with the Mir space station. While the windows were small on the Soyuz capsule, Helen found the views totally mesmerising and spent what time she could gazing out. At one point she had caught a glimpse of Mir, a brilliant white T-shaped structure floating against the black sky. It had been a breathtaking sight. Now they were going to approach and dock.

As preparations began, the crew struggled back into their space suits and then into their seats. There was considerable work for the crew as they went down the long list of checks, and there were a couple of technical hitches on their final approach. But apart from a gentle bump, the docking was smooth, and suddenly Helen heard in her headset clapping and cheers from mission control.

Nothing was fast, but after many more procedures and checks, Helen slowly moved up and floated through the connecting hatch to enter Mir. Despite the mock-ups Helen had visited in training, Mir was a surprise. Looking around, it was larger than she expected. It was also packed with a mass of equipment with no spare space anywhere.

Helen had travelled to Mir as part of the crew transfer. Her companions on the way out would replace two of the existing crew who would in turn travel back with Helen in six days' time. They all had work to do to prepare for the change and the time sped past in a fascinating routine. There was no chance of getting bored as nothing could be done quickly on the space station; Helen was kept busy with technical tasks, checks and various experiments; every action, including clothing and eating, had to be done carefully in the weightless environment. Helen also spent time in contact with earth, including being involved in a school project helping students learn about orbits and radio technology. But she took what time she could to look out of the little window. The earth, so far below, looked stunningly beautiful. They were orbiting the earth every ninety-two minutes, and in that time Helen could spot many of the features of the world, from the high snow-capped mountain ranges to the outlines of the various continents and islands. But more than anything, Helen's overall impression was one of a deep intense blue from the oceans and a startling bright white from the clouds. At night, Helen could spot the lights shining up from big cities and, on the occasions when they flew over an electric storm, looking down on the lightning discharge over a wide area and then seeing it set off another flash was dramatic. These were memories that would stay with her forever.

There was one early moment of drama for Helen during her stay on Mir, when the noisy fans stopped and then the lights went out. As Helen later described, it was as if the station had suddenly died. But the crew all knew this was a temporary problem that would be rectified as soon as the batteries in Mir's solar panels could be recharged. This is exactly what happened, and when the sun appeared over the horizon, everything started to work again.

The few days sped past quickly and suddenly it was time to say goodbye to Mir. It had all gone too fast and this was difficult for Helen. Her visit had been the culmination of two years of incredible effort and she didn't want to leave! After preparations and a final farewell, Helen slowly floated out of Mir and made her way down through the hatch, into the Soyuz craft and then into her seat for her trip back to earth. There were three hours of checks to work through but finally these were completed and it was time to separate.

Travelling back to earth was not easy and carried multiple dangers. It was also very uncomfortable. There were G forces to be reckoned with and other physical problems as the feeling of weight returned. Looking out through the small window, because of increased friction as the craft entered the upper atmosphere, there was some luminescence with flashes of orange, yellow and almost white suddenly appearing. Helen spotted extreme bursts of light almost like fireballs racing past the window. As the capsule descended, three parachutes opened, causing really violent oscillation. Then, suddenly, with a bone-shattering jar, they were down, tipping over, spinning across empty scrubland in the Karaganda region of Kazakhstan, as Soyuz bounced its way to a stop. Strapped in tightly and hanging at violent angles in their seats, it was a difficult and very uncomfortable time for the team. Also, Helen felt so heavy, just trying to lift her arm was a major effort.

But soon the arrival team approached and opened the hatch. It was no speedy matter to extract the crew, and it was forty minutes before Helen finally managed to get out of the capsule, smell fresh air and feel warm sun on her face. Someone gave her a bunch of red roses; others helped her to walk as she was escorted to a chair for medical checks. Her sense of balance took a while to return, but then it was back to Star City for more checks and then, finally, home. Her mission had been accomplished.

Helen never particularly enjoyed being in the limelight, but on her return to the UK she was of course showered with awards and acclaim. As things quietened down, she continued with all her key interests, giving talks about science and space and also working at the National Physical Laboratory and Kingston University before becoming operations manager for the Department of Chemistry at London's Imperial College. Probably none of the new roles in her life, though, quite matched up to the excitement of being Britain's first ever woman in space.

16

NOT ALONE: OTHER BRITISH WOMEN WHO HAVE MADE SIGNIFICANT CONTRIBUTIONS TO AVIATION

This book has concentrated on key British women who achieved notable firsts in their field of aviation. However, there have also been many other courageous and inspiring British women who have played major roles in helping to move flight forward and open up aviation for future generations of women.

GERTRUDE BACON, 1900

Aeronautical pioneer

Gertrude was never an aeronaut, parachutist or pilot; nevertheless, she made an enormous contribution to aviation thanks to her strong talent for writing great stories. Brought up in Newbury at the end of the nineteenth century, she shared her learned father's interests in astronomy and aeronautics and soon became involved in his fascinating world. In November 1899 she accompanied him and leading aeronaut Stanley Spencer on a gas balloon trip to observe a special meteor shower.

Gertrude wrote about this adventure in detail and the nation was enthralled. After that, she wrote about numerous other activities including going up in an airship in 1904 and in a seaplane in 1912. While she never flew an aircraft herself, in the years before the First World War she had certainly enjoyed more flying experiences than most women of that era.

DOLLY SHEPHERD, 1904

The best-known female Edwardian parachutist

When young Dolly Shepherd heard that the great American military march musician John Philip Sousa was coming to play at London's Alexandra Palace, the only way she could get in to see a concert was to become a waitress there. She managed to get a job and was able to watch the entire show standing at the refreshment counter.

While working at 'Ally Pally', as it was known, Dolly met balloonist and parachutist Auguste Gaudron who gave aviation displays across the country. With Dolly's exuberant personality and immediate interest, he realised he had found a new potential female parachutist for his shows, and the deal was done. Dolly, at just 17, agreed to do a jump. She was paid £2 10*s*, much more than waitressing would ever bring, and was happy to do some more jumps. For the next eight years Dolly devoted herself to parachuting, giving professional displays up and down the country and becoming one of the most famous parachutists of the era.

ELEANOR TREHAWKE DAVIES, 1911

The first woman to cross the English Channel in an aircraft and the first British woman to loop the loop

Eleanor Trehawke Davies was never a pilot, but she managed to make such a contribution to early flight that in 1913 she was awarded a trophy by the Women's Aerial League for her services for aviation. It started when she was 31 years old in 1911 and she hired a pilot to fly her from Hendon to Brighton and back. She loved the excitement of flying and the next year she arranged to fly with another early British aviator, Gustav Hamel. This flight was from north London's Hendon Aerodrome to Paris, giving Eleanor the distinction of being the first woman to fly in a plane across the English Channel.

She then accompanied other leading pilots to take part in air races and other events, including winning an altitude competition in 1912. Just before the First World War, in January 1914, she joined Gustav Hamel in a Morane-Saulnier monoplane where they flew a vertical circle in the plane, or looped the loop, as it is often called, giving Eleanor the record of becoming the first British woman to experience this manoeuvre, albeit as a passenger.

WINIFRED BULLER, 1912

The first female test pilot

Winnie Buller never made huge headlines but her contribution to flight started when she became the third woman in Britain to obtain her aviation licence, certificate number 848 in May 1912. She trained alongside French army pilots and from the start showed tremendous skill and also what was then termed a 'cool head'.

For a short time, as the First World War developed, she joined the British Caudron Aircraft Company in Cricklewood. Some of her work included doing check flights on new aircraft, which could enable her to be named the first female test pilot. She had some interesting experiences, including once when the control wires on her aircraft had been badly fitted and she had to lean out of the cockpit and pull on them to control the flight. Somehow, she managed to make a perfect landing. She served in a land-based role with the Women's Royal Air Force for a period immediately after the war.

MAY ASSHETON HARBORD, 1912

The first woman granted an Aero Club Aeronaut's Certificate

Australian-born May Cunningham quickly integrated into British society after marrying her second husband Captain Assheton Harbord in London. In 1906, she was invited to go for a balloon flight and she became an immediate enthusiast. Within the year she had ordered and taken delivery of her own 45,000 cubic ft balloon and just a few weeks later flew with a pilot across the English Channel. Four days later she crossed the Channel again, this time in another balloon flown by well-known aeronaut Griffith Brewer. May was soon a very active member of the fledgling Aero Club of Great Britain, flying in many different balloons, although never solo.

After taking delivery of her biggest balloon yet, the 60,000 cubic ft *Valkyrie*, May went on to fly with various pilots to compete well in some of the major balloon races of the day, including winning the Mortimer Singer Plate for distance flight. In May 1912 May Assheton Harbard became the first woman and the sixteenth person overall to be awarded an official Aeronaut's Certificate.

FLORENCE WILSON, 1928

The pioneer pilot who helped develop aviation in East Africa

Florence was born into a family of shipping magnates, and after her marriage she arrived in Kenya with her husband Major Wilson to run a farm. He died in 1928, leaving her a wealthy widow. Soon after, she linked up with charismatic pilot Tom Campbell Black, who soon excited her with the idea of aviation in Kenya.

With Tom's advice and help, Florence bought a de Havilland Gipsy Moth and set up Wilson Airways, operating from the very basic Ngong Landing Field in Nairobi, an airstrip which was often shared with cattle. Tom helped to advise her on business matters, plus he worked as her chief pilot. Bookings for the plane came in quickly, not only for passengers but also for delivering mail across

East Africa. The next year the business moved to the current site of Wilson Airport and more permanent facilities were built. After Tom became involved with another woman Florence continued with her business, employing other pilots and flying more and more passengers. Wilson Airport is today Nairobi's main international airport, named in official recognition of Florence's outstanding contribution to early aviation.

LADY ANNE SAVILE AND ELSIE MACKAY, 1927 AND 1928

The first British women to attempt to fly the Atlantic

In early aviation, so often things seemed to come in pairs. This was certainly the case in the late 1920s when two intrepid society girls decided independently to try to become the first ever woman to fly across the Atlantic.

First to make the attempt was Lady Anne Savile. Anne, born in 1864, was the daughter of the 4th Earl of Mexborough. When her husband died, Anne became excited by all the developments in aviation. As the First World War approached, she managed to persuade a pilot to take her on a flight across the Channel. After that, she arranged to be taken up as a passenger as often as she could, and by 1922 had bought her own Airco DH.9C plane, although she never learned to fly.

In May 1927, American Charles Lindbergh flew his *Spirit of St Louis* monoplane across the Atlantic from New York to Paris, and this created huge news. A friend of Anne's, Captain Leslie Hamilton, decided he would try to fly the Atlantic from east to west. Anne was hugely supportive and offered to finance the attempt, and then made a sudden decision; she would join Captain Hamilton as a passenger to become the first woman to fly across the Atlantic. They took off from Upavon in Wiltshire on 31 August 1927 and were last spotted off the west coast of Ireland. They were never seen again.

Young Elsie Mackay showed similar courage when she attempted the same route just seven months later. Elsie was the daughter of Lord and Lady Inchcape and was brought up in the fabulous Glenapp Castle in south-west Scotland. She escaped the traditional society life and took acting jobs in London under the false name of Poppy Wyndham before flying caught her eye. Elsie learned to fly at the De Havilland Flying School in August 1922, becoming the seventh woman in Britain to be granted a pilot's licence. Buying her own aircraft, she started doing acrobatics as well as general flying. It hadn't escaped her notice that no woman had ever flown across the Atlantic, and Elsie decided she wanted to be the first. She made detailed preparations and enlisted the help of experienced pilot Captain Hinchcliffe. On 14 March 1928 they set off from Cranwell Airfield in Lincolnshire to fly to America. They were last spotted 170 miles off the west coast of Ireland heading out into the wide stormy Atlantic and were never seen again.

MARY, DUCHESS OF BEDFORD, 1929

Holder of the distance record to India

Mary Tribe wasn't expecting to become the Duchess of Bedford when she married Lord Herbrand Russell in January 1888. She was a well-brought-up 22-year-old looking forward to a normal married life. It wasn't to be. Herbrand's father, the Duke of Bedford, developed pneumonia and, in a state of high fever, shot himself; Herbrand's older brother later died of diabetes. Unexpectedly, Mary's husband became the new Duke of Bedford. They moved into the family seat at Woburn Abbey and, as a duchess, life for Mary was pleasant but not particularly fulfilling. In 1926, she went for her first flight and was immediately hooked. From then on, Mary started hiring various pilots and planes to fly to events around the country and then started doing many long-distance flights, including a record-breaking flight to Karachi in 1929 and to Cape Town and back in 1930.

After this success, and with so many hours in the air, Mary decided it really was time she learned to fly herself. In May 1933, at the age of 67, she finally achieved her pilot's licence and continued to fly. Five years later, at the age of 72, she flew off from Woburn and was believed to have come down in the North Sea. She never returned.

GRACE DRUMMOND HAY, 1929

The first woman to circumnavigate the world in an airship

When Grace Drummond Hay heard that the German *Graf Zeppelin*, the world's largest passenger-carrying airship, was going to attempt the first ever round-the-world flight, she knew she had to be on it. She had already had some experience as a journalist, and she managed to strike a deal with the trip's sponsor, William Randolph Hearst. In return for a berth on the airship, she would write some stories for the Hearst-owned *Chicago Herald and Examiner*.

The *Graf Zeppelin* was due to leave Lakehurst in New Jersey, America, on 8 August 1929. As Grace clambered on board with the other twenty or so passengers, there was a buzz of excitement as they saw the level of luxury that awaited them. The charming main dining room was carefully furnished with round cloth-covered tables featuring elegant glassware and fresh flowers; there was a comfortable sitting room with four large windows, and the passenger cabins had been designed in the style of the first-class 'Pullman' compartments on trains. It was just like a hotel in the air, and Grace settled in happily, writing reports, chatting to guests and staring out of the window as they gained height and headed east.

The airship could cruise at around 80mph and after a fifty-five-hour flight across the Atlantic they reached Germany, where they stopped to refuel. Then off the airship went again, purring eastwards across Russia and making it to Tokyo 101 hours later. Here it landed for more refuelling and checks before it went on again, heading right across the Pacific Ocean. Reaching America, it finally landed safely back at Lakehurst on 29 August. The flight, which covered around 20,651 miles, had taken just three weeks, and Grace had become the first woman ever to go round the world by air.

WINIFRED SPOONER, 1930

Champion racer and the first truly commercial British woman pilot

Winifred Spooner may not be recognised for any breakthrough firsts in aviation, but without doubt she was one of the most outstanding pilots of the time.

When she started learning to fly at the London Aeroplane Club in Stag Lane she showed her skills immediately. In August 1927 she achieved aviator certificate number 8137, the sixteenth woman in Britain to get a licence. After that, aviation took over her life. In her de Havilland DH.60 Cirrus Moth, G-EBOT, she set up a taxi service, flying passengers anywhere they wanted to go for £4 an hour. She also entered air pageants and races around the country, often beating many of the famous male pilots of the era. When, in summer 1929, she entered the FAI International Challenge in Paris, there were fifty-five entries from six countries. Having a female entry caused a lot of attention. With impeccable flying skills and navigation over the 4,000-mile route, Winnie came seventh. That year she was awarded the Harmon Trophy as the world's most outstanding aviatrix.

The following year Winnie continued to enter numerous races and air challenges, and in that year's FAI International Challenge, despite appalling weather across the 4,600-mile route, she came fourth overall. Now she was awarded the title of World's Champion Airwoman, plus the Gold Medal of the German Aero Club and other awards. She was one of the best competitive female pilots of the time.

She achieved fame when, through no fault of her own, her plane crashed into the Mediterranean. She swam in darkness through the cold sea for over two hours before she reached the Italian coast. The authorities quickly organised a search and her co-pilot was found clinging to a piece of wreckage. Winnie arrived back home to a heroine's welcome.

This attracted the attention of Sir Lindsay Everard, MP for Melton Mowbray in Leicestershire, who was looking for a private pilot plus someone to manage his private airfield and his three aeroplanes. It was the perfect job for Winnie and established her as one of the very first fully commercial female pilots. When she took time off to visit a brother in America, she also took her American pilot's licence, certificate 8045, which was signed by Orville Wright.

Sadly Winnie was struck down by pneumonia and died in January 1933, when she was just 32. Her old school in Sherborne set up a scholarship in her memory to be given to a girl showing courage, enterprise, independence and generosity. The Winifred Spooner Memorial Scholarship is a perfect tribute to one of the outstanding female pilots of the time.

CONSTANCE LEATHART, 1930S

Set up a maintenance business, and built and flew an experimental glider

Constance Leathart, born in 1903, showed an early interest in aviation and started taking flying lessons in 1925 at Newcastle Aero Club. She crashed after her first solo flight but this didn't deter her and she eventually obtained her pilot's licence in 1927. She then took part in many aviation activities and races. In the early 1930s, together with a friend, Leslie Runciman (later Viscount Runciman II), she set up Cramlington Aircraft Ltd in Northumberland. The aim of the business was to repair and overhaul aeroplanes for their yearly airworthiness certificate. It became successful and their work was well respected. The company then started making a new single-seat glider called the Cramcraft. These were designed mainly for simplicity, robustness and low cost rather than for aerodynamic performance, and Connie must have been one of the first female pilots to fly an experimental glider.

MRS VICTOR BRUCE, 1930

The first woman, with ocean crossings by boat, to fly around the world

Right from her early years at her childhood home in Essex, Mildred Mary Petre had demonstrated a love of adventure bordering on the reckless. She had to wait, however, until she was 15 before she had her first real taste of speed on her brother's Matchless motorbike.

It was then a natural progression to cars and, after marrying the Hon. Victor Bruce, the first Briton to compete in the prestigious Monte Carlo car rally, she had an ally in her love of speed. Inevitably Mary progressed to an interest in aeroplanes. When she heard, in May 1930, that Amy Johnson had reached Australia, she decided to go one better. With her mind set and definitely not lacking in confidence, Mary first bought a plane, a Blackburn Bluebird IV, and then she took flying lessons at Brooklands. On 26 July 1930 she achieved her pilot's licence, number 2855.

Just two months later, with minimal experience, she took off from London's Heston Aerodrome and headed east. A crack in the fuel tank; following a railway line that suddenly went into a tunnel on the face of a tall cliff; torrential monsoon rains that brought her down in remote north-east Thailand: Mary was gaining knowledge and experience the hard way. But on she went. By the time she reached Shanghai she was becoming a very capable pilot. Then Mary flew for eight hours across the Yellow Sea to South Korea to claim the record of being the first person to cross the Yellow Sea by air.

Going on to Japan, Mary and her plane then travelled by ocean liner across the Pacific to arrive in Vancouver. There were various incidents as Mary continued across America. Another sea voyage followed from New York to Le Havre, where Mary and her plane disembarked so they could fly the final leg to the UK. She arrived back at Lympne Airfield in Kent on 19 February 1931. Albeit with many stops and covering much of the distance by sea, Mary had managed to fly around the world.

PAULINE GOWER AND DOROTHY SPICER, 1930S

Pioneer female barnstormers and professionals

Pauline Gower and Dorothy Spicer both grew up determined to fly, and when they met at London's Stag Lane Aerodrome early in 1931 they quickly became friends. They both loved their flying so much that they were keen to see if they could earn their living in aviation. Qualifications were important and neither woman held back. Along with gaining their pilot's licences, in 1931 Pauline achieved a B licence so she could carry passengers for reward while Dorothy qualified as a ground engineer. Then they were set to go.

Initially they decided to try to earn their living by joining one of the air circuses which were touring Britain at the time. In the summer of 1932, they were involved in a relentless agenda of 200 shows up and down the country to help support British hospitals. While many women had given displays before, Pauline and Dorothy were Britain's first official all-female team of barnstormers, travelling full time around the country giving aerial displays, and it must have been a hectic, fun and exhausting time. Pauline was flying a British Spartan biplane aircraft and Dorothy was stripping it down and undertaking repairs whenever necessary.

But while air circuses offered a sense of adventure and fun, Pauline and Dorothy really wanted to run their own aviation business. They decided to set up a proper company, Air Trips Ltd, offering passenger flights and air taxi services. They based themselves in a flat field near Hunstanton, and over two seasons they carried nearly 3,000 passengers, an astonishing success for a fledgling aviation business.

By the mid 1930s both women had succeeded in becoming well-respected and well-known professional pilots. As it became more and more likely there would be a war, Pauline started campaigning for female pilots to be allowed to help. She met a great deal of resistance but with her experience and knowledge of aviation, her diplomacy and her determination, she continued to argue the case and finally, at the end of 1939, she was given the job of organising a woman's section of the Air Transport Auxiliary. The organisation under her leadership made an enormous contribution to the war effort and in 1942 Pauline was awarded an MBE.

Sadly, neither Pauline nor Dorothy lived long enough to see the exciting onward progression of women in aviation. Pauline died in 1947 soon after giving birth to twin boys; and Dorothy died in a passenger aircraft in Brazil when bad weather forced the plane down to crash into a mountainside. It was an unfortunate ending for both groundbreaking women who had contributed so much to British aviation.

WINIFRED DRINKWATER, 1932

The youngest fully qualified female pilot

Another Winifred in 1930s aviation was Winifred Drinkwater, who decided to take up flying at a time when very few Scottish ladies were involved in flight. Born in Waterfoot, south of Glasgow, Winifred joined the Scottish Flying Club near Renfrew in the summer of 1930 when she was just 17. She qualified for her private pilot's licence later that year, becoming the youngest Scottish pilot at the time and then, just two years later at the age of 19, she was awarded her B licence. This made her one of the youngest pilots in the world authorised to take up passengers. As if that was not enough for Winifred, she went on to gain her instructor's certificate later the same year and her ground engineer's licence in 1933. By the age of just 20, Winifred had become one of the most qualified female pilots.

She was taken on as a commercial pilot by Midland and Scottish Air Ferries, first flying a de Havilland Fox Moth but then changing to a de Havilland Dragon when she started to fly scheduled routes from Glasgow down to London. Winifred was not a record seeker but simply loved flying, and her work included a variety of assignments including at one time flying photographers low over Loch Ness to search for the Loch Ness Monster.

BERYL MARKHAM, 1936

The first woman to fly across the Atlantic from east to west

Beryl Markham is remembered for her record-breaking trip of flying east to west across the Atlantic, the first woman to achieve this challenging route. But in fact her whole life was one long adventure, starting in 1906 when she was 4 and her family moved to Africa. Her father was a racehorse trainer and Beryl became the first woman in Africa to receive a racehorse trainer's licence when she was 18.

Very social and part of the Nairobi set, she enjoyed the company of men and had many liaisons as well as three marriages. Tom

Campbell Black, one of the loves of her life, helped to teach her to fly. Buying her own Avian IV aeroplane, she started taking freelance pilot jobs, taking groups on safari, transporting passengers to remote farmsteads and delivering goods and mail.

She steadily became a very efficient pilot and when a friend suggested an east-to-west flight across the Atlantic, Beryl thought it would be an excellent way to support her idea of an Atlantic air service. On the evening of Friday 4 September 1936, in a Percival Vega Gull monoplane with extra fuel tanks and some sandwiches, she set off from Abingdon near Oxford. The weather was rough from the beginning, with headwinds reducing her speed to around 90mph. She flew on, initially in total darkness and without any radio contact, for hours and hours. After nineteen hours her fuel situation became crucial. Luckily she managed to reach Cape Breton Island, Nova Scotia, and put down in a soft bog, damaging the plane but creating the record she had hoped for. She had become the first woman to fly west across the Atlantic.

ANN WELCH, 1930S TO 1980S

A lifetime of service to aviation

As a young child, Ann Welch used to keep a diary of every aeroplane that flew over her Kent home. When, in 1930, at the age of 13, she was given a flight in an Airspeed Ferry plane, the scene was finally set. She knew she wanted to make a future in aviation. She obtained her pilot's licence at the age of 17, and then, three years later, started gliding at the London Gliding Club in Dunstable. In 1938, she helped to start the Surrey Gliding Club and became a gliding instructor.

As the Second World War got underway, Ann joined the ATA and, like all the female pilots there, flew a wide range of aircraft around Britain. After the war, she returned to gliding and became an outstanding pilot and a member of the British team. Thanks to her organisation and administrative skills as well as her flying experience, she was asked to manage the British gliding teams. She was so successful she continued to do this for twenty years.

Despite her dedication to gliding, Ann was also fascinated by all forms of flight and early in 1970, after a visit to California where she saw some youngsters gliding down hills under a basic Rogallo flexible type of wing, she became very enthusiastic about hang gliding. She became founder president of the FAI's Hang Gliding and Paragliding Commissions and also served as president of the British Hang Gliding and Paragliding Association and the British Microlight Aircraft Association. During her life, Ann was given numerous recognitions and awards including an OBE in 1966.

SHEILA SCOTT, 1971

The first woman to fly around the world via the North Pole

For someone who failed her driving test three times, it was remarkable that Sheila Scott could fly at all. The fact that she went on to become a knowledgeable pilot and break several aviation records is extraordinary.

Sheila Hopkins was born in Worcester in 1922 and, with ambitions to be an actress, she changed her name to Sheila Scott. This was to no avail; her career plans, together with her marriage, failed. In 1958 her world changed dramatically when she learned to fly and then bought her first plane, a converted Tiger Moth. After that, there was nothing else Sheila wanted to do but fly. In 1966, she set off on a 31,000-mile journey around the world. Then she set off to break various records, including flights in 1967 between London and Cape Town and across the North Atlantic and a flight over the South Atlantic in 1969. In 1971 Sheila achieved another record, becoming the first pilot in a light aircraft to circle the globe on a route that included flying over the true North Pole.

Sheila was awarded the Harmon International Aviation Trophy in 1967 and the Royal Aero Club Gold Medal in 1968 for her achievements in aviation.

BARBARA HARMER, 1992

The first woman to fly a supersonic commercial airline

With three older sisters, it wasn't surprising that Barbara Harmer was introduced early into the world of fashion and beauty. In 1968, when she was 15, she left her school in Bognor Regis to become a hairdresser and it took five years before she realised she might be capable of wider adventures. After that, there was no stopping her. First Barbara trained as an air traffic controller and studied privately for A-level qualifications; then she started to learn to fly. With a massive bank loan and working as an instructor at Goodwood Flying School, she managed to study and then obtain her commercial pilot's licence. All this was a stunning achievement, but it was just the beginning. Then it was a long route starting with a small commuter airline before finally joining British Airways in 1987, when she was 34. At that time she was one of only sixty female pilots employed by BA, compared with over 3,000 men.

In 1992 Barbara was selected for a six-month conversion course to fly Concorde, the world's first and only supersonic passenger-carrying aircraft. She loved it, describing it as an extraordinary plane, surprisingly smooth with a very special aura. Most of the flying she did was on the London-to-New York route, flying at 60,000ft at 1,350mph, offering unique views of the world below.

Barbara stayed with Concorde until it was withdrawn from service, ten years later, and then she continued to fly on other planes until 2009, when she left BA.

JENNIFER MURRAY, 1997

The first woman to fly around the world in a helicopter

Jennifer had already led a full and exciting life, living in various places around the world. When she was in her fifties and settled into a comfortable life in England with children and grandchildren, her husband bought a half share in a helicopter. However, he was having problems finding the time to learn to fly, so Jennifer decided to learn. As soon as she got into the air, she showed excellent skills and she loved it more than anything. She quickly started building up her hours, flying the helicopter whenever she could, and then she decided a long flight could be a great way to raise money for charity.

In a little single-engine piston Robinson R44 helicopter, with co-pilot Quentin Smith to help, Jennifer set off on 10 May 1997 and travelled through twenty-eight countries before arriving back on 8 August. This earned Jennifer a few world records, including the first woman and grandmother to circumnavigate the globe in a helicopter.

Instead of being satisfied, this achievement just inspired Jennifer to see if she could do more. She might have been approaching 60, but this wouldn't stop her plans. In 2000 she sorted out her fuel, her routes, the weather and all the complex arrangements of flying a small helicopter on long distances to become the first women to fly a helicopter solo around the world.

Jennifer's love of flying continued. Following an aborted attempt in 2003 to fly across the South Pole, in 2006–7, along with a co-pilot, Jennifer became the first pilot to fly around the world in a helicopter via the South and North Poles.

KATHARINE BOARD, 2005

Britain's first female commercial airship pilot

Some 100 years after the first woman, Britain's Rose Spencer, took control of a powered airship, Kate Board was busy building up hours to become Britain's first female professional airship pilot.

Like Rose, Kate hadn't been dreaming of flying airships in her childhood. In 1994, when her father gave her five flying lessons for her 19th birthday, it was the start of a new venture that would change her life. Gaining her pilot's licence at her local flying club at Manston in Kent, she wanted to make a career in aviation but felt being an airline pilot wasn't for her. She started to work as ground crew for Virgin, a company involved in hot-air balloons and airships. Kate realised that, in the modern world, lighter-than-air flight offered something refreshingly new. She went over to Kissimmee in Florida to train as an airship pilot and then, in 2005, she was back in Europe, flying an American Blimp Corporate A-60+ for the Lightship Group, a partnership that had been formed earlier between Virgin Lightships and Lightship America.

Kate enjoyed the mix of technical excellence and slow speed. The A-60+ airship, carrying 68,000 cubic ft of helium and cruising at around 32mph, was a perfect combination of challenge and fun. Kate then moved to California where she joined Airship Ventures which was operating a commercial passenger Zeppelin airship. The German Zeppelin company had incorporated new ideas in design and technology to develop a modern airship which it called the Zeppelin NT. Kate was the first woman in the world to qualify on these Zeppelin airships, and for Airship Ventures she flew passenger trips up and down the Californian coast. She loved it. One day she spotted whales out in the ocean. She put the airship into a low hover and sat there with her passengers, watching the fascinating whales play just below.

Kate steadily accumulated experience and flying hours and became fully certified by the CAA, LBA and FAA as a commercial airship pilot. In 2012, she wanted to return to Europe for family reasons and she applied to the Zeppelin company, which was offering commercial flights from its base in Friedrichshafen in southern Germany. Kate moved over to join them as a pilot and she loved it from the start, explaining to excited passengers the basics of how the airship flies and helping them achieve wonderful photographs by flying slowly at low level over the most picturesque scenery. However the new era of airships develops in the future, Kate will now always have the record of being the first British woman to qualify as a commercial airship pilot.

BIBLIOGRAPHY AND SOURCES

Babington Smith, Constance: *Amy Johnson*, Collins (London) 1967

Bacon, Gertrude: *How Men Fly*, Cassell and Co. (London) 1911

Bowman, Gerald: *Stories of the Caterpillar Club*, White Lion (Aldershot) 1955

Bowyer, Chaz: *Handley Page Bombers of the First World War*, Aston Publications (Birmingham) 1999

Burchard, Peter: *Pioneers of Flight*, St Martin's Press (New York) 1970

Burge, C.G: *Complete Book of Aviation*, Isaac Pitman and Sons (London) 1935

Buxton, Meriel: *The High-Flying Duchess*, Woodperry Books (Stanton St John) 2008

Cadogan, Mary: *Women with Wings*, MacMillan (London) 1992

Davies, Mark: *King of All Balloons: The Adventurous Life of James Sadler, the First English Aeronaut*, Amberley (Stroud) 2018

Dwiggins, Don: *Bailout*, MacMillan (New York) 1969

Ellis, Mary: *A Spitfire Girl*, Frontline Books (Yorkshire) 2016

Falloon, Jane: *Throttle Full Open*, Lilliput Press (Dublin) 1999

Frater, Alexander: *Beyond the Blue Horizon*, William Heinemann (London) 1986

Gardiner, L.: *Lunardi: The Story of Vincenzo Lunardi*, Airlife (Shrewsbury) 1984

Gregory, Howard: *The Falcon's Disciples*, Pageant Press (New York) 1967

Hale, Julian: *Women in Aviation*, Bloomsbury (London) 2019

Hearn, Peter: *Sky High Irvin*, Robert Hale (London) 1983

Hewlett, Gail: *Old Bird: The Irrepressible Mrs Hewlett*, Matador (Leicester) 2010

Highfill, Philip H., Burnim, Kalman A. and Langhans, Edward A.: *A Biographical Dictionary of Actors, Actresses, Musicians, Dancers, Managers and other Stage Personnel in London 1660–1800*, Vols 7 and 13, Southern Illinois University Press (Carbondale) 1982

Hoare, R.J.: *The Story of Aircraft*, A&C Black (London) 1958

Holmes, Richard: *Falling Upwards: How We Took to the Air*, Harper Collins (London) 1913

Inglis, Lucy: *Georgian London, Into the Streets*, Penguin (London) 2013

Hodgson, J.E.: *The History of Aeronautics in Great Britain*, Oxford University Press (Oxford) 1924

Jackson, Donald Dale: *The Aeronauts*, Time Life Books (Alexandria, VA) 1980

Jarrett, Philip: *Another Icarus*, Smithsonian Institution Press (Washington) 1987

Johns W.E.: *Some Milestones of Aviation*, John Hamilton (London) 1936

Kim, Mi Gyung: *The Imagined Empire: Balloon Enlightenments in Revolutionary Europe*, University of Pittsburgh Press (Pittsburgh) 2017

Learmonth, Bob, Nash, Joanna and Cluett, Douglas: *The First Croydon Airport 1915 to 1928*, Sutton (Stroud) 1977

Lebow, Eileen F.: *Before Amelia*, Brassey's (Washington, DC) 2003

Lucas, John: *The Big Umbrella*, Elm Tree Books (London) 1973

Lucas, John: *The Silken Canopy*, Airlife (Shrewsbury) 1997

Lynn, Michael R: *The Sublime Invention, Ballooning in Europe*, Routledge (Abingdon) 2010

Meager, George: *My Airship Flights*, William Kimber (London) 1970

Meggitt, George: *Winifred Brown*, Pitchpole Books (Cheshire) 2013

Moggridge, Jackie: *Spitfire Girl*, Head of Zeus (London) 2014

Morgan, Albert: *Airborne for Pleasure*, David & Charles (London) 1975

Mortimer, Charles: *Brooklands and Beyond*, Goose and Son (Norwich) 1974

Naughton, Lindie: *Lady Icarus*, Ashfield Press (Dublin) 2004

Ovington, Adelaide: *An Aviator's Wife*, Dodd, Mead and Company (New York) 1929

Pegasus: *Parachutist*, Jarrolds (London) 1943

Predergast, Curtis: *The First Aviators*, Time Life Books (Alexandria, Va) 1981

Rolt, L.T.C: *The Aeronauts*, Longmans (London) 1966

Sage, L.A.: *A Letter Addressed to a Female Friend*, 3rd ed., Gale ECCO (Farmington Hills) 2010

Sellick, Bud: *Parachutes and Parachuting*, Prentice-Hall (Englewood Cliffs) 1971

Sharman, Helen and Priest, Christopher: *Seize the Moment*, Victor Gollancz (London) 1993

Shayler, David J. and Moule, Ian: *Women in Space: Following Valentina*, Praxis (Chichester) 2005

Shepherd, Dolly: *When the Chute Went Up*, Robert Hale (London) 1984
Stuart, S.E. and Potts, W.T.W.: *Early Balloon Flights and the Lancaster Balloon Mystery*, The Council for British Archaeology (York) 1919
Thomas, Nick: *Naomi the Aviatrix*, Incline Village (Nevada) 2011
Trunum, John: *Nine Lives*, John Hamilton (London) 1933
Visser, Margaret: *The Rituals of Dinner*, Penguin (New York) 1991
Volkersz, Veronica: *The Sky and I*, W.H. Allen (London) 1956
Walker, Diana Barnato: *Spreading My Wings*, Grub Street (London) 2003
Walker, Mike: *Powder Puff Derby*, John Wiley and Sons (Chichester) 2004
Ward, Valerie: *Amy and the Aviatrices*, Zeteo (Leeds) 2012
Wilson, Nancy: *Queen of Speed*, Ex Libris Press (Bradford-on-Avon) 2012
Wright, Sharon: *Balloonomania Belles*, Pen & Sword (Barnsley) 2018

ARCHIVES, OFFICIAL BODIES AND COLLECTIONS

Aero-Club de France (Paris)
Aeroscopia Aeronautical Museum (Toulouse)
Airship Association
Airship Heritage Trust
Air Transport Auxiliary Association
Amy Johnson Arts Trust
Bodleian Library, Oxford
British Aircraft Preservation Council
British Balloon and Airship Club
British Balloon Museum and Library
British Gliding Association
British Hang Gliding And Paragliding Association
British Library
British Newspaper Archive
British Pathé
British Parachute Association
British Women's Pilots' Association
Brooklands Museum
Burney Collection, British Library
Civil Aviation Authority
Cuming Museum, Southward
English Heritage
Farnborough Air Sciences Trust
Fédération Aéronautique Internationale (Lausanne, Switzerland)
FlightGlobal
Flight International
Friends of Richmond Park
Gliding Heritage Centre, Lasham
Helensburgh Heritage Trust
Historic Croydon Airport Trust
Institute of Historical Research
Institute of Women of Aviation Worldwide
Monash University (Melbourne, Australia)
Museums Association
National Aeronautics and Space Administration (Washington DC, USA)
National Aerospace Library
National Archives
National Balloon Museum (Indianola, Iowa, USA)
National Library of Australia
National Library of Scotland
National Maritime Archives (The Hague, Holland)
National Museum of Flight
National Portrait Gallery
Naval Airship Association (Edgewater, Florida, USA)
Pau Wright Aviation Association

RAF Museum
Royal Aero Club
Royal Parks Guild
Shuttleworth Collection
Smithsonian Libraries (Washington, US)
Smithsonian National Air and Space Museum (Washington, US)
Suffolk Aviation Heritage Group
The Old Bailey
The Royal Aeronautical Society
Vintage Glider Club
Victoria and Albert Museum
Women in Aviation International (West Alexandria, Ohio, US)

INDEX